W9-CEZ-416

Editorial and Advisory Board

NUTSHELL SERIES

JESSE H. CHOPER
Professor of Law
University of California, Berkeley

DAVID P. CURRIE
Professor of Law
University of Chicago

YALE KAMISAR
Professor of Law
University of Michigan

ROBERT E. KEETON
Professor of Law
Harvard University

RICHARD C. MAXWELL
Professor of Law
University of California, Los Angeles

MICHAEL I. SOVERN
Dean and Professor of Law
Columbia University

CHARLES ALAN WRIGHT
Professor of Law
University of Texas

II

COMMERCIAL PAPER

IN A

NUTSHELL

By

CHARLES M. WEBER

Member of the New York Bar and
Professor of Business Law at the
Wharton School of the University of
Pennsylvania

Second Edition

ST. PAUL, MINN.
WEST PUBLISHING CO.
1975

COPYRIGHT © 1965 CHARLES M. WEBER

COPYRIGHT © 1975
By
WEST PUBLISHING CO.
All rights reserved

Library of Congress Catalog Card Number: 75–2535

Weber Comm. Paper
1st Reprint—1975

To

Ida Elizabeth

*

PREFACE

The purpose of this book is to introduce the law of commercial paper in a way that promotes understanding and remembering and furnishes a sound foundation for any further study of the subject that the reader may pursue.

As used in the title and throughout the book, "commercial paper" refers to promissory notes, drafts, checks and certificates of deposit—the subject matter of Article 3 of the Uniform Commercial Code. It does not purport to treat any other types of documents that often are used in commercial transactions such as bills of lading, warehouse receipts, security devices, letters of credit, or stocks and bonds, all of which are treated in other articles of the Code.

This is a revised and enlarged edition of my book, COMMERCIAL PAPER, first published in 1965.

Additional space has become available in this edition as the result of the more flexible format of the NUTSHELL SERIES and the fact that the transition from the Negotiable Instruments Law to the Code is almost complete so that it is possible now to omit all but a few of the many references to the Negotiable Instruments Law that were included in the first edition.

The additional space has made it possible to treat more thoroughly some matters treated inadequately in the first edition and to include some matters reluctantly omitted from the first edition for lack of space. Also, it has made it possible to increase substantially the number of short cases used to illustrate principles discussed in the text. These short cases have proven to be an efficient means of helping students to understand and recall the principles discussed. Most of the cases are based on one or more court decisions which have been freely edited in the interest of clarity, brevity, and relevance which are so important to a NUTSHELL. Others are based entirely on my own understanding of the principles stated in the Code.

To help the reader focus on the important facts in the short cases, I have usually followed the common practice of using convenient symbols to identify the parties who most frequently come into contact with commercial paper. As the reader probably would infer, M stands for maker, P for payee, R for drawer, E for drawee, H for holder (who may or may not be a holder in due course) and HDC for holder in due course.

In the spirit of the NUTSHELL emphasis continues to be on basic principles. In the same spirit, citations have been limited mainly to Code sections and Official Comments. One who knows the number of a Code section can, with the aid of a fully annotated copy of the Code, quickly locate virtually all of the reported cases decided under it. Those who wish to pursue the subject in greater depth and to deal with some of the truly knotty problems that relate to commercial paper will find a plethora of materials in a large number of scholarly articles, most of which are listed in the INDEX TO LEGAL PERIODICALS; in a number of excellent textbooks and casebooks; in UNIFORM LAWS ANNOTATED, UNIFORM COMMERCIAL CODE, MASTER EDITION (West 1968) and Annual Supplement; and in the many reports that were prepared for state legislatures when they were considering adopting the Code.

In a work as brief as this, it is not possible to set forth all of the provisions of Article 3. At appropriate points in the text, however, a limited number of its provisions with identifying section numbers are set forth in full. Some provisions are quoted because they are fundamental and are referred to many times. This is true, for example, of Section 3–104(1) which states the requisites of a negotiable instrument, and Section 3–302(1) which states the requisites of a holder in due course. Other provisions are quoted because it is thought that quick access to the provision itself should make the discussion of its subject matter easier to understand. Usually, however, the reason for quoting a provision is that it seems to speak quite clearly for itself. When a statement in the text is based on a Code provision which is not quoted, the section number usually is shown in brackets.

Occasionally, statements in this book are made in reliance upon the Official Comments that follow the sections to which they relate in the official texts. In these instances, the number of the Code section to which the comment relates, preceded by the word "Comment" and the comment number, if any, is enclosed in brackets following the statement that it supports. It is true that the comments have never been enacted into law and that some of them have been questioned. Nonetheless, they were prepared by and are sponsored by the American Law Institute and the Conference of Commissioners on Uniform State Laws and they are often a primary source of light when one is uncertain about the meaning or rationale of a Code provision. Moreover, it is natural for a court, confronted by a borderline case not treated clearly in the Code, to consult and give weight to any relevant comment that has logical appeal; and many courts appear to have done so.

Even a small book is rarely written without help. I renew my thanks to all those who helped with the First Edition. I owe thanks to the members of the banking community and other friends who generously helped with the Second Edition. In particular, I thank Pam Porter for the thoughtful views of a second year law student; and I thank Stephen and Gwen Weber for their help with legal research and in many other ways. I give special thanks to Professor Thomas M. Quinn of the Fordham University School of Law, Editor of the UNIFORM COMMERCIAL CODE LAW

PREFACE

LETTER, for his fine review of the first edition and for his many useful suggestions for improving it. Most of all, I thank Professor William D. Hawkland of the College of Law of the University of Illinois, author of many leading books and articles on commercial paper, commercial transactions, and bank deposits and collections, who reviewed the original manuscripts of both the first and second editions, for his invaluable help.

CHARLES M. WEBER

February, 1975

*

OUTLINE

OUTLINE

CHAPTER 5. ISSUE—Continued

CHAPTER 6. TRANSFER AND NEGOTIATION _____ 90

CHAPTER 6. TRANSFER AND NEGOTIATION—Continued

CHAPTER 7. LIABILITY OF PARTIES ON THE INSTRUMENT
—Continued

CHAPTER 8. PRESENTMENT, DISHONOR, NOTICE OF DISHONOR AND PROTEST 164

CHAPTER 8. PRESENTMENT, DISHON-OR, NOTICE OF DIS-HONOR AND PROTEST
—Continued

CHAPTER 8. PRESENTMENT, DISHONOR, NOTICE OF DISHONOR AND PROTEST
—Continued

CHAPTER 9. LIABILITY BASED ON WARRANTIES _____ 198

CHAPTER 10. HOLDERS IN DUE COURSE—Continued

CHAPTER 10. HOLDERS IN DUE COURSE—Cont'd

CHAPTER 11. DEFENSES AND CLAIMS 272

CHAPTER 11.   DEFENSES AND CLAIMS
—Continued

CHAPTER 12.   DISCHARGE

CHAPTER 12.   DISCHARGE—Continued

CHAPTER 13.   SPECIAL CHARACTERISTICS OF CHECKS AND RELATIONSHIP BETWEEN BANK AND ITS CHECKING ACCOUNT CUSTOMER

TABLE OF CASES

References are to Pages

TABLE OF CASES

TABLE OF REFERENCES TO U.C.C. PROVISIONS AND COMMENTS

TABLE OF REFERENCES

TABLE OF REFERENCES

TABLE OF REFERENCES

TABLE OF REFERENCES

TABLE OF REFERENCES

XXXVI

TABLE OF REFERENCES

TABLE OF REFERENCES

TABLE OF REFERENCES

TABLE OF REFERENCES

TABLE OF REFERENCES

†

COMMERCIAL PAPER

CHAPTER 1

INTRODUCTION

§ 1. Importance of Commercial Paper

Checks, drafts, and promissory notes—the principal kinds of commercial paper—perform vital functions in the business community, serving as the means of payment in most significant transactions and facilitating the free movement of goods and services. In our society, which does most of its business on credit, they are the instruments by which business normally is financed. Promises represented by the several forms of commercial paper are among the most important promises that people live by, and the law which determines the rights and liabilities of those who deal with such paper concerns us all.

§ 2. What "Commercial Paper" Encompasses

The Uniform Commercial Code does not expressly define "commercial paper." In legal and business circles, however, the term usually refers to notes, drafts, checks and certificates of deposit; and these instruments furnish the subject matter of Article 3 which is entitled "Commercial Paper." [Comment 1, 3–103] Usually "commercial paper" is used to refer to instruments that are negotiable, but it sometimes is used broadly to include instruments that are not negotiable. Although Article 3 is concerned primarily with instruments that are negotiable, it is concerned also with instruments that are not negotiable. Similarly, the study of commercial paper is concerned primarily with notes, drafts, checks and certificates of deposit that are negotiable, but it is also concerned with such instruments when they are not negotiable. (For the requisites of a negotiable instrument see Chapter 4.)

§ 3. Commercial Paper as a Contract

Whether or not an instrument is negotiable, it represents a contract and is governed by most of the principles that govern other forms of contracts. For example, a person usually is not charged with an obligation on a note, check, or draft unless he has manifested his willingness to be bound. Similarly, there usually is need for consideration, capacity, and a legal object. Nonetheless, these instruments are special forms of contracts, and the major portion of the law of commercial paper is concerned with their special rather than their general characteristics.

§ 4. Commercial Paper as Property

Like other kinds of contracts, commercial paper is property, and it has most of the attributes of other property and is governed by most of the same legal principles that govern other property. It is transferable by sale, gift, will or intestacy; it is subject to the legal process of creditors to satisfy debts; it can be possessed, loaned, converted, lost, stolen, and taxed; and, as is true of other property, it represents bundles of rights, privileges, powers and immunities that are recognized by the courts. But just as commercial paper represents a special form of contract, so also, it represents a special form of property and it may be subject to a number of special legal principles that do not apply to most other forms of property. All of this will appear more clearly from later discussion.

§ 5. Early History of Commercial Paper

Since trading began, merchants have found it convenient to substitute certain forms of documents for money for various commercial purposes. Instruments roughly similar to those we know were used as early as 2000 B.C. More modern forms were used by medieval merchants in various parts of northern Europe, including the British Isles, from which they came to us in America. Because most of the law governing commerce, including the law governing the creation and transfer of these instruments, originated primarily in the practices and customs of these merchants, this body of law came to be known as the *law merchant*. For a long time these merchants had their own courts to settle disputes which arose among them; the law merchant was not part of the common law of England, nor was it recognized by the King's common law courts. Eventually, however, largely through the efforts of an aggressive eighteenth century judge, Lord Mansfield, the common law absorbed the law merchant. Today the law governing commercial paper and commercial transactions is as much a part of the law of the land in England and America as is any other branch of the law. (For a brief history of the law of commercial paper, see Chapter 12, Kempin, Historical Introduction to Anglo-American Law in a Nutshell, Second Edition, this series 1973).

§ 6. Uniform Negotiable Instruments Law

In 1896, the National Conference of Commissioners on Uniform State Laws promulgated the Uniform Negotiable Instruments Act which is often referred to as the Negotiable Instruments Law or the N.I.L. Like the British Bills of Exchange Act (1882), after which it was in most respects modeled, the N.I.L. was largely declaratory of the common law. By 1924 it had been adopted with only minor variations in all states.

§ 7. Uniform Commercial Code

Eventually, the N.I.L. was found to contain serious defects which resulted primarily from its failure to provide for changing commercial practices. Also, differences in interpretation among the courts tended to destroy the uniformity which it was intended to provide.

Similar weaknesses appeared in other areas of commercial law. Some legal authorities felt that these difficulties should be overcome by piecemeal amendments of existing statutes; others thought that a comprehensive statute to deal with the various areas of the law governing commerce was necessary. The efforts of the latter group during several decades resulted in the Uniform Commercial Code—usually referred to as the "Code."

The Code was primarily the joint work of the American Law Institute and the National Conference of Commissioners on Uniform State Laws. In preparing the Code, these organizations used the knowledge, experience, and talents of literally hundreds of judges, lawyers, law professors, bankers, merchants, and many other persons, from various parts of the country. However, the 1952 Official Text, the first, was adopted in only one state, Pennsylvania. It was not adopted in other states largely because the legislature of New York, a key state in commercial matters, referred the Code to its Law Revision Commission which, after making an intensive study over a period of several years, reported to the New York Legislature in 1956 that "the Code is not yet ready for enactment." (Legislative Document 1956 No. 65(A) 5)

The New York Law Revision Commission Report contained a large number of detailed criticisms and suggestions. After studying these, the Code editorial board recommended a large number of amendments of the 1952 Official Text, which were reflected in the 1957 Official Text. Many of these amendments related directly to the provisions treating commercial paper. Later Official Texts (1958, 1962, 1972), however, made few significant changes in the Code provisions relating to commercial paper.

As of January 1, 1975, the Code has been adopted so as to be effective in all states, except Louisiana (which has adopted Articles 1, 3, 4, 5), as well as in the District of Columbia and the Virgin Islands. Thus far, although Congress has enacted the Code for the District of Columbia, it has refused to adopt it as general federal statutory law.

The Code deals with not only commercial paper, which is covered in Article 3, but also with sales of goods (Article 2), bank deposits and collections (Article 4), letters of credit (Article 5), bulk transfers (Article 6), documents of title (Article 7), investment securities (Article 8), and secured transactions (Article 9). Article 1 contains a number of general provisions including a large number of general definitions and general rules of construction and principles of interpretation. Article 10 provides the effective date of the Code and also repeals the Negotiable Instruments Law and a number of other state laws. Article 11, which is added by the 1972 Official Text, is a transition provision that indicates when the original version of Article 9 continues to govern secured transactions in states in which that Article has been substantially revised after the particular secured transaction was consummated by the parties.

The following discussion is based primarily on Article 3, entitled "Commercial Paper," which has earned the approval of almost all legal scholars, the courts, and lawyers, as well as bankers and other businessmen. There are several reasons why Article 3 serves well as a basis for a discussion of the law of commercial paper. One reason is that it is basically a restatement, clarification, and modernization of such law, and embodies and retains virtually all of the sound principles of its predecessor, the N.I.L., and of the cases decided before and after the adoption of the N.I.L. Another reason is that in most situations in which the courts were divided under the prior law, the Code ended the division by adopting one view or the other, or a third view. Also, the Code, to a far greater degree than almost any other comprehensive statute, was carefully thought out and anticipated possible problems of interpretation as well as deviations from normal business conduct. Finally, the Code dealt with these problems and deviations directly and expressly rather than leaving them to be decided by the courts in the painful process of litigation.

§ 8. Non-Code Law

Despite the breadth of its title, the Code does not deal with all of the legal aspects of commercial transactions. Similarly, although Article 3 is the primary source of the law governing commercial paper, it does not deal with all aspects of such law. This is emphasized by Section 1–103 which provides:

> Unless displaced by the particular provisions of this Act, the principles of law and equity, including the law merchant and the law relative to capacity to contract, principal and agent, estoppel, fraud, misrepresentation, duress, coercion, mistake, bankruptcy, or other validating or invalidating cause shall supplement its provisions.

As Section 1–103 indicates, the areas of law specifically mentioned therein are not exclusive. As seen earlier, commercial paper is a form of *property* and is governed by most of the principles that govern other forms of property; similarly, commercial paper represents a form of *contract* and is governed by most of the principles that

[*8*]

govern other forms of contract. Occasionally, principles in these areas of the law must be mentioned in discussing the law of commercial paper.

Among the areas of non-Code law that are of major importance in the law of commercial paper is the portion of the common law of contracts that is known as *assignments*. This body of law governs many aspects of commercial paper that are not treated by the Code, especially matters relating to instruments that are not negotiable. For this reason, and others that will be explained, the common law of assignments furnishes a natural starting place for the study of commercial paper and is the subject matter of Chapter 2.

The subject matter of Chapters 3 through 12 are based primarily on the provisions of Article 3 of the Code. Chapter 13, which treats the law governing the relationship between a bank and its checking account customer, is based largely on Part 4 of Article 4.

CHAPTER 2

ASSIGNMENTS

§ 1. Need to Consider Assignments

The law of assignments is the natural starting place for the study of the law of commercial paper for several reasons. First, the transferability of an instrument that is not negotiable normally is governed by the law of assignments. Further, even if an instrument is negotiable (for the requirements of a negotiable instrument, see Chapter 4), there are many situations in which the rights and duties of the parties are governed by the general law of assignments. Most important, as the following brief discussion of the law of assignments will show, this area of the law furnishes a convenient basis for making comparisons and illustrating some of the unique characteristics of the law of negotiability which explain why negotiable commercial paper—our primary concern—plays such an important part in the modern business world.

§ 2. Nature of Assignment

In a broad sense, an assignment is a voluntary transfer of any kind of rights from one person to another. The purpose of most assignments, however, is to transfer a contract right to receive money. Since the creation and transfer of commercial paper, whether negotiable or not, has this same purpose, the following discussion will relate primarily to assignments of this kind.

§ 3. Requirements

In the business world almost all true assignments are contracts and are governed by the same principles that govern other contracts. Although, like other contracts, assignments of the right to receive money normally need not be in writing, in practice they almost always are; and if they are not evidenced by a writing, they are not enforceable, "beyond five thousand dollars in amount or value." [1–206]

§ 4. Terminology and Analysis

Even the simplest contract is a two-sided affair: One party, the *obligee,* has one or more rights and the opposite party, the *obligor,* has one or more duties. If only one party has rights, as where A lends B $100, there is only one obligee, A, and only one obligor, B. If both parties have rights, as is commonly the case, there are two obligees and two obligors.

Generally, the person by whom a right is transferred is the *assignor,* and the person to whom it is transferred is the *assignee.* Assume that A delivers a machine to B and that, in return, B contracts to pay A $100. If A transfers to C the right to receive the $100, A is the assignor and C the assignee. Once the assignment is made, A ceases to be the obligee. C, his assignee, becomes the obligee. B remains the obligor, but as soon as he learns of the assignment, he becomes bound to pay C rather than A—assuming of course that the obligation has matured and that B has no defense against the claim.

In the preceding paragraph the right in a simple contract was transferred by an assignment, which is the only way such a right can be transferred. The rights embodied in a negotiable instrument might be transferred either by assignment or by negotiation. (See pages 90–91). Whether a transfer is made by assignment or by negotiation the person who makes the transfer properly may be called a *transferor* and the person to whom it is made may be called the *transferee*. In other words, a transferor may be an assignor or someone who negotiates a negotiable instrument and a transferee may be either an assignee or a holder to whom a negotiable instrument is negotiated.

§ 5. Assignability of Right to Receive Money

Except when an attempt to assign is ineffective because of public policy, any right is assignable unless it is *personal,* that is, unless requiring performance for some new obligee might materially change the nature of the duty or impose some new risk on the obligor. For example, if A and B enter a contract which binds A to support B during the latter's lifetime, B cannot effectively assign his right under the contract so as to require A to support C, for this might materially change the nature of A's duty.

The right to receive money is never considered personal and is therefore freely assignable. This is usually so, even when the contract which creates the right expressly forbids assignment. [See 2–210(2), 9–318(4)] The law does not consider the nature of a debtor's obligation materially changed by requiring him to pay an assignee rather than the original creditor. Any distaste he may have for such a change is considered outweighed by the commercial advantages of recognizing the assignment. The law is not concerned with the possibility that a claim against a poor widow will pass from a kindhearted creditor to an oppressive one.

§ 6. Rights Acquired by an Assignment

A. GENERAL RULE GOVERNING TRANSFER OF RIGHTS

The general rule governing the transfer of almost all forms of property is that a person can transfer no greater interest than he owns. Thus, if A finds, steals, or borrows B's watch and sells it to C, no property interest will pass to C, and B will be entitled to recover his watch from C even if C proves that he acted in good faith and paid fair value. C's only remedy is to recover from A, either on the basis of fraud or on the basis of the seller's implied warranty that the title conveyed is good and its transfer rightful. [2–312(1)(a)]

B. ASSIGNMENTS FOLLOW GENERAL RULE

It is fundamental that any attempt to transfer rights by assignment follows the general rule, which sometimes is expressed by stating that the assignee steps into the shoes of the assignor.

For example, assume that A, owed $100 by B, gives C a written assignment of the right to receive the money and the assignment is stolen from C. If the thief thereafter attempts to transfer the right to the money by delivering the writing to D, the latter will acquire no right against B even though it is proved that D acted in good faith and paid fair value. The thief acquired no rights by his theft, and under the general rule he could transfer no greater interest than he owned. The result is the same if D purchases a written assignment from a finder rather than from a thief.

In contrast, in an analogous transaction involving a negotiable instrument that is in such form as to be negotiable by delivery alone, a person who lacks title, even a thief or finder, can transfer a

[14]

good title to a *holder in due course* and thus deprive the original owner of his property even though he is free of fault. Later, it will be necessary to consider when an instrument is negotiable by delivery alone (see pages 91–98) and who is a holder in due course. It is sufficient here to realize that many instruments are negotiable by delivery alone and that most persons who purchase negotiable instruments qualify as holders in due course because they purchase *for value, in good faith, and without notice that it is overdue, or has been dishonored, or is subject to any defense or claim.* (See Chapter 10)

The general rule that a person cannot transfer more than he owns also governs assignments in cases wherein the assignor is the original obligee rather than a finder or a thief. For example, assume that A contracts to sell goods to B and assigns to C the right to receive the purchase price. Under the general rule, C acquires no greater rights than A had and is charged with knowing all the terms, conditions, and limitations relating to A's right to receive the purchase price. Consequently, if it appears that A had induced B to enter the contract by fraud or duress, or if any other defense arose from the making or performance of the contract, B can assert it just as effectively against C as he could have asserted it against A.

Here again, there usually is a different result when the law governing negotiable instruments is applied in an analogous case. Assume that A induces B to purchase goods under circumstances which result in a defense and that, in payment, B delivers to A a note or other negotiable instrument. If A thereafter negotiates the instrument to C, a holder in due course, the latter normally is *not* affected by any defense that B has against A. C is entitled to collect from B at maturity merely by proving that he is a holder in due course. B's remedy is to sue A. (The extent to which this result may be modified by special statutes intended to protect *consumers* is discussed at pages 262–271).

Just as an assignee steps into the assignor's shoes and is subject to any defenses that result from the making or performance of the contract, an assignee usually is subject also to any counterclaims or set-offs which the obligor might have asserted against the assignor at the time of the assignment.

> A owes B $10,000. A sells B a machine for $25,-000 on credit. A delivers the machine to B and then assigns C the right to receive the purchase price. C holds the assignment subject to B's right to set off A's $10,000 debt as a counterclaim and partial defense. Consequently, C is entitled to recover only $15,000 from B. (In this case, C usually has rights against A, either on the basis of A's implied warranty that the assigned right is not subject to any defense or counterclaim or on the basis of fraud.) (See assignor's warranties pages 18–21.)

[*16*]

In contrast, one who acquires a negotiable instrument as a holder in due course normally takes it free of any counterclaims that the obligor holds against the transferor.

It should not be assumed that it is never possible to obtain by an assignment substantially the same advantages acquired by purchasing a negotiable instrument. An ordinary obligor may agree with his obligee to give up his right to plead defenses or counterclaims against an assignee [9–206(1)], but he normally does not do so. Such agreements usually are enforceable if the parties are businessmen, but increasingly the states are striking them down on the ground of public policy if the obligor is a *consumer*. In most of the same states, however, even a holder in due course may be deprived of the advantage of being free from defenses and counterclaims when he sues a consumer on a negotiable instrument. (See pages 262–271)

§ 7. Notice of Assignment

As explained above, an assignee normally receives an assignment subject to any defense or counterclaim that the obligor may have against the assignor *at the time* the assignment is made. The assignee is subject also to defenses and counterclaims that arise *after* the assignment is made, if they arise *before* the obligor becomes *aware* of the assignment. To protect himself against the

[*17*]

risk that he may become subject to defenses or counterclaims that arise *after* the assignment is made the assignee must give the obligor prompt notice of the assignment.

> A owes B $5,000. B assigns the right to receive payment to C. While unaware of the assignment, A pays the $5,000 to B. A is not liable to C. To protect himself against the risk that his rights against A might be cut off, C should have notified A of the assignment before A paid B. (Of course, B is liable to C. See assignor's warranties pages 18–21)

In contrast, one who receives a negotiable instrument as a holder in due course is not required to give the obligor notice of the transfer to avoid the risk of being subjected to a defense or counterclaim which might arise after he acquires the instrument. If A holds a negotiable note made by B, and negotiates it to C, a holder in due course, C is entitled to recover from B on the note even though B can prove that before he learned of the transfer he paid the amount due on the note to A or entered into some other transaction giving rise to a defense or counterclaim against A. (For possible statutory protection given to *consumers*, see pages 262–271).

§ 8. Warranties of Assignor

When the assignee cannot obtain full performance from the obligor because of a defense, counterclaim, or any other reason, it becomes important to determine if he has any right to relief against the assignor. Whether or not this right exists depends upon the contract between the assignor and the assignee. Obligations assumed by the assignor usually are called warranties. If a warranty of the obligor is stated in the contract itself, it is said to be express; otherwise it is implied.

In the absence of contract terms or surrounding circumstances showing a different intention, one who for consideration purports to assign a contract right impliedly warrants that:

1. the right actually exists;

2. the right is not subject to any defense or counterclaim;

3. any writing evidencing the right that is delivered to the assignee or shown to him to induce him to accept the assignment is genuine and is what it purports to be;

4. he will do nothing to impair the value of the assignment; and

5. he has no knowledge of any fact that would impair the value of the assignment.

It is important to notice that normally there is no implied warranty that the obligor will perform for the assignee. If the assignor does not expressly warrant that the obligor will perform, it is usually held that no warranty to this effect arises.

> A owes B $10,000. B assigns the right to receive payment to C. At maturity, A flatly refuses to pay C, even though A has no defense or counterclaim. C is entitled to recover from A, but C has no right against B unless B expressly warranted that A would pay.

One who transfers a negotiable instrument for consideration by an *unqualified indorsement*—which is by far the most common type of indorsement, encompassing virtually any indorsement which does not show by the use of the words "without recourse" that it is qualified (see page 156), gives warranties that are roughly equivalent to those given by an assignor. But unlike the assignor's warranties, the warranties of an indorser normally run to successive transferees. Even more important, the unqualified indorser agrees that if, following a proper demand, the person who is expected to pay fails to do so—with or without justification—he, the unqualified indorser, will himself make the payment if he is given due notice of the failure. And this secondary, or backup liability, like his warranty liability, normally runs to the advantage of successive later transferees.

> M makes a negotiable note payable to P. By unqualified indorsements, P negotiates the note to A and A negotiates the note to H. At maturity

H makes due demand for payment upon M. M, without any defense or other justification, refuses to pay. If H duly notifies P and A, he is entitled to recover from either of them on their secondary liability even though neither made any express agreement to this effect.

§ 9. Advantages of Receiving Negotiable Instrument

As seen above, the holder in due course of a negotiable instrument may enjoy certain advantages not available to one who acquires rights by assignment. He may hold a good title although his transferor had none. He normally takes the instrument free of all counterclaims, set-offs, and most other defenses which might have been asserted against his transferor. He is not required to give notice of receipt of the instrument to protect himself against the risk that the obligor will acquire some counterclaim or defense prior to learning of the transfer. He normally is entitled to recover from his transferor if the obligor fails to pay, whether or not the obligor had any justification for his failure.

In addition, there are several rules of procedure which render it easier to recover on a negotiable instrument than on an assignment. Furthermore, a negotiable instrument is in an easily recognized form, and its legal status is subject to far less guesswork on the part of one who receives it than is true of an assignment. Finally, the law governing negotiable instruments—namely, Article 3 of the Code—is clearer and better developed to meet modern needs than the law of assignments which, with respect to some matters, is haphazard, antiquated, and far from uniform. Commercial planning, therefore, is better facilitated by using negotiable instruments than by using simple contracts or other paper that is not negotiable.

One who is aware of these advantages can easily understand why an instrument in negotiable form is readily acceptable in the business community as a commercial medium of exchange, and why anyone would normally prefer to receive an instrument under circumstances in which the laws of negotiability rather than the laws of assignment apply.

CHAPTER 3

FORMS AND USES OF COMMERCIAL PAPER AND TERMINOLOGY

It is helpful in acquiring a sound understanding of the legal principles governing commercial paper to learn to recognize quickly the various forms of such paper and the different capacities in which the names of the parties may appear on it, and to become acquainted with the different uses of each kind of instrument.

§ 1. Forms of Commercial Paper and Parties

A. PROMISSORY NOTE

The most elementary form of commercial paper is the *promissory note*, which usually is referred to simply as a *note*. A note is a written promise other than a certificate of deposit. (See page 29) to pay money signed by the person making the promise, who is called the *maker*. [3–104(2)(d)] In the short form cases that appear throughout this book the maker is usually identified by a capital "M." In banking circles and in some courts the term "maker" commonly refers to the drawer of a check. (See e. g. Wilson Supply Co. v. West Artesia, 505 S.W.2d 312 (Tex.Civ.App. 1974)) But in the Code and other statutes, "maker" refers exclusively to one who issues a note or a certificate of deposit. In this book it will be used only in this latter sense. Like other forms of commercial paper, a note may be made payable to a named person, to his order, or to bearer. If a note or any other form of instrument when first issued is made payable to a named person or to his order, he is called the *payee*. In the short form cases mentioned above the payee usually is identified by a capital "P."

The promissory note is the only kind of commercial paper that undertakes to express the obligation of the party who issues it. As we shall see later, the obligation of the drawer of a check or draft is not so expressly revealed and neither is the obligation of the maker of a certificate of deposit.

A note may take any of a number of different forms, depending on its purpose, the understanding of the parties and other factors. A simple note might take the following form.

$5,000.00   New York, N. Y.   July 1, 1974.

One year after date I promise to pay to the order of Paul Payee five thousand dollars.

Due   July 1, 1975   (Signed)   Michael Maker

The above note is payable at a definite time. A note might instead be payable on demand. (See pages 44, 58) It is common to refer to a note that is payable at a definite time as a *time* note or time instrument and to refer to one that is payable on demand as a *demand* note or demand instrument. If an instrument is payable on demand, the holder normally is entitled to demand payment at any time after it is issued. If a demand instrument is post-dated, however, the holder must wait until the date shown on the instrument arrives.

Usually, a note is prepared on a printed form which originally contained blank spaces for the date of issue, the place, the amount, the name of the payee, and the signature of the maker. If the payee is a bank or other lending institution, the name of the payee is likely to appear on the original printed form. Typically, the form also contains the words "value received" and "with interest at the rate of" and leaves blanks for the interest rate, the due date, the place of payment, the number of the note, a memorandum of the transaction, the address of the maker and for other details. A note might also contain provisions relating to security, payment in instalments, acceleration, renewals, other notes in the same series, and many other matters. Very little of what might be included is necessary for a valid and enforceable note. An instrument that provides, "I will pay John Jones $1,000," may be enforced as a non-negotiable note if it is signed by a maker. (For a wide range of examples of forms that commercial paper might take under Article 3, along with useful commentary, see Uniform Laws Annotated, Uniform Commercial Code, Master Edition, Vol. 4 Forms, Henson & Davenport, West Publishing Company 1968, with Annual Supplement.)

B.   DRAFT

Draft and *bill of exchange* are synonyms. [3–104(2)(a)] However, since the Code uses *draft,* and since *bill of exchange* is rarely used except in international trade, we will use the word *draft.*

A draft is an *order* to pay money. The person issuing the order is the *drawer* and the person to whom the order is addressed is the *drawee.* In the short cases that appear herein, the drawer usually is identified by a capital "R," and the drawee is usually identified by a capital "E." In virtually all drafts, the order to pay is expressed by the word "pay." A draft is basically different from a note because it does not contain a promise. The drawer of a draft does not expressly promise to pay it. Indeed his normal expectation is that he will not have to pay it. He orders the drawee to pay. However, if the drawee does not pay, the drawer, under circumstances that will be discussed later, may be required to pay. Like a note, a draft may be payable to bearer or to some specific person or to his order. Sometimes the drawer names himself as payee, but normally he names a third party. Like a note, a draft may be payable on demand or at a definite future time. (See pages 44, 58)

A simple draft might take the following form.

Miami, Florida   May 1, 1974

One year from date pay to the order of Payee & Company

$20,000.00   Twenty thousand ..... Dollars.

(Signed)   David Drawer
DAVID DRAWER

To: DANIEL DRAWEE
10 Broad Street
Rome, Georgia

Like a note, a draft usually is prepared on a printed form. Although a draft might contain many terms and furnish much information, most drafts are simple in form.

C.   CHECK

By far the most widely used form of commercial paper is the check. Each year the Federal Reserve Banks alone process about ten billion checks that total about five trillion dollars.

A check is a *draft* which is drawn by the drawer on a *bank*, as drawee, and is payable *on demand*.

[3–104(2)(b)] All other forms of commercial paper may be payable either on demand (for example, a demand note) or at some definite future time (for example, a 60-day note). It is interesting to notice that when the drawee of a "traveler's check" is not a bank, as is sometimes the case, it is really not a check. Although a check is one kind of draft, it is common to refer to a draft that is drawn on a bank and is payable on demand as a "check"; and it is common to refer to any other draft simply as a "draft", although occasionally in the interest of precision, it is called an "ordinary draft" or a "non-check draft." When the word "draft" is used without qualification in the statement of legal principles, however, the term includes checks as well as other kinds of drafts unless the context indicates otherwise.

Below is a simple form of check.

September 15, 1974

Pay to the order of Paul Payee $1,000.00

One Thousand .... Dollars

ALLINE BANK   DRAWER CORP.
Alline, Ohio   By (Signed) Daniel Drawer,
                            Treasurer

To facilitate passage through banking channels, however, most checks contain also, in the upper right hand corner a hyphenated number over another number. Most checks contain, in addition in the lower lefthand corner, a combination of numbers and symbols which are required by the Magnetic Ink Character Recognition check collection system pursuant to which checks are passed through a computer which sorts the checks and charges each check to its proper account. Farnsworth, Commercial Paper 185 (1968). In addition, for the convenience of the depositor, most checks that are furnished by banks contain the customer's name and address printed on the face, a space for the number assigned to the check by the customer, and a space for recording the reason for issuing the check. In contrast with notes, the vast majority of checks show little variation with respect to the provisions that affect the rights and duties of the parties.

D. CERTIFICATE OF DEPOSIT

A certificate of deposit, often referred to as a "CD," is the acknowledgement by a *bank* of a receipt of money and an express or implied promise to repay it. [3–104(2)(c)] Thus, it resembles an ordinary note in that the party who issues it promises to pay; and it resembles a check in that the person who is expected to pay is always a bank. The bank that issues a certificate of deposit may properly be referred to as the "maker."

[29]

A certificate of deposit may take any one of a number of forms. The following is typical.

NEGOTIABLE TIME CERTIFICATE OF DEPOSIT

FIRST CITY BANK OF ARIZONA

No. 5693   Tucson, Arizona   June 1, 1974

THIS CERTIFIES THAT THERE HAS BEEN DEPOSITED with the undersigned the sum of $200,000.00
Two hundred thousand .... Dollars Payable to the order of PAYEE DEPOSI-TOR CORPORATION on December 1, 1976 with interest only to maturity at the rate of TEN per cent (10%) per annum upon surrender of this certificate properly indorsed.

FIRST CITY BANK OF ARIZONA
By (Signature) Dirk Duer, Vice-President
Authorized Signature

---

§ 2.   Uses of Commercial Paper

A.   PROMISSORY NOTES

A promissory note may be used for many different purposes, but generally these purposes fall into one of the following categories: (1) a means of borrowing money, (2) a means of buying on credit, or (3) a method of evidencing a pre-existing debt.

1. MEANS OF BORROWING MONEY

The first purpose mentioned is probably the most obvious. For example, assume that a businessman borrows $50,000 from a bank to help finance the purchase of raw materials. As evidence of the loan, he is required to sign and deliver to the bank a negotiable note in which he promises to pay to the order of the bank six months after date the sum of $50,000.

The bank computes the amount of interest on $50,000 for six months at the agreed rate, deducts this amount from the $50,000 and places the balance as a credit in the maker's checking account. The bank may hold this note until it is paid, or rediscount it at another bank where a lower rate of interest is charged, thus obtaining cash or credit and netting a profit for the difference between the two rates of discount.

In order to induce a second bank to rediscount the note, the payee bank will have to *indorse* (*or endorse*) it, so as to assume secondary liability. (The indorser's secondary liability is discussed on pages 153–156) Normally, one indorses an instrument by signing one's name on the back of it. By indorsing, the payee bank becomes an *indorser*. The bank to whom the note is transferred is the *indorsee*. While the payee bank is in possession of the note as payee, it is the *holder*. (In the short cases that appear in this book, the holder usually is identified by capital "H.") After the instrument is duly indorsed and delivered, the transferee bank becomes the new holder. (The precise meaning of "holder" is discussed on pages 94–95.)

Very often the lender insists, before making a loan, that a note be signed by someone other than the maker. If the additional party signs along with the borrower he is co-maker. More frequently, he is merely required to indorse the instrument on the back. In either case he is called an *accommodation* party if he did not receive the consideration for the instrument. The borrower, who received the money, is the *accommodated* party. (Accommodation parties are discussed on pages 158–162) When a small or newly formed corporation wishes to borrow money, the lender usually insists that one or more of the maker's principal stockholders or officers sign as accommodation maker or indorser.

One form of note commonly used for borrowing money is the collateral note, which enables the borrower to offer as security for the repayment of the loan, not only his personal credit in the form of a negotiable note, but also some other negotiable or quasi-negotiable instrument or instruments, such as stocks, bonds, bills of lading, or warehouse receipts. (For the Code treatment of secured transactions, see Articles 9 and 11.) If the borrower's note is payable at a specified future time, as it usually is, the bank may discount it in advance or charge interest when it becomes due. An enormous amount of money is loaned on the basis of collateral notes. In some states it is common to use a note to evidence a loan made to purchase land. Such a note usually is secured by a real estate mortgage.

2. MEANS OF BUYING ON CREDIT

In a common transaction, a merchant sells goods, and in payment, receives the buyer's thirty-day note naming the seller as payee. The note is definite evidence of the debt and is more satisfactory to the seller than having merely a charge on his books against the buyer. Also, the seller may indorse the note to some other firm in payment of goods he has purchased or he can raise money on the note at his bank. When the seller indorses, he normally binds himself to pay if the buyer does not. Sometimes a note passes through a number of hands before maturity, gaining credit by virtue of the secondary liability assumed by each indorser. At present, a vast amount of credit is extended to consumers of goods and services on the basis of notes, particularly installment notes which often are secured by liens on the goods purchased.

3.   MEANS OF EVIDENCING PREVIOUSLY EXISTING DEBT

Very often a debtor who is short of funds can obtain temporary relief by giving his creditor a promissory note payable at a later time.   From the creditor's point of view this is often more satisfactory than bringing suit to collect because he can maintain the good will of his debtor, who is often a customer, and secure undisputable evidence of the debt.   The creditor may use the note, in turn, to pay his own debts, to sell, or to deliver as security to bolster his own credit with his bank.

B.   DRAFT

Ordinary or non-check drafts, usually referred to simply as "drafts," are used extensively in business for a variety of purposes, most commonly to collect accounts, finance the movement of goods, and transfer funds.

1.   MEANS OF COLLECTING ACCOUNTS

Although the effectiveness of a draft as a means of collecting accounts is sometimes questioned, it is often used for this purpose.   Suppose a creditor in Nebraska has sold goods to a debtor in Florida and is having difficulty in collecting.   After trying other means to persuade the debtor to pay, the creditor may decide to draw a time draft on the debtor, thereby definitely putting it up to him to agree to pay by a certain time. The draft may be payable at a fixed future date or a stated time after demand or sight. The creditor (drawer) will name his bank in Nebraska as payee and will deliver the draft to this bank for collection. The creditor's bank will then forward the draft to its correspondent bank in Florida. The Florida bank will then present the draft to the debtor (drawee) and request his acceptance. "Acceptance is the drawee's signed engagement to honor the draft as presented." [3–410(1)] (See page 149) In other words, the debtor (drawee) can accept by merely signing the draft. The debtor is, of course, not obligated to accept the draft because the owing of a debt imposes no duty to assume a new form of contract for its payment. If he values his business reputation, however, he may not wish to go on record as being unwilling to pay his debts. If he chooses to accede to the demand made, he usually will write across the face of the draft, "Accepted," sign his name, and possibly indicate the date and the bank at which it is payable. (See pages 149–150) The debtor thereby becomes an *acceptor* and the draft may be referred to as an *acceptance*. Depending upon its instructions, the correspondent bank either returns the accepted draft to the forwarding bank or holds it for collection. In the latter event, it presents the draft for payment at maturity. If paid, it remits to the forwarding bank which credits the credi-

tor's account. (For further discussion of the
part played by banks in the collection process see
pages 117–125. See also Article 4 of the Code.)
If the debtor accepts the draft but refuses to pay
when it falls due, the creditor at least possesses
evidence of the debt and has the procedural
advantages that attend the holder of a negotiable
instrument. If the debtor refuses to accept the
draft, the creditor is no worse off than he was
originally, since he can still sue on the original
debt.

2. MEANS OF FINANCING THE MOVEMENT OF GOODS

Businessmen who ship goods constantly face the
problem of obtaining payment of the purchase
price as promptly as possible. One of the most
common and at the same time, one of the most
satisfactory, methods of financing the shipment of
goods involves the use of a draft.

Assume that a merchant in Wilmington is selling goods to a merchant in Cleveland. The shipment is large and the seller is not entirely satisfied with the buyer's credit rating; or perhaps
the seller must keep his funds liquid by quick collections. He therefore contracts for payment by
having the buyer honor a demand draft for the
price plus charges, upon delivery of a bill of lading
for the goods. Accordingly, when he ships the
goods, he obtains from the railroad a negotiable

bill of lading representing the goods. He then draws a sight, or demand, draft for the price plus charges, naming the buyer as drawee. He delivers the draft, with the bill of lading attached, to his own bank, which he names as payee in the draft, and directs that the draft with the bill of lading attached be forwarded to the Cleveland correspondent bank for presentment to the buyer (drawee). The seller's bank complies. When the Cleveland bank receives the draft and bill of lading, it notifies the buyer. If he wishes to obtain the goods, he pays the draft and the correspondent bank surrenders the bill of lading to him. The bill of lading entitles him to require the railroad to deliver the goods to him. Meanwhile the Cleveland correspondent remits the proceeds, less its charges, to the forwarding bank which credits the seller. When papers such as a bill of lading are attached to a draft which is forwarded to the drawee, as in the above case, the draft commonly is called a *documentary* draft. (For a fuller treatment of documentary drafts, see Sections 4–501–504 of the Code.) When no papers accompany the draft, it is called a *clean* draft.

A common procedure for financing the movement of goods if the seller does not consider immediate payment essential is the *trade acceptance*, which arises when a purchaser of goods agrees to pay at a *future* time by accepting a *time* draft drawn on him by the seller. The procedure is the

[*37*]

same as when a sight draft is used, except that the buyer need not make payment before he receives the bill of lading, but he must bind himself to pay at a later time by writing his acceptance on the draft. When a trade acceptance is returned to the seller, he may hold it until maturity or indorse it and discount it at his bank, thereby obtaining ready cash for the sale. Such paper is highly regarded by banks because it has behind it the credit of the acceptor *and* the drawer.

Still another form of draft used to finance the shipment of goods is the *banker's acceptance,* which is simply a draft that has been accepted by a bank. For example, a buyer in Austin, Texas, wishes to buy goods from a merchant in Baltimore, Maryland. The buyer's credit may not be good enough to enable him to buy goods on credit outside of Austin, but his credit is good at First Bank of Austin, which agrees to finance him. The seller is willing to sell upon the well-known credit of First Bank. Accordingly he ships the goods and draws a time draft for the amount of the shipment on First Bank. He forwards the draft, with the bill of lading attached, to First Bank, which writes its acceptance across the face and returns the draft to the seller. This draft is readily salable because of the high standing of the acceptor. Meanwhile, the buyer has agreed to provide First Bank with funds to pay the draft when it falls due and First Bank has given him the bill of lading entitling him to possession of the goods. In some cases First Bank will insist on receiving some form of security from the buyer.

It will be noted that the bank acceptance accomplishes the following useful purposes: It enables sellers to make sales which they otherwise would be unwilling to make; it secures payment in a highly desirable negotiable form; it enables buyers to buy in places where their credit is unknown; and like other forms of drafts, it serves as a means of transferring funds.

C. CHECK

Serving primarily as means of payment and as vehicles for the transfer of money, checks make possible an enormous amoun⁺ of business activity with a minimum amount of currency. Occasionally, a postdated check is used as a short term credit device. A check also furnishes a receipt, aids in keeping records, serves as evidence, reduces the risk of loss, destruction and theft of currency, and in other ways serves as a great commercial convenience.

Normally the issuance of a check is preceded by a contract between the bank and the drawer under which the latter makes a deposit and the bank agrees to honor his order for making payments in such amounts as he sees fit, up to the amount of deposits. (Some special problems that arise from the relationship between the bank and its checking account depositor are discussed in Chapter 13.)

A seller or other creditor who is unwilling to take his debtor's check is entitled to insist on payment in legal tender. Such a creditor, however, may be willing to take instead a demand draft naming him as payee and drawn by the debtor's bank on the creditor's bank. If so, the debtor purchases such a draft from his bank and remits it to the creditor who obtains payment from the drawee bank which charges the drawer bank. An instrument of this kind, by which one bank draws on another, usually is referred to as a "bank draft;" but it is also a check because it is drawn on a bank and is payable on demand. (Bank drafts are used also in the process of collecting checks deposited by bank customers, in which case they are called "remittance drafts.") The demands of a creditor who is unwilling to take his debtor's check might also be met by the debtor's purchasing from his bank, and sending to his creditor, a cashier's check, or official check, by which the debtor's bank draws on itself. Sometimes a creditor who is otherwise unwilling to take his debtor's check will take it if it has been certified by the drawee bank which becomes liable as *acceptor* of the check. (See pages 149–150.)

D. CERTIFICATE OF DEPOSIT

A firm having a temporary excess of cash may wish to invest it on a short term basis in some liquid form. An individual faced with this problem would be likely to deposit his funds in a savings account, but by law a corporation is not permitted to draw interest on savings accounts, nor on demand deposits in commercial banks. The corporation's needs may be conveniently satisfied, however, by a time certificate of deposit. Since it carries the primary obligation of a bank and bears a stated rate of interest, it is a sound investment and may serve as an effective means of making payment, as a convenient form of security, or as an asset which can be quickly liquidated if necessary.

During recent years, time certificates of deposit, usually for one or two years, have been used increasingly as a device for encouraging individuals to deposit funds in commercial banks. In return for the depositor giving up his right to withdraw his funds on short notice, the bank is willing to pay a higher rate of interest than it pays on its ordinary savings accounts.

The foregoing is, of course, only a brief and summary description of the forms and uses of commercial paper. There are many other less common uses. In fact, attorneys, bankers and other business people are constantly challenged to

[41]

devise new ways to have commercial paper serve the needs of business.

This chapter has considered the special characteristics and uses of each of the various forms of commercial paper and, in doing so, has emphasized the differences among them. Therefore it seems appropriate to emphasize, before proceeding further, that most of the principles in the law of commercial paper apply equally to notes, ordinary drafts, checks, and certificates of deposit. In the discussion that follows, when this is not so, it will be clear from the context.

Although most of the instruments set forth above happen to be negotiable, the general descriptions that have been given apply to notes, drafts, checks, and certificates of deposit whether they are negotiable or not. Also, the instruments that are not negotiable may serve the same general purposes as those that are, but usually not as well. The special requirements that must be satisfied in order to render an instrument negotiable will be discussed in Chapter 4, which follows.

CHAPTER 4

REQUISITES OF NEGOTIABILITY

To be a negotiable instrument under Article 3 of the Code, an instrument must possess certain requisites, and if *one* requisite is missing, it is not negotiable. It may still be a valid contract and as such assignable from person to person; but with few exceptions, it is subject to all the disabilities of assignment which were discussed in Chapter 2. On the other hand, if the instrument possesses all the requisites of negotiability, it becomes transferable by the process of negotiation and is attended by many important legal consequences, some of which have been mentioned.

§ 1. Requisites of Negotiability under Article 3

The commercial purposes of the merchants who first used commercial paper required clear, concise expression, which could be quickly recognized and easily understood by commercial people and which would facilitate the transfer of such paper in the course of trade. In the contemporary world the need for concise language in promissory notes, checks, and drafts is increased greatly because of the velocity of their circulation.

These basic needs of commerce are recognized by the Code just as they were recognized by common law and under the N.I.L. Section 3–104(1) of the Code states the requisites of negotiability as follows:

> Any writing to be a negotiable instrument within this Article must
>
> (a) be signed by the maker or drawer; and
>
> (b) contain an unconditional promise or order to pay a sum certain in money and no other promise, order, obligation or power given by the maker or drawer except as authorized by this Article; and
>
> (c) be payable on demand or at a definite time; and
>
> (d) be payable to order or to bearer.

Assuming that a writing is signed by a maker or drawer, the answer to the question whether it satisfies the requirements of Section 3–104(1) so as to be a negotiable instrument is always to be determined by what appears on the face of the instrument alone. [Comment 5, 3–119] A separate agreement, oral or written, never affects the negotiability of an instrument. [3–119(2)] With Section 3–104(1) in mind and the instrument in hand, it usually is possible to determine immediately whether an instrument is negotiable. Since many consequences hinge upon negotiability, this Section is the logical starting place when considering many of the problems which arise in the law of commercial paper, and therefore should be studied carefully. As the following discussion will show, however, there always will be some instruments which cannot be categorized as negotiable or not negotiable solely on the basis of the broad language of this Section.

Upon close examination, it appears that there are in fact nine basic requisites which must be satisfied if an instrument is to qualify as being negotiable under Section 3–104(1). They will be discussed below separately.

A. MUST BE IN WRITING

The need for a writing rarely presents any problem. Although commercial paper usually is executed on printed forms drafted by lawyers with the requisites of negotiability in mind, the requirement of a writing may be satisfied also by engraving, stamping, lithographing, photographing, typing, longhand writing in pencil or ink, any similar process, or any combination of these.

B. MUST BE SIGNED BY MAKER OR DRAWER

This requirement is equally easy to satisfy. Normally it is met by a person's writing his name in longhand in ink. It also may be satisfied by adopting any symbol affixed to the instrument by hand, machine or in any other manner, if it is done with the present intention of authenticating the instrument. [1–201(39)] The symbol may consist of a name, initials, trade name, assumed name, mark, or even a thumb print. [3–401 and Comment 2] Although there is no clear limit to the ways in which a signature may be affixed, anyone considering receiving an instrument which has been signed in some unusual way should remember that whenever a signature is denied the burden of proving the signature is on the person who claims under it. [3–307(1)(a)] Also, an unusual signature may decrease the marketability of an instrument by raising questions and suggesting uncertainty.

C. MUST CONTAIN A PROMISE OR ORDER

To be negotiable, a note or certificate of deposit must contain a *promise* to pay, whereas a draft or check must contain an *order* to pay.

1. PROMISE

Notes usually contain an *express promise* such as "I promise to pay," but any language of similar meaning is sufficient. Mere acknowledgment of a debt, however, is not adequate. [3–102(1)(c)] Accordingly such statements as "I.O.U. $100" and "Borrowed $100" have been held not to be promises. But it has been held that if such words as "to be paid on demand" or "due on demand" are added, the need for a promise is satisfied. The fact that such cases have reached the courts, however, is good reason for avoiding doubtful language. A *certificate of deposit* is different; here the requirement of a promise is satisfied by the fact that the bank's acknowledgment of the deposit and the other terms of the instrument clearly *imply* a promise to pay.

2. ORDER

An order is a direction to pay. [3–102(1)(b)] The usual way of expressing the order is to use the imperative form of the verb "pay." "Pay bearer" is clearly an order. The mandatory character of the order is not altered by the fact that it is couched in courteous form such as "please pay" or "kindly pay." However, there must be more than an authorization or request. [3–102 (1)(b)] Such uncertain language as "I wish you would pay" would not qualify as an order. The commercial world wants no uncertainty about the right to be paid. Moreover, to operate as an effective order, the direction to pay must identify with reasonable certainty the person who is ordered to pay. [3–102(1)(b)] (The person ordered to pay is the *drawee*.) In an ordinary draft, this requirement is usually satisfied by inserting the drawee's name immediately following the word "To" on the printed form. In the case of an ordinary check it is satisfied by having the drawee bank's name printed on the face of the check.

a. Drawer Named as Drawee

Occasionally, the drawer orders himself to pay; that is, the drawer and drawee are the same person. Typically this happens when an agent in one department or branch of a corporation draws on the corporation and addresses the order to another department or branch. For example, an adjuster acting for a claims department of a corporation may pay a claim by issuing a draft naming the corporation as drawee and addressing it to the treasurer's office. When the drawer and drawee are the same person, the instrument is effective as a promissory note. [3–118(a)] Consequently, the drawer's liability is the same as normally is imposed on the maker of a note rather than that normally imposed on a drawer. This means that there is no need for presentment, dishonor and notice of dishonor which normally are required to charge the drawer as explained in Chapter 8.

b. Multiple Drawees

Although an order must identify the drawee with reasonable certainty, it may be addressed to more than one drawee, either *jointly* (To A *and* B) or in the *alternative* (To A *or* B). [3–102(1) (b)] In either case the holder is required to present the draft only once. If the instrument is not paid or accepted as drawn when it is presented to any one of the drawees named, it is dishonored, and the holder may proceed immediately against the drawer without presenting it to the remaining drawees. [3–504(3)(a) and Comment 3] This enables a large corporation to issue a negotiable dividend check naming a number of independent drawees in the alternative in different parts of the country. This is a convenience to the stockholder who can present the check to any drawee, and if that drawee dishonors it, he can proceed immediately against the drawer. Naming drawees in *succession* (To A, and if A fails to pay, to B) prevents negotiability because in this case a holder has no right to proceed against the drawer until the draft has been dishonored by all drawees. [3–102(1)(b) and Comment 3]

D. PROMISE OR ORDER MUST BE UNCONDITIONAL

Two major functions of commercial paper are to serve as currency and to serve as a suitable basis for credit. If commercial paper is to perform either function effectively, businessmen must be assured that there are no strings attached to payment. Therefore, an instrument is not negotiable unless it contains an unconditional promise or order. [3–104(1)(b)] That is, the obligation must be expressed in terms which are absolute and not subject to contingencies, provisos, qualifications, or reservations which may impair the obligation to pay. It must be a "courier without luggage." (Overton v. Tyler, 3 Pa. 346, at 347 (1846))

1. TERMS OF INSTRUMENT DETERMINE PRESENCE OF CONDITION

As far as negotiability is concerned, determining if a promise or order is conditional *requires an examination of the instrument itself and nothing else*. No matter what anyone has said about the instrument, for the purpose of determining negotiability the promise or order it contains is unconditional unless something in the instrument itself expresses the contrary. For example, assume that M hands P a note which provides, "I promise to pay $1000 to the order of P on demand. (Signed) M," and while doing so, M says, "This money will not be paid unless a bond is delivered to me." The note is negotiable because *the promise contained in the note itself* is unconditional and all other requirements are satisfied. (See pages 85–89, for the effect of the extrinsic condition.) In contrast, if the note *itself* provides that payment is to be made only if the bond is delivered, the note is not negotiable.

2. EFFECT OF ANOTHER WRITING

Negotiable instruments are rarely issued in isolation. Usually they are issued pursuant to or as part of some underlying agreement between the parties. For example, a check may be delivered to carry out the terms of a sales contract executed some time earlier, or a note may be issued according to the terms of a loan agreement which provides for other notes as well as for security.

When determining the respective rights and duties of the *original* parties to transactions of this kind, the Code follows the common law rule that writings executed as part of the same transaction are to be read together as a single agreement. Negotiability, however, is concerned primarily with the rights of those who are not parties to the original transaction. Consequently, *regardless of what any outside writing may provide, it does not destroy the negotiability of an instrument which otherwise satisfies the requirements of negotiability.* [3–119(2)] When the instrument itself makes express reference to an outside agreement or document, however, the effect on negotiability may vary considerably from case to case depending upon the *nature of the reference.*

3. IMPLIED CONDITIONS NOT RECOGNIZED

In treating such references, the Code strongly favors negotiability by providing that a promise or order which is otherwise unconditional is not rendered conditional by the fact that the instrument is subject to implied or constructive conditions. [3–105(1)(a)] The Code thus rejects the theory that a recital in an instrument disclosing that it is given for an executory promise creates an implied condition that the instrument is not to be paid unless the promise is performed and so destroys negotiability. Commercial paper often refers to contractual arrangements still to be performed. Usually such recitals are intended as statements of consideration without implications of any kind. If the maker or drawer intends to condition his liability, the Code requires him to do more than leave it to inference. Thus, if an instrument otherwise negotiable provides that it is given as payment in accordance with or "as per" some collateral contract, the possible inference that payment is conditioned on performance of the other contract is not permitted to destroy negotiability. [3–105(1)(b)] Rather it is treated merely as a recital of the origin of the instrument or as an informational reference to another contract. In like vein, a statement in a draft that it is drawn under a letter of credit does not state a condition but merely identifies the occasion for the issuance of the instrument. [3–105(1)(d)] Also, the statement in an instrument that it is secured by a mortgage or other security device does not render it conditional. [3–105(1)(e)] The existence of the security, rather than detracting from the obligation, fortifies it.

4. "SUBJECT TO" OR SIMILAR WORDS NEGATE NEGOTIABILITY

If the instrument expressly states that it is "subject to" or "governed by" any other agreement, or contains any other words which, fairly construed, convey the same meaning, the promise or order is conditional and negotiability is destroyed. [3–105(2)(a) and Comment 8] Here the limitation appears in the instrument itself and no inference is necessary. The fact that the terms of payment cannot be determined by looking at the instrument itself, that it is necessary to look to an outside agreement, is contrary to the concept of negotiability. This is so even though it appears by hindsight that the outside document, to which the instrument is expressly made subject, contains no conditions or other provisions that are contrary to the requirements of negotiability. United States v. Farrington, 172 F.Supp. 797 (D.C. Mass.1959)

If, however, the instrument unconditionally provides terms of payment to which the holder is entitled, the promise or order is not prevented from being unconditional by the fact that it also declares that a right of *prepayment* or *acceleration* is provided in a separate writing. [3–105(1)(c)] In this case the reference can only speed up the right to payment provided in the instrument and cannot provide any impediment to the right. In substance, the reference operates much like an acceleration clause which, as will be explained, does not destroy negotiability by rendering the instrument indefinite as to time.

5. REFERENCE TO ACCOUNT OR FUND

The fact that an instrument indicates a particular account to be debited or any fund or source from which reimbursement is *expected* does not render a promise or order conditional. [3–105 (1)(f)] For example, the drawer of a bill may direct the drawee to pay the money to the order of the payee and "charge the same to the account of the drawer" or to the "merchandise account" or the like. Such directions are for accounting purposes, and the drawer's obligation is in no way contingent upon a credit balance in the account.

It is the general rule, however, that a promise or order is conditional if the instrument states that payment is to be made *only* out of a particular fund or source. [3–105(2)(b)] In that case, the obligation to pay is necessarily contingent upon the sufficiency of the fund. To be unconditional an order or promise must carry the *general credit* of the maker or drawer.

The Code recognizes two exceptions to the rule that a promise or order to pay only out of a particular fund destroys negotiability. The first is recognized if an instrument is issued by a government agency or unit. [3–105(1)(g)] Govern-

[54]

ment agencies often find it necessary to issue commercial paper which provides for payment only out of special assessments of the property benefited. By rendering such instruments negotiable, it is possible to avoid disappointing purchasers who normally consider such paper to be negotiable. The second exception is recognized if an instrument is issued by a partnership, unincorporated association, trust, or other estate, and provides that payment is to be made only out of the assets of the issuing party. [3–105(1)(h)] So far as negotiability is concerned such entities are treated as if they were corporations. It should be recognized, however, that this exception relates only to negotiability. It does not change any state law which declares void any provision limiting the liability of a partner, association member, trustee, or estate representative. [Comment 7, 3–105]

E. MUST SPECIFY A SUM CERTAIN

As a general rule, the term *sum certain* means a sum which the holder himself can determine from the instrument itself by any necessary computation at the time the instrument is payable, without reference to any outside source.

For example, an instrument which contains a promise to pay a stated sum on demand with interest at six per cent provides for a sum certain because, even though the amount to be paid is not known when the note is issued, it can be computed readily by the holder by examining the instrument when a demand for payment is made. [3–106(1)(a)] Similarly, the sum payable is certain if it is subject to a fixed discount or increase if paid before or after the date provided for payment. [3–106(1)(c)] Also, the sum is certain even though it is to be paid with different stated rates of interest before and after default or on a specified date. [3–106(1)(b)] And the fact that an instrument makes no reference to interest does not make the sum uncertain since such an instrument simply draws no interest. Nor is the sum rendered uncertain by the fact that the instrument provides for payment "with interest," without mentioning the rate, for in that case the rate is the same as the judgment rate which is declared by law. [3–118(d)] It seems to be assumed that everyone knows this rate. The sum is not certain, however, if the instrument is payable with interest "at the *current* rate" because the current rate of interest cannot be determined from the instrument itself without reference to an outside source. [Comment 1, 3–106]

Commercial needs sometimes require some relaxation of the rule that a *sum certain* is a sum which the holder can determine from the instrument itself with any necessary computation at the time the instrument is payable. For example, promissory notes often provide for collection charges to make certain the holder will receive his principal sum without impairment due to collection costs. The Code states that if an instrument provides for payment with costs of collection or an attorney's fee or both on default, the sum payable is a sum certain. [3–106(1)(e)] If the cost or rate is not stated, it usually is supplied by local law or custom. Where the instrument itself expressly provides the amount of the attorney's fee, the amount must be reasonable or the provision will be held to be a penalty and void because it is against public policy. The Code relaxes the general rule also by providing that negotiability is not destroyed by making the instrument payable with, or less, *exchange* at the *current* rate [3–106 (1)(d)], "exchange" being the difference between the values of the two currencies which is determined by supply and demand and fluctuates from day to day so that it can be known only by looking beyond the instrument.

F. MUST BE PAYABLE IN MONEY

An instrument is payable in money if it is stated as payable in a medium of exchange authorized or adopted by a domestic or foreign government as part of its official currency at the time the instrument is issued. [1–201(24); 3–107(1); and Comment 1, 3–107] The Code rejects the view of some early cases that money is limited to legal tender which an obligee is required to accept in discharge of his obligation. [Comment 1, 3–107]

It also rejects the contention that a commodity used as money, such as gold dust or beaver pelts, is money. [Comment 1, 3–107] An instrument which is payable in "currency" or "current funds," however, is payable in money. [3–107(1)] If an instrument is payable in sterling, francs, lira, or other recognized currency of a foreign government, it satisfies the requirement of money even though it is payable in the United States. [Comment 1, 3–107] However, such an instrument normally may be satisfied by the payment of dollars at the appropriate rate.

G. MUST BE PAYABLE ON DEMAND OR AT A DEFINITE TIME

The basis for this requirement is that the time of payment of commercial paper is important for all parties concerned and uncertainty in this matter is commercially objectionable.

1. PAYABLE ON DEMAND

An instrument is payable on demand if it contains a promise or order to pay "on demand," "at sight," or "on presentation," or *if no time for payment is stated*. [3–108] Most instruments that are payable on demand, including virtually all checks, are so payable because they make no express provision for the time of payment.

2. PAYABLE AT A DEFINITE TIME

An instrument is payable at a definite time if by its terms it is payable on or before a stated date or at a fixed period after a stated date. [3–109(1)(a)] For example, an instrument would be payable at a definite time if it were payable "on July 1, 1975," "thirty days after date" (assuming, of course, the instrument is dated), or "on or before March 1, 1975." Although "on or before" may suggest indefiniteness, there is no reason to deny such instruments negotiability because there is no more uncertainty involved in such an instrument than in an instrument which is payable on demand. [Comment 4, 3–109] Similarly, an instrument payable at a fixed period after sight is payable at a definite time. [3–109 (1)(b)] The holder controls the matter and may, by presenting it for acceptance, have maturity promptly determined.

3. ACCELERATION CLAUSES

If the time provided for payment is otherwise definite, the fact that the instrument provides that the time of payment is subject to *acceleration* does not render the time indefinite. [3–109(1) (c)] This is so whether the acceleration is at the option of one of the parties or is automatic upon the occurrence of some event. [Comment 4, 3–109]

4. EXTENSION CLAUSES

Also, an instrument is payable at a definite time if, by its terms, it is payable at a definite time subject to (1) extension at the option of the *holder*, or (2) extension to a further definite time at the option of the *maker or acceptor*, or (3) extension to a further definite time automatically upon or after a specified act or event. [3–109 (1) (d)]

As indicated above, where the extension is at the option of the *holder*, the time is definite even though no time limit is stated for the extension. Unless otherwise specified, however, a consent to an extension authorizes a single extension for not longer than the original time period. [3–118(f)] Furthermore, a holder may not exercise his option to extend the time over the objection of the maker or acceptor or other party who duly tenders full payment when the instrument is due. [3–118(f)] This prevents a holder from refusing payment or keeping interest running against the wishes of a maker or acceptor or another party even though the instrument expressly states that the holder has the option to extend the time for payment. [Comment 7, 3–118]

A provision allowing the *maker* or *acceptor* to extend for a further definite period does not interfere with negotiability because it is as if the instrument were payable at the ultimate date with the possibility of acceleration. [Comment 5, 3–109] If it is expressly provided that there is no limit on the time the maker or acceptor may extend, however, the instrument is payable neither on demand nor at a definite time and so is not negotiable. But if the instrument provides simply that the maker or acceptor has a right to extend the time of payment without stating a time, the time is definite because, unless otherwise specified, consent to an extension authorizes a single extension for not longer than the original period. [3–118(f)]

5. EVENT CERTAIN TO HAPPEN

Before the Code, an instrument payable at the death of a named individual was payable at a definite time. Notes so payable are often issued by persons who anticipate their inheritances. Such notes are not commercially important. The Code renders these and similar instruments not negotiable by providing that an "instrument which by its terms is otherwise payable *only* upon an act or event uncertain as to time of occurrence is not payable at a definite time even though the act or event has occurred." [3–109(2)] (Emphasis added.) This change eliminates one inroad into the concept of definiteness. Nonetheless it is still possible to accomplish the usual purpose of such instruments without destroying negotiability by specifying a date in the distant future when the instrument is payable and then adding that the time of payment will be accelerated by death.

H. MUST BE PAYABLE TO ORDER OR TO BEARER

To be negotiable an instrument must be payable *to order* or *to bearer*. [3–104(1)(d)] Words which satisfy this requirement are called *words of negotiability*. The phrases "to order" and "to bearer" are the most common earmarks of negotiability and they most clearly indicate the intention of the maker or drawer to issue an instrument which is negotiable and subject to all the incidents which attach to this form of contract. They are not the only words that can satisfy the requirement, but for other words to be sufficient, they must be clear or recognized equivalents to these phrases. [Comment 5, 3–104] (For the legal significance of the fact that an instrument is payable to order rather than to bearer, see Chapter 6.)

1. PAYABLE TO ORDER

The Code provides that "an instrument is payable to order when by its terms it is payable to the order or assigns of any person therein specified with reasonable certainty, or to him or his order, or when it is conspicuously designated on its face as 'exchange' or the like and names a payee." [3–110(1)] The usual expressions are "to the order of X" or "to X or his order."

The phrase "or assigns" seems merely to be tolerated as an intended equivalent of "or order." The reason an instrument conspicuously designated "exchange" and naming a payee is recognized as being payable to order is that it is so recognized by the Geneva Convention on international usage and is likely to be so understood by businessmen using such instruments. New York Law Revision Commission Report Legislative Document No. 65D (1955) 51.

An instrument may be made payable to the order of anyone, including the maker, drawer, or drawee. [3–110(1)(a)(b)] An instrument may be made payable to the order of two or more persons together as "A, B, *and* C," or in the alternative as "A, B, *or* C." [3–110(1)(d)] Multiple *payees* should not be confused with multiple *drawees*. (For a discussion of multiple drawees see pages 48–49. For further discussion of multiple payees see pages 110–111.)

The Code provides that an instrument may be made payable to the order of an estate, trust, or fund, without regard to whether or not it is a legal entity. [3–110(1)(e)] Such instruments are held to be payable to the estate representative. He, of course, must account to the estate. Similarly, it may be made payable to the order of a partnership or unincorporated association, for example, "Local 10, United Plumbers." In this case it may be indorsed or transferred by any duly authorized person. [3–110(1)(g)] Also, an instrument may be payable to the order of an office or officer by his title as such, for example, the County Treasurer. If so, it is payable to the principal, but the incumbent of the office or his successor may act as if he were the holder. [3–110(1)(f)]

2. PAYABLE TO BEARER

An instrument is payable to bearer when by its terms it is payable "to bearer," "to the order of bearer," to a specified person "or bearer," "to cash," "to the order of cash," or to any other designation which does not purport to refer to a specific payee. [3–111] Perhaps the most common of these is "to bearer." "To the order of bearer" or "to the order of cash" or similar language is usually the result of inserting "bearer" or "cash" in the space provided for a payee's name in a check or other printed form originally containing the words "to the order of." [Comment 1, 3–111] Typical designations, in addition to "cash," which do not purport to refer to specific payees are "cash for payroll," "sundries," "accounts payable," "petty cash," and "bills payable." Where an instrument contains the words "to the order of" followed by blank space, the instrument is not payable to bearer; it is an incomplete order instrument. [Comment 2, 3–111] Although, as indicated above, an instrument that is payable to "John Jones, or bearer," is payable to bearer, an instrument payable to "John Jones, bearer," is not, and is therefore not negotiable.

Sometimes a person signs an instrument in which the name of the payee appears between "Pay to the order of" and "or bearer." Whether such an instrument is held to be an order instrument or a bearer instrument depends upon additional facts. If all of the words except the name of the payee are printed on a form (which is usually the root of the problem) the instrument is payable to order on the assumption that the party issuing it overlooked the words "or bearer" and that his intention was probably to sign an order instrument. If the word "bearer" is either handwritten or typewritten this is deemed to be a sufficient indication of a contrary intention and so it is held to be a bearer instrument. [3–110(3) and Comment 6] Of course, in determining whether the instrument is negotiable it makes no difference whether it is payable to order or to bearer so long as it is payable to one or the other. It is necessary to classify it as order or bearer paper, however, to determine what is required for further negotiation. (See pages 91–92.)

I. MUST CONTAIN NO OTHER PROMISE, ORDER, OBLIGATION OR POWER

Even assuming that an instrument fully satisfies all of the requirements of negotiability already discussed, it is prevented from being a negotiable instrument if, in addition to the promise or order to pay money, the maker or drawer gives any other "promise, order, obligation or power * * * *except as authorized by (Article 3)*." [3–104(1)(b)] (Emphasis added.)   For example, an instrument is not negotiable if, in addition to the promise or order to pay money, it contains a promise or order to render services or to sell goods or gives an option to acquire property or services.   The principal exceptions authorized by Article 3 are expressly stated in Section 3–112 which provides that negotiability is not destroyed by giving the holder power to realize on or dispose of collateral, or by giving the power to confess judgment on the instrument if it is not paid when due, or by assuming an obligation to waive the benefit of any law intended for the benefit of the obligor.   Other exceptions are provided by Section 3–105 which authorizes a provision that empowers or orders a drawee to debit a particular account;   by Section 3–106 which authorizes the inclusion of a promise to pay the cost of collection or attorney's fees upon default;   and by Section 3–109 which authorizes a provision giving the holder an option to extend or accelerate the time of payment.   It should be noticed that each of these exceptions is intended to strengthen the promise or order to pay money and has no independent value of its own.

§ 2. Instrument Declared to be Negotiable

After patiently examining the requisites of a negotiable instrument, one might well ask whether it is not possible to shortcut the matter and create a negotiable instrument simply by declaring in an instrument otherwise not negotiable that it is intended to be negotiable.

Prior to the Code the courts were divided. (See Foley v. Hardy, 122 Kan. 616, 253 P. 238, 50 A.L. R. 422 (1927)) Since the Code has not dealt with the question directly, any quick resolution of the problem seems unlikely. It would seem, however, that the effect of designating as negotiable an instrument otherwise not negotiable depends mainly on what requisite is involved. It seems likely that such a designation would not render negotiable an instrument that provides that it is payable in something other than money or provides a condition to payment. But it seems likely that an instrument that is not negotiable only because it lacks other words of negotiability might be rendered negotiable by including "negotiable" on the face of the instrument. This appears to be consistent with Section 3–110(1) which declares that an instrument is payable to order if it is payable to "assigns" of a specified person or if it is conspicuously designated on its face as "exchange," "or the like," and names a payee. Additionally, the formal requisite that a negotiable instrument contain words of negotiability is said to be based on the need to show that the parties intend the consequences that usually accompany the concept of negotiability. The words "bearer" or "order" or the like are usually a clear indication of this intention. But this intention seems to be indicated also by the use of the word "negotiable." (See also Comments 2 and 5, Section 3–104 and Comment 3, Section 3–112)

§ 3. Instrument Lacking Only Words of Negotiability

Special treatment is accorded to an instrument that satisfies all of the requirements of negotiability except that it lacks words of negotiability, in that it is not payable to either order or bearer. Such an instrument is governed by all of the special principles that govern negotiable instruments under Article 3 except that there can be no holder in due course of such an instrument. [3–805] In contrast, instruments that fail to satisfy any of the other requirements of negotiability are treated in most respects as simple contracts. [Comment, 3–805] Although some courts commonly refer to an instrument that is not negotiable for any reason as a "non-negotiable instrument", other courts reserve the term "non-negotiable instrument" to refer exclusively to an instrument which is not negotiable only because it is not payable to order or bearer. Usually, the context clearly indicates the sense in which the term is used.

§ 4. Terms and Omissions Not Affecting Negotiability

There are many terms that normally are not included that might be included without affecting negotiability. For example, negotiability is not destroyed by providing that by indorsing or cashing a check the payee acknowledges full satisfaction of some obligation owed to him. (For other examples, see Chapter 3 dealing with forms and uses of commercial paper.)

Also, many matters often mentioned in commercial paper may be omitted without destroying negotiability. For example, it is not necessary to mention the place where the instrument is issued or payable. Nor is it necessary to mention the consideration paid for the instrument even though its lack is a good defense against one who does not have the rights of a holder in due course. In fact it is not necessary to include any provision that is not expressly required by Section 3–104(1).

The negotiability is not prevented by including a term that purports to waive the benefit of a law intended to protect the obligor. [3–112(1)(e)] Even when such waiver clauses are unenforceable, they do not destroy negotiability.

Nor is an instrument which otherwise meets the requisites of negotiability prevented from being negotiable by the fact that it is declared to be void because it contains a provision that is against public policy or because it arises from a transaction that is against public policy. This is so even though such a defense is good against a holder in due course. The reader might well ask what difference it makes that an instrument is classified as negotiable if it cannot be enforced even by a holder in due course. The answer is that the instrument may be acquired later by parties who are not involved in the illegality; and a determination of the rights and duties of these later parties is likely to depend to a large degree on the fact that the instrument is negotiable.

> M issues P an instrument that satisfies the requisites of negotiability in payment of a gambling debt in a state wherein such notes are held to be void. If P negotiates the note to A who negotiates it to B who negotiates it to HDC, none of these parties can recover on the note against M even though it is negotiable. But only M can assert the illegality as a defense, and the rights and duties of P, A, B, and HDC among themselves are determined on the assumption that the note is negotiable.

§ 5. Incomplete Instruments

Even though an incomplete instrument is signed it cannot be a negotiable instrument until it is completed. When it is completed, however, assuming that it is completed so as to satisfy the requirements of negotiability, it becomes a negotiable instrument. This is so even though it is completed without, or contrary to, the signer's authority. [3–115, 3–407] To say that an instrument that has been completed without or contrary to authority is negotiable, however, does not mean that the rights and duties of the parties are the same as if the instrument had been completed in a manner that was authorized. (The legal consequences of completing an instrument without or contrary to the signer's authority are discussed more fully at pages 139–142.)

§ 6. Omitting Date, Antedating, and Postdating

The negotiability of an instrument normally is not affected by the fact that it is undated. [3–114(1)] If a person, inadvertently or otherwise, omits a date, there usually is no good reason to deny the instrument negotiability. If, for instance, it is payable "on July 1, 1975," a date for the instrument is immaterial. The same is true if the instrument is payable "on demand." If a date is essential to fix maturity, however, as in an instrument payable "thirty days after date," the absence of a date prevents the instrument from being payable at a definite time and so bars negotiability until a date is inserted. [3–115; Comment 2, 3–114]

Negotiability is not affected by the fact that the instrument is antedated or postdated. [3–114(1)] The time when postdated and antedated instruments are payable is determined by the stated date if the instrument is payable either on demand or at a fixed period after date.   [3–114 (2)]   For example, a demand note issued on May 1 but dated May 5 would not be due until May 5; and a note dated April 20 and stated to be payable one week after date but not issued until May 1 would be due when issued.   The usual reason for issuing a postdated check is to obtain an extension of credit.   By issuing such a check, a drawer promises in effect to have funds on deposit when the check falls due.   It has been held that, unless there is an intent to defraud when the check is issued, issuing a postdated check knowing that there are not then sufficient funds on deposit to cover it is not a violation of a worthless check statute even though the check is dishonored for lack of funds on the date stated. Commonwealth v. Kelinson, 199 Pa.Super. 135, 184 A.2d 374 (1962)

§ 7. "Instrument," "Note," "Draft," and "Check" Presumed to Refer to Instrument that is Negotiable

Although the study of commercial paper is concerned with instruments that are not negotiable as well as with those that are, its primary concern is negotiable instruments.   Therefore, in the discussion that follows it should be assumed that "instrument" refers to a negotiable instrument, rather than to one that is not, unless the context indicates otherwise. [See Section 3–102(1)(e)] This is consistent with the usage that prevails throughout Article 3 of the Code, and in the business community as well. For similar reasons, it should be assumed that "note," "draft," "check," or "certificate of deposit" refers to one that is negotiable rather than not negotiable. [See Section 3–104(3)]

CHAPTER 5

ISSUE

The forms and requisites of a negotiable instrument have been discussed. Now we are concerned with its career in the business community. Its life span normally resembles that of a person. It is born, travels, dies, and is forgotten. For example, a check is born when it is issued, passes about by a process of transfer and negotiation, dies at the bank as the result of payment, and takes its place in the graveyard of cancelled checks. In this Chapter we are concerned primarily with only the first stage—the issue of commercial paper and the rights and duties of the *original parties* vis-a-vis each other. In later chapters, transfer and negotiation and the rights and duties of all of the parties—later holders and transferors as well as original parties—will be considered in their various combinations.

§ 1. Meaning of "Issue"

The signing of a negotiable instrument obviously is important. As stated in Chapter 4, a writing cannot be a negotiable instrument unless it is signed by a maker or drawer. Also, as will be explained more fully in Chapter 7, a person cannot be liable on a negotiable instrument unless he is charged with having signed it. Nonetheless, signing alone creates no liability. A maker or drawer, or anyone else, incurs no liability on an instrument unless he *delivers* it. The *first delivery* of an instrument, which is almost invariably by the maker or drawer, is called *issue*. [3–102(1)(a)]

Although the legal relationship between the maker or drawer and the person to whom a negotiable instrument is issued is governed in most respects by the law of simple contracts, this is not so of the requirement of delivery. The requirement that there be delivery in order to render a maker or drawer liable on a negotiable instrument to the person with whom he deals is imposed as a rule of law. In contrast, in the law of simple contracts, although delivery may be important as evidence of an intention to be bound or because the parties have determined that it is necessary to the creation of a contract, delivery is not required in all cases.

A person who issues a negotiable instrument normally does so in order to effect a contract on the instrument with the person to whom it is delivered. Often the instrument is required by the terms of some underlying contract. For example, a contract for the sale of goods might provide that the buyer is to issue his 30-day note for the price. If the buyer signs such a note but refuses to deliver it, he becomes liable for the breach of the underlying contract, but he incurs no liability on the note to the party with whom he is dealing. However, the fact that he has not delivered the note does not shield him from liability on the instrument if it is later stolen and delivered to someone who qualifies as a holder in due course. The fact that the maker did not deliver the note is not a valid defense against a holder in due course. If a person qualifies as a holder in due course, it makes no difference who delivers the note to him.

§ 2. Meaning of "Delivery"

The meaning of "delivery" requires a brief comment. Section 1–201(14) declares that *delivery* with respect to commercial paper and certain other documents means, "voluntary transfer of possession." By this deceptively simple statement the Code adopts, with all of its subtleties, a concept of delivery which has been evolving for centuries with a decreasing emphasis on the movement of the thing transferred and an increasing emphasis on the intention of the parties. Consequently, under the Code, the question whether there has been a delivery of a negotiable instrument is likely to be answered by what appears to be the likely understanding of the parties with respect to giving the instrument legal effect.

As might be reasonably expected, an actual manual transfer of possession is not required, nor is it conclusive evidence of the required intention. Delivery might be symbolical, as where a person

turns over the keys to his strongbox with the
intention of transferring the possession of the instrument it contains. Delivery is often con
tive. For example, if a payee requests th
instrument be mailed to him, the instrum
delivered as soon as it is properly mailed.
an instrument is mailed without the pric
thorization of the payee, delivery is not eff
until the instrument is received by the payo
a payee requests that delivery be made
agent, delivery is effective as soon as the p
agent receives the instrument. But delivery
complete when a maker or drawer hands
strument to his own agent. For examp
Leigh v. Horsum, 4 Me. (Greenl.) 28 (182€
defendant made a note payable to his son's
itor and handed it to his son with instructi
take it to the creditor, but the son was kil
the way. The court denied the creditor the
to recover on the note on the ground that
not been delivered. Suppose that an em
draws a check payable to an employee ar
the purpose of embarrassing the employee
it to his wife, with whom he has been in
in litigation. Is the employer liable for cc
ing the employee's check? In Caviness v.
& Roberts, 508 S.W.2d 253 (Mo.App.1974)
held that no conversion had occurred. The court
stated that delivery was essential to the validity
of the check and that under the facts of this case

the employee's wife could by no stretch of the imagination be considered the employee's agent to receive possession.

There is a rebuttable presumption that an instrument in the possession of someone other than the maker or drawer has been delivered. Conversely, the fact that one who signs an instrument retains physical control over it creates a rebuttable presumption that delivery was not intended. Predicting the outcome of cases of this kind, however, may be hazardous. (See, e. g., Marten's Estate, 226 Iowa 162, 283 N.W. 885 (1939) and First National Bank in Fort Lauderdale v. Hunt, 244 So.2d 481 (Fla.App.1971))

§ 3. Effect of Delivery—Contract Between Immediate Parties

Normally an effective delivery not only gives rise to a contract based on the instrument but also suspends whatever right there was to sue on the underlying obligation for which the instrument is given unless and until the instrument is dishonored. [3–802(1)] (See pages 296–302.)

The legal relationship of the two immediate parties on the basis of the contract on the instrument is in most respects the same as if they had entered a simple contract. True, certain procedural advantages are enjoyed by a party to whom a negotiable instrument is issued. (See pages

290–295) Also, the rights and duties of the parties are governed by Article 3. But, with few exceptions, the provisions of Article 3 are consistent with what the parties probably expected, and the law of simple contracts applies in most situations not expressly covered by Article 3. Moreover, virtually all of the defenses that are available against one who sues on a simple contract also are available to the maker or drawer against the person to whom the instrument is issued.

Furthermore, in determining the rights and duties of the immediate parties following the issuance of a negotiable instrument, one must consider not only the instrument itself but also any other documents or writings that were executed at the time the instrument was issued. This is in accordance with the principle that writings that are executed as part of the same transaction must be read together as a single agreement—at least, as between the immediate parties. This is the substance of Section 3–119(1) which provides:

> As between the obligor and his immediate obligee or any transferee the terms of an instrument may be modified or affected by any other written agreement executed as a part of the same transaction, except that a holder in due course is not affected by any limitation of his rights arising out of the separate written agreement if he had no notice of the limitation when he took the instrument.

So long as they are part of the same transaction, the two instruments may be read together even though they do not expressly refer to each other. (See, e. g., Texas State Bank of Austin v. Sharp, 506 S.W.2d 761 (Tex.Civ.App.1974))

As between the *immediate parties*, the existence of other *writings* executed as part of the *same transaction* as a negotiable instrument have created few problems. (At this point it may be well to recall that a separate writing does not affect the negotiability of an instrument) [3–119(2)] (See pages 50–51.)

Problems arise, however, when one of the parties tries to show that the rights and duties arising from the instrument are somehow altered by an *oral* statement made at the time it was issued or by a *written* or *oral* statement made *before* it was issued. The legal effect of such statements on the rights and duties of the original parties to the instrument depends very largely on the *parol evidence rule*, and to a lesser extent, on the express provisions of Article 3 which sometimes limit, even more than the parol evidence rule, the freedom of either party to affect their rights and duties by introducing such evidence. (See pages 83–84) Here we are concerned mainly with the effect of the parol evidence rule on such statements.

§ 4. Parol Evidence Rule and Its Application to Commercial Paper

The parol evidence rule applies to negotiable instruments in much the same way that it applies to other written contracts.

According to the parol evidence rule—actually a rule of substantive law rather than a rule of evidence—when two parties reduce their agreement to writing, being under no mistake with respect to what the writing provides, with the intention of adopting the writing as the final and complete expression of their contract, neither party may thereafter introduce parol, or outside, evidence—that is, evidence of an oral agreement made at the time the writing was signed, or evidence of a prior oral or written agreement—for the purpose of showing that the terms they actually agreed upon were different from those expressed in the writing. It is reasoned that all of the prior or simultaneous agreements or understandings that are entitled to legal effect are embodied or merged in the one integrated writing, which is sometimes called an "integration," or "merger." In short, the parol evidence rule simply prevents either party from going back in time and re-writing the instrument.

The parol evidence rule applies not only when the parties adopt a writing as the final and complete expression of their *total* agreement but also when they adopt a writing as the final and complete expression of *only a part* of their agreement. In the latter case, the writing is called a "partial" integration. Depending on the facts, a writing in the form of a negotiable instrument may constitute either a complete or a partial integration of the agreement between the parties. In either case, its terms usually are protected by the parol evidence rule. Accordingly, with only minor exceptions which will be explained, neither the issuing party nor the party to whom the instrument is issued is permitted to introduce any evidence, written or oral, of what occurred prior to signing or any oral evidence of what was agreed at the time of signing for the purpose of changing, adding to, or deleting, any terms of the instrument. For example, such evidence would not be admitted for the purpose of changing the promise or order, the time or place of payment, the amount to be paid, or the words of negotiability.

A. LIMITATIONS ON OPERATION OF PAROL EVIDENCE RULE

Although the parol evidence rule plays an important part in protecting a negotiable instrument against proof that it is not what it appears to be, there are a number of serious limitations on the operation of the rule. One limitation allows a person to have an instrument reformed, to express what the parties intended to have it express, if he can prove by clear and convincing evidence that, as the result of a mutual mistake in reducing the agreement to writing, it provided something different from what they thought it provided when it was signed. [See Comment 1, 3–118] Likewise, the parol evidence rule does not prevent a party from showing that *after* the instrument was signed, the parties agreed to change it. Nor does it prevent a party from introducing evidence to *avoid*, or set aside, an instrument, rather than vary it, by proving fraud, mistake, duress, undue influence, infancy or ordinary incompetency. Also a party who signs an instrument may show that he later was discharged from liability by an agreement or in any of the other ways recognized by law. Finally, he may introduce evidence to show that the instrument never took effect so as to impose liability on him because it arose from an illegal transaction or for some other reason. It will be noted that except for the limitation allowing reformation, none of the limitations admits evidence intended to vary the terms of the instrument.

The relationship of the parol evidence rule to ambiguous terms merits special consideration. Sometimes, even though there is no mistake in reducing an agreement to writing, the words selected and used by the parties are ambiguous. The application of the parol evidence rule does not preclude evidence offered to resolve such ambiguity because such evidence merely explains and does not vary the terms used by the parties. Mainly to increase certainty in commercial dealings, however, the Code provides rules of construction to deal with several common ambiguities and to exclude parol evidence intended to resolve them even though such evidence might be admitted under the normal operation of the parol evidence rule. Most of the rules of construction provided by the Code deal with special matters which are discussed elsewhere in this book. It should be sufficient here to mention only two of these rules which are of a general nature. The first is that "handwritten terms control typewritten and printed terms, and typewritten control printed." [3–118(b)] The second is that "words control figures except that if the words are ambiguous figures control." [3–118(c)] Ambiguities which are governed by the rules of construction are resolved without giving any consideration to parol evidence. In short, although the Code, like the parol evidence rule, would not preclude parol evidence to reform an instrument the terms of which are, as the result of a mistake, not what the parties intended, and would admit parol evidence to resolve most ambiguities in the words chosen by the parties, it does preclude the admission of parol evidence to resolve ambiguities with respect to matters and terms that are governed by rules of construction. (Comment 1, 3–118)

B. CONDITIONAL DELIVERY AND THE PAROL EVIDENCE RULE

Conditions Precedent and Conditions Subsequent. In applying the parol evidence rule to agreements made *at or before* the delivery of a negotiable instrument, the courts make a vital distinction between conditions *precedent* and conditions *subsequent.* A condition precedent is intended to prevent an instrument from taking effect until the occurrence of the condition. A condition subsequent is intended to terminate the liability of a party on an instrument *after* it has taken effect.   Courts have consistently held that the parol evidence rule does not exclude parol evidence that an instrument was delivered on a condition precedent, but a large majority of the courts have held that it does exclude evidence of delivery on a condition subsequent. It is reasoned that proof of a condition precedent is not offered to contradict a contract; rather it is offered to prove that no contract ever came into existence. In contrast it usually is reasoned that proof of a condition subsequent assumes the existence of a written contract and is offered to show that although the promise contained in a writing appears to be unconditional, actually it is qualified by the condition subsequent.   Since this would contradict the writing, it is excluded by the parol evidence rule.

[*85*]

Of course, there are many cases in which it is clear from the parol evidence that the parties agreed that the occurrence or non-occurrence of some event is intended to be a condition to the liability of the signing party, but it is difficult to determine whether the occurrence is a condition precedent to liability or the non-occurrence is a condition subsequent.

Typical cases in which a person who signs and delivers a negotiable instrument is *permitted* to prove by parol evidence the existence of a condition *precedent* that will shield him from liability are those in which a party signs a note as maker and delivers it with the understanding that he is not to become liable on it until some other named person signs as co-maker, or where a maker signs and delivers a renewal note with the understanding that it is not to take effect until the original note is returned, or where a buyer signs and delivers his check as part payment of the price with the understanding that it will not bind him unless and until he is able to obtain a loan for the balance from a third person. In these cases the evidence of the condition is introduced to show that the instrument never took effect as a contract, and not to contradict the writing, and so it is admissible. (See, e. g., Weirton S. & L. Co. v. Cortez, 203 S.E. 2d 468 (W.Va.1974)¹)

Typical cases in which a person who signs and delivers a negotiable instrument is barred from introducing parol evidence of a condition *subsequent* are those in which the maker of a note offers to prove that, at the time of delivery, it was orally agreed that the maker would be discharged from liability by rendering some performance other than the payment of money or that, at the time of delivery, it was orally agreed that the maker would be liable only until some other specified person signed the note at which time the maker would be discharged. In cases such as these, the instrument is assumed to be an integrated writing that represents the true contract of the parties and the parol evidence is inadmissible because it is offered to change that contract.

C. UNDERSTANDING SIGNER IS NOT TO BE BOUND

Occasionally, a person sued on a negotiable instrument tries to avoid liability altogether by proving that, when he signed, it was agreed that he would not be liable *under any circumstances*. Various reasons have been given for such understandings. For example, it has been claimed that the instrument was signed as a mere formality, or was intended to conceal the identity of the true party or that it played a role in bookkeeping procedures. (See, e. g., Arizona Cotton Ginning Co. v. Nichols, 9 Ariz.App. 493, 454 P.2d 163 (1969).) Sometimes it has appeared that there was a plan to deceive a third party such as a bank examiner. Obviously, to accept such a defense too readily would go far to undermine the stability of commercial paper. However, parol evidence offered to prove an agreement that a signer is not to be liable on an instrument under any circumstances seems to be no more contradictory of the terms of the instrument than parol evidence of a condition precedent, which is clearly admissible. Nonetheless, in a large majority of the cases, parol evidence of such an understanding has been excluded on the ground that it would contradict the writing and so violate the parol evidence rule. (See, e. g., Blake v. Coates, 292 Ala. 351, 294 So. 2d 433 (1974).) One rationalization of this result is that such evidence would contradict the writing by reducing the stated amount to zero. Britton, Bills & Notes 126 (Second Edition 1961). In some cases courts have asserted public policy as an additional reason for excluding such evidence. In most cases where evidence of an oral agreement that a signer is not to be bound at all is admitted into evidence despite the objection that it violates the parol evidence rule, it appears that the evidence is properly admissible to prove fraud or some other defense.

Perhaps the reader should be reminded that in this Chapter we have been discussing the rights and duties of the *original parties*. What has been stated would not necessarily apply with respect to a later party who is a holder in due course. For example, a party who is liable on an instrument normally would not be entitled to have the instrument reformed on the ground that a mutual mistake had been made in reducing it to writing, nor could he effectively assert a claim to an instrument if this would work to the detriment of a later holder in due course. Similarly, conditional delivery and most other defenses that could be asserted against an original party could not be asserted against a later holder in due course. (For a discussion of defenses that might be asserted against a holder in due course, see Chapter 11.)

§ 5. Similar Principles Apply to Subsequent Delivery

The foregoing discussion relates primarily to the *issue* or *first delivery* of an instrument and to the liability of the maker or drawer to the first holder. However, with exceptions applicable to a later holder who is a holder in due course, the same general principles apply in determining the effect of later deliveries that occur in the process of transfer and negotiation, the subject to which we now turn.

CHAPTER 6

TRANSFER AND NEGOTIATION

A key characteristic of commercial paper is the ease with which it may be transferred from person to person after it has been issued. Transfer and negotiation deals with the many problems incident to these transfers. This is a technical subject, and it is sometimes difficult. But the time spent studying it should be worthwhile because it furnishes the key to many problems in the law of commercial paper.

§ 1. Negotiation and Assignment

After issue, a negotiable instrument may be transferred by negotiation or by assignment. (For a discussion of assignments, see Chapter 2.) Whether a transfer is by negotiation or assignment, a transferee normally acquires whatever rights his transferor had, in accordance with a general principle of property law embodied in the Code (3–201(1). If a transfer falls short of being a negotiation, the transferee receives no more than his transferor had and does not enjoy the special advantages accorded a holder. If the transfer is by negotiation, the transferee becomes a holder. [3–202(1)] (For the meaning of holder see pages 94–95) As a holder, whether or not he is the owner, he has the legal power to transfer the instrument further by assignment or negotiation; he normally has the power to enforce it in his own name (3–301); he can discharge the liability of any party on the instrument by receiving payment or in a number of other ways (see pages 303–318) and he enjoys several procedural advantages. In addition, one who is a holder and satisfies the remaining requirements for being a holder in due course—he pays value and takes the instrument in good faith and without notice that it is overdue or has been dishonored or is subject to any claim or defense (see Chapter 10)—he takes the instrument free of all claims and most defenses that might have been asserted against his transferor or any prior party (see Chapter 11) and enjoys the other benefits of being a holder in due course. In taking an instrument free of claims and defenses that might have been asserted against prior parties, a holder in due course acquires more than his transferor had. This idea that a negotiation might confer upon a transferee greater rights than were held by the transferor is a key feature of negotiability. For the above reasons, as well as others, it is important to know what is required in order to make a transfer that is a negotiation.

§ 2. Requisites of Negotiation

The essential ingredients of negotiation depend upon whether the instrument is payable to *bearer* or to *order* at the time of transfer. If it is payable to bearer, *delivery alone* suffices for a complete negotiation. If it is payable to order, a complete negotiation requires, first, an indorsement by the appropriate party, and second, delivery. [3–202 (1)] As a requisite of negotiation, "delivery" has the same meaning and is governed by the same principles as were set forth when it was considered as a requisite of issue. Basically it means voluntary transfer of possession. See Chapter 5.

§ 3. Bearer and Order Paper Distinguished

An instrument is payable to *bearer* if (1) it is payable to *bearer on its face* (see page 64) and carries no indorsement by an appropriate party or (2) it carries one or more indorsements and the last of these made by an appropriate party is *in blank*. An instrument is payable to order if (1) it is payable *to order on its face* (see page 62) and it carries no indorsement by an appropriate party or (2) it carries one or more indorsements and the last of these by an appropriate party is *special*.

§ 4. Blank and Special Indorsements Distinguished

A *blank* indorsement is one which does not name an indorsee. [3–204(2)] Usually it consists of only the indorser's signature. A *special* indorsement specifies a person to whom or to whose order payment is to be made. [3–204(1)] Assume that Arthur Adam, the payee of an instrument, transfers it to Ben Barrow, who transfers it to Carl Cater, and that on the reverse side of the instrument the following indorsements appear:

(1) Pay Ben Barrow

(Signed) Arthur Adam

(2) (Signed) Ben Barrow

Arthur Adam's indorsement is special because it names the transferee; Ben Barrow's indorsement is blank because it does not. The effect of Arthur Adam's indorsement would have been the same if instead of providing "Pay Ben Barrow," it had provided "Pay Ben Barrow or Order" or "Pay to the order of Ben Barrow."

§ 5. Appropriate Party to Indorse

An indorsement can affect the character of an instrument as bearer or order paper or the character of a transfer as a negotiation or as an assignment only if it is made by an *appropriate* party. An indorsement by an inappropriate party must be ignored when considering these matters. (Such an indorsement, however, normally would impose liability on the indorser. This is so regardless of whether he signs his own name or forges someone else's name. (See page 138.) The appropriate party to indorse is always the *holder* of the instrument or someone authorized to indorse on his behalf. [3–202(2)]

A.   HOLDER

A *holder* is a person who has *possession* of an instrument that *runs* to him.

A *bearer* instrument *runs* to any person who has possession of it.   This is so whether he acquired possession by original issue from the maker or drawer, by delivery alone from the holder of a bearer instrument, by delivery plus blank indorsement from the holder of either a bearer or an order instrument, or *even without delivery*, as is true of possession acquired by a finder or a thief. Since a bearer instrument always runs to the person in possession of it, that person is always a holder.   A bearer instrument retains its character as bearer paper and runs to anyone in possession of it until it is indorsed specially;   then it becomes order paper and runs to the special indorsee.

At the outset, an instrument which originates as *order* paper *runs* to the payee.   If it is issued directly to the payee he becomes the *holder*.   But if it is issued to someone else, that person is called the *remitter*;   he is not, however, the holder.   At this point there is no holder.   When the remitter delivers the instrument to the person named as payee, the latter becomes the holder.   If the payee indorses the instrument specially, it continues as order paper and runs to the special indorsee who, on obtaining possession, becomes the holder, and as such, the appropriate party to indorse. If the payee or special indorsee indorses the instrument in blank, it becomes a bearer instrument which runs to anyone who happens to acquire possession of it, just as if it had been issued originally as a bearer instrument. This was recognized by Lord Mansfield in 1781 in deciding Peacock v. Rhodes, 2 Doug. 633, 97 Eng.Rep. 871, wherein he said, "I see no difference between a note indorsed blank and one payable to bearer. They both go by delivery and possession proves property in both cases."

§ 6. Requisites of Negotiation Illustrated

The foregoing principles are illustrated by the following cases each involving a *negotiable* instrument.

Case 1. A bearer instrument is issued to P. Without indorsing, P delivers it to A. Result: The transfer to A was by negotiation and A became a holder. A bearer instrument can be negotiated by delivery alone and anyone in possession of a bearer instrument is the holder.

Case 2. P has an instrument which names him as payee. Without indorsing, P delivers it to A. Result: The transfer to A was an assignment and not a negotiation, and A does not become a holder, because the instrument runs to P. Negotiation of an order instrument requires indorsement by an appropriate party (P in this case), in addition to delivery.

[*95*]

Case 3.   A bearer instrument is issued to P. T steals
it from P and delivers it to B. Result: The transfer to B was by negotiation and B became holder.
T did not acquire the instrument by negotiation
because it was not delivered to him.   However, a
bearer instrument runs to anyone who acquires
possession of it, even a thief.   Therefore, T was
a holder.   As holder, T had power to negotiate
the instrument to make B holder.   This is so even
though T, the thief, never was owner of the instrument.

Case 4.   P has an instrument which names him as
payee.   T steals the instrument from P, indorses
it in blank, and then delivers it to B.   Result:
Neither T nor B were holders.   An order instrument can be negotiated only after it has been indorsed by an *appropriate* party.   Since P, the
payee, had not indorsed, no later party could become a holder.   Notice also that since T was not
the appropriate party to indorse, his indorsement
could not affect the character of the paper so that
it remained order paper that ran to P even though
T's indorsement was in blank.

Case 5.   P has an instrument naming him as payee.
He indorses it in blank.   It is stolen from P by T
who sells and delivers it to B.   Result: The transfer to B was by negotiation and B became a holder.
Although the instrument started out as order
paper, it became bearer paper when it was indorsed
in blank by P, the appropriate party to indorse.
Thereafter anyone who acquired possession of the
instrument, even a thief, became holder and had
the power to negotiate it by delivery with or without indorsement.   If B had indorsed the instrument specially to C, the instrument would again

have become order paper because it is the nature
of the last indorsement by an appropriate party
that determines the character of an instrument as
bearer or order paper.

§ 7. "Holder" Not Synonymous With "Owner"

Perhaps it should be emphasized that although
the holder and the owner are usually the same
person, they frequently are two different persons.
For example, a holder may be a thief, finder,
agent, or other bailee who happens to have possession of an instrument that runs to him; and the
owner may not be a holder because he never acquired possession, or because he gave it up, or
because, although he has possession, the instrument does not run to him—for example, X purchases a note from the payee and obtains possession, but the payee neglects to indorse the note.

§ 8. Risks of Bearer Paper

Bearer paper entails obvious risks. As we have
seen, since bearer paper runs to whoever acquires
possession of it, even a finder or a thief of such
paper can become a holder and, as such, has the
power to negotiate it to a third party so as to
deprive the true owner of his property in the instrument. Also, as holder, he normally has the
power to discharge any person from liability on
an instrument by obtaining payment or satisfaction. All this is so even though the finder or the

thief never becomes the owner. Because bearer paper carries much of the circulation potential and risks of money, it should be treated with the same caution usually exercised when handling money.

A. USING ORDER PAPER TO AVOID RISKS

Fortunately the risks of bearer paper can be largely avoided by the use of order paper. The drawer or maker can start by issuing the instrument as order paper, and usually does. Also, the Code permits a holder of bearer paper to avoid the risks simply by indorsing the instrument specially to himself, thus converting the paper into order paper which thereafter can be negotiated only if he indorses it. This is so, regardless of whether the paper originates as bearer paper or as order paper. If the instrument is payable to bearer because the last indorsement is in blank, the holder can convert it into order paper merely by inserting "Pay" followed by his own name directly above the blank indorsement, thereby converting it into a special indorsement. [3–204(3)]

Whether the foregoing principles lead to justice in a given case is likely to depend on one's point of view. But it can hardly be denied that in most cases they lead to reasonably predictable results and so they are of great importance in the business world. For example, they mean that a drawer can safely mail his check to the payee because he knows that if it is stolen and the payee's signature is forged and the bank overlooks this and pays the check, it will not be allowed to charge his account because the drawer ordered the bank to pay the holder and the bank paid someone else. They mean that if a note is stolen from the payee or special indorsee who has not indorsed, the maker remains liable to the victim of the theft regardless of whether he pays the thief. They mean that if a good faith purchaser acquires an instrument relying on a forged indorsement of the payee, the innocent purchaser, and not the person whose signature is forged, must bear the loss. Usually, once the facts are determined these principles are relatively easy to apply. But there are two cases which pose more difficult problems because justice and expediency combine to require a *special* application of these principles. One case involves the *fictitious payee* and the other involves the *impostor*.

§ 9. Fictitious Payee Problem

The *fictitious payee* is a favorite device for those who practice skulduggery, especially the employee who wishes to swindle his employer by padding bills or payrolls.

Suppose that X, a merchant, gives Y, his employee, general authority to issue checks drawn on B Bank to pay creditors and employees. Intending to cheat X, and enrich himself, Y draws a check for $3,000 on B Bank payable to the order of F, and signs X's name as drawer. F is neither a creditor nor an employee, and Y intends F to have no interest in the check. Y indorses the check in the name of F naming himself as indorsee. Y promptly cashes the check at B Bank and retains the proceeds. B Bank charges X's account for the $3,000. When X learns of Y's duplicity, he demands that the bank recredit his account $3,000. When B Bank refuses, X sues B Bank.

Both X and B Bank agree that X was liable on the check and that B Bank had a right to charge X's account if, but only if, Y was a *holder*. [3–603(1)] (See Chapter 12.) X contends that Y was not a holder because the check was payable to the order of F, who was therefore the only appropriate party to indorse, and that it was never indorsed by F, so Y could not become holder. Logically, there is much to be said for X's position.

However, as a matter of policy, the Code favors B Bank. It does so by providing that "an indorsement *by any person* in the name of a named payee is effective if * * * a person signing as or on behalf of a maker or drawer intends the payee to have no interest in the instrument." [3–405 (1)(b)] (Emphasis added) By virtue of this provision the indorsement of Y, the defrauder, (or his confederate or anyone else), in the name of F, the named payee, had, in these special circumstances, the same effect as if F, the named payee, had indorsed. Consequently, Y was in possession of an instrument that ran to him and therefore was the holder. When a person draws a negotiable draft or check he orders the drawee to pay the holder. Therefore when the bank in good faith paid Y, it was obeying X's order and so was entitled to charge his account.

Just as the above provision protects one who *pays* relying on a signature in the name of a named payee in these fictitious payee cases, so also it protects one who *purchases* such an instrument in good faith. Assume that instead of cashing the check himself, Y had promptly indorsed the check in F's name either in blank or naming H as indorsee and had sold the check for value to H. Assume further that the bank, acting pursuant to X's instructions, had refused to pay H when the latter presented the check for payment, and that H sued X on the check. By virtue of Section 3–405(1)(b), H would have qualified as a holder and if he met the other requirements he would have been a holder in due course and, as such, entitled to recover from X despite Y's fraud.

In the above case, the dishonest employee was the "drawer" of the check in the sense that he signed it with the authority of the employer who was named as drawer. Suppose that, instead of actually *signing* the check, Y merely *prepared* it for X's signature and that X signed it thinking that F was a business creditor. Or suppose that instead of preparing the check, Y merely prepared a payroll or other voucher on which F's name falsely appeared as creditor. In these situations, the Code again favors the drawee bank if it pays, this time by providing that "an indorsement by any person in the name of a named payee is effective if * * * an agent or employee of the maker or drawer has *supplied him with the name of the payee* intending the latter to have no such interest." [3–405(1)(c)] (Emphasis added) And, as shown above, it also favors a holder in due course who takes the instrument through the indorsement of the defrauder or anyone else.

Fictitious payee fraud may take many forms. Sometimes there is an actual person or company bearing the name of the payee, sometimes not. It makes no difference. Sometimes the defrauder is a corporate officer, such as the treasurer, sometimes he is only a clerk. Again, it makes no difference, although the corporate officer is more likely to be signing the instrument, and the clerk is more likely to be furnishing the name of the payee. The important factor is that the defrauder intends the named payee to have no interest in the instrument.

Behind the Code provisions governing fictitious payee frauds is the feeling that the risk of the employee's fraud in these cases should fall on the employer drawer or maker rather than on the paying good faith drawee or purchaser because (1) the employer is in a better position to avoid the risk by exercising proper care in the selection and supervision of his employees; (2) he is better able to protect himself by fidelity insurance; and (3) the cost of such insurance is properly an expense of the employer. [Comment 4, 3–405] However, in United States v. Bank of America National Trust, 288 F.Supp. 343 at 348 (D.C.N.D. Cal.1968), this rationale was declared to be inapplicable to the federal government because "the Government, especially with respect to military personnel, cannot be expected to exercise the same control as a private enterprise over its employees." The court also declared that the United States is not bound by the Code by analogy or otherwise and that, in the absence of a governing federal statute, the first duty of a federal court dealing with the rights and duties of the United States in commercial transactions is to choose a federal rule that protects a federal right. In this case, in which two storekeepers had prepared checks, naming a fictitious payee, for the signature of their disbursing officer, the court held that the United States was entitled to recover from the bank that paid the checks the amount the bank had collected from the United States Treasury.

Suppose that a bank acts in good faith but is *negligent* in paying a check indorsed in the name of a fictitious payee, does its negligence deprive it of the benefit of the fictitious payee principle? In Prudential Ins. Co. v. Marine Bank, 371 F.Supp. 1002 (E.D.Wis.1974) the court favored the bank and held that in a case such as this so long as the payor acted in good faith, it is intended by the Code that the loss should fall on the employer and that the payor's negligence is not relevant.

§ 10. Impostor Problem

The fictitious payee problem discussed above usually arises from an *inside* job. In contrast, the impostor problem is almost always an *outside* job. Typically, a confidence man, by impersonating a respectable citizen and making some promise which he has no intention of keeping, induces a drawer or maker to deliver his check or note made payable to the order of the respectable citizen. After indorsing in the name of the payee, he practices his lowly art again to induce a second trusting party to purchase or pay the instrument. Finally, he departs with his loot, and the law must determine which of the two innocent and defrauded parties must bear the cost of his leech-like existence.

Before the Code the outcome of these cases usually depended on what the court found to be the *dominant intent* of the defrauded party. If he dealt face to face with the impostor, his dominant intent was usually found to be to deliver the instrument to the impostor. Consequently, the impostor was treated as *holder*, and the party who gave the instrument to the impostor bore the loss rather than the person who purchased the instrument or paid the impostor. If the parties dealt by mail or telegram, it usually was reasoned that the defrauded party intended to deliver the instrument to the person the impostor pretended to be. Consequently, the impostor did not become the holder and so the loss was borne by the person who purchased the instrument or paid the impostor.

The *dominant intent* test was criticized as a fiction because in the eyes of the deceived drawer or maker, the payee named and the defrauder are the same person so that there is only one intention, or if there are two, they are so intertwined as to be inseparable. The framers of the Code therefore rejected the test of dominant intent and refused expressly to distinguish between imposture face to face and by correspondence by providing that "an indorsement *by any person* in the name of a named payee is effective if * * * an impostor *by use of the mails or otherwise* has induced the maker or drawer to issue the instrument to him or his confederate in the name of the payee." [3-405(1)(a)] (Emphasis added)

Under the Code, regardless of how the imposture is carried out, when the impostor or his confederate or anyone else indorses the instrument it is as if the payee of an ordinary order instrument indorsed it. If the indorsement is in blank, the instrument immediately becomes payable to bearer so that the impostor or anyone else in possession of it becomes the holder and the proper person to negotiate it or to receive payment. If the instrument is indorsed specially, by anyone, and delivered to the special indorsee, the latter becomes the holder, and if he meets the other requirements, he becomes a holder in due course who is entitled to enforce the instrument against the defrauded maker or drawer. If a drawee pays the holder, whether he be the impostor or anyone else, the drawee is entitled to charge the drawer's account because a payment to the holder is in accordance with the drawer's order. The net result is that the ultimate loss is normally borne by the defrauded maker or drawer rather than by the transferee from the defrauder or by the drawee who pays the impostor or a transferee.

Even under the Code, however, if the defrauder, instead of misrepresenting himself to be another, misrepresents himself to be the *agent* of another, and thereby induces a maker or drawer to issue him a negotiable instrument made *payable to his alleged principal,* there can be no effective negotiation of the instrument unless the alleged principal, himself, indorses the instrument. Under the Code, the underlying reason for this result is the feeling that the maker or the drawer who takes the precaution of making the instrument payable to the principal is entitled to the principal's indorsement. [Comment 2, 3–405]

At this point, the reader might well ask whether an instrument that is payable to a fictitious payee or to an impersonated payee is payable to order or to bearer. It is arguable that it is payable to bearer, to order, or to neither. Perhaps it is best to recognize that such an instrument is anomalous and that although it is governed by some well established principles in the law of commercial paper it is treated in a way that cannot be reconciled with some other equally well recognized principles. The Code starts with a desire to help the good faith purchaser or drawee who pays. It might have done this simply by declaring such paper to be payable to bearer so as not to require any indorsement. But if it had done this it would have favored even those who did not insist on even the appearance of a regular chain of indorsements and it did not wish to go this far. [Comment 1, 3–405] So it required that at least someone appear to sign on behalf of the person named as payee before anyone could become a holder of it. (See Wright v. Bank of California, 276 Cal.App.2d 485, 81 Cal. Rptr. 11 (1969), in which the court refused to accept any proposed "equivalents" for an indorsement.)

§ 11. Incomplete Negotiation

Occasionally, an order instrument is delivered for value by the payee or an indorsee without his indorsement. When this occurs, the transferee's status may be summarized as follows: (1) The transferee is not a holder. (2) The transferee acquires only the rights of the transferor against prior parties. (3) Unless the transferor and transferee have agreed otherwise, the transferee has the right to the *unqualified* (see page 114) indorsement of the transferor and if necessary may obtain a decree of specific performance ordering the transferor, under pain of punishment for contempt of court, to indorse. Because this order is issued by a court of equity, the transferee is sometimes said to have equitable title prior to obtaining the indorsement. Actually, he is the true owner even though he is not yet the holder. (4) When the transferor completes the negotiation by indorsing, the transferee becomes the holder. The transferee's status as holder is determined as of the time of the indorsement. [3–201 (3) and Comment 7]

> P, payee, obtains a note from M, maker, by fraud. Before maturity, P delivers the note without indorsement to H, a good faith purchaser for value who is unaware of the fraud. H is entitled to P's unqualified indorsement. H becomes a holder in due course who is free of M's defense of fraud if he obtains P's indorsement before the note is overdue and before learning of the fraud; but otherwise not.

§ 12.   Depositary Bank's Power to Supply Missing Indorsement to Complete Negotiation

Occasionally, through oversight or otherwise, a payee deposits a check or other item in a bank for collection without indorsing it. If ordinary principles applied, the bank could not become a holder without getting the depositor's indorsement. For the bank to return the item for indorsement in this situation, however, delays collection with little advantage to the drawer and none to the depositor or bank. Still, some drawers are more concerned with having the payee's indorsement as convenient evidence of payment than they are with speeding up the collection process. Reflecting a balancing of these conflicting interests, Section 4–205(1) of the Code provides:

> A depositary bank which has taken an item for collection may supply any indorsement of the customer which is necessary to title unless the item contains the words "payee's indorsement required" or the like. In the absence of such a requirement a statement placed on the item by the depositary bank to the effect that the item was deposited by a customer or credited to his account is effective as the customer's indorsement.

Under this Section a depositary bank that receives an item for collection without the depositor's indorsement may indicate on the item that it has been credited to the depositor's account and this normally has the same effect as if the depositor had indorsed. The bank becomes a holder and, if it otherwise qualifies, it becomes a holder in due course. Also, if a drawee bank pays such an item, it is entitled to charge the drawer's account. However, if a check or other item shows that a payee's or indorsee's indorsement is required, no later party can become a holder without such indorsement.

§ 13.   Negotiation by Multiple Payees

As stated earlier (page 63), an instrument is not prevented from being negotiable by the fact that it names several payees either in the alternative, as "A, B, or C," or together as "A, B and C."   [3–110(1)(d)]

If the instrument is payable to two or more payees in the alternative, it is payable to any one of them and it may be negotiated, discharged or enforced by any one of them who has possession of it.   [3–116(a)]   To negotiate such an instrument, the indorsement of only one of them is required.

If the instrument is payable to several payees together, it may be negotiated, discharged, or enforced only by all of them acting together.   [3–116(b)]   To negotiate an instrument that names several payees together, it must be indorsed by all of them.   [3–116(b)]

The naming of several payees together is often a convenient device for a person who owes one obligation to several persons. If all such named payees indorse an instrument to negotiate it or if all sign a receipt for payment, the distribution of the proceeds need not concern the party issuing the instrument. But the case in which one of such payees, allegedly without authority, has purported to act on behalf of the others, in signing or negotiating the instrument or in obtaining payment, has been the source of much litigation involving not only the payees, but also the issuing party and others as well.

§ 14. Effect of Attempt to Negotiate Less than Balance Due

If an instrument has been paid in part it may be negotiated as to the balance due. To be effective as a negotiation, however, an indorsement must transfer the entire instrument or the entire unpaid balance. If the indorsement purports to transfer less, it operates only as a *partial assignment* [3–202(3)] and the partial assignee does not become a holder or acquire his advantages. Whether the partial assignee can sue to enforce his rights, and if so, the conditions under which he may do so, are left by the Code to local law. [Comment 4, 3–202]

§ 15. Place of Indorsement on Instrument

Normally an indorsement appears on the reverse side of an instrument, but it may appear elsewhere. To cover cases where the capacity in which a person signed is uncertain the Code provides that unless the instrument clearly indicates that a signature is made in some other capacity, it is an indorsement. [3–402] To provide for the unusual case in which there are so many indorsements that there is no room on the back for more, the Code provides that an indorsement may be written on the instrument "or on a paper so firmly affixed thereto as to become a part thereof." [3–202(2)] A paper so affixed is called an *allonge*.

§ 16. Negotiation when Name is Misspelled or Misstated

Occasionally an instrument is made payable to a payee or indorsee under a misspelled name or name other than his own. In this case, an indorsement in the name that appears on the instrument is legally sufficient for an effective negotiation, but this alone is commercially unsatisfactory because of the difficulty a later holder might have in proving the identity of the indorser. An indorsement in his true name alone also is legally sufficient for a negotiation, but this is unsatisfactory because a later transferee may be uncertain about the state of title. To avoid this difficulty, the Code provides that any person paying or giving value for the instrument may require the indorser to sign both names.   [3–203]

§ 17.   Effect of Negotiation that may be Rescinded

If a transfer satisfies the described requirements, it is an effective negotiation even if it may be rescinded on the grounds of incapacity, fraud, duress, or illegality, or because it was made in breach of trust [3–207(1)], and even if it is made by a thief, a finder, or someone else acting without authority.   In fact, although the transaction in which it occurs is held to be entirely void because of illegality, an adjudication of incompetency, or on any other ground, a transfer meeting the requirements is an effective negotiation. [Comment 1, 3–207]   Consequently, the transferee of an instrument in any of these transactions is a holder with full power to negotiate it further as long as he retains possession; and the transferor loses all of his rights in the instrument until he recovers it.   [Comment 2, 3–207]   If the instrument falls into the hands of a holder in due course, even the right to reclaim it is lost.   [3–305(1)]   (For a discussion of claims and defenses, see Chapter 11.)

§ 18.   Unqualified and Qualified Indorsements Affect Liability

As explained earlier, indorsements are classified as either blank or special to ascertain whether an instrument is bearer or order and thus determine if any indorsement is necessary for an effective negotiation of the instrument. Whether or not an indorsement is blank or special, it may be classified a second way—*unqualified* or *qualified*—to indicate the nature of the indorser's liability. An unqualified indorser's liability normally is of two types: (1) *secondary*, by which he is obliged to pay if the party expected to pay fails to do so and certain other conditions are met, and (2) *warranty*, by which he incurs liability if the instrument has been altered or if certain other special circumstances have arisen. If he indorses in the usual way, by either blank or special indorsement, the indorsement is said to be unqualified, as the indorser incurs both types of liability. To disclaim his secondary liability, however, an indorser can include the words "without recourse," or words of similar meaning, in his indorsement; in which case, his indorsement, and consequently his liability, is said to be qualified. (See Chapters 7, 8, 9)

§ 19.   Restrictive Indorsements

In addition to being classified as blank or special, to determine what is necessary for further negotiation, or unqualified or qualified to determine whether the indorser incurs secondary liability, any indorsement can be classified as unrestrictive or restrictive to determine whether it limits the rights and powers transferred in any of the ways specifically provided by Section 3–205 which defines restrictive indorsements.

Section 3–205 provides that an indorsement is restrictive which either (a) is conditional; or (b) purports to prohibit further transfer of the instrument; or (c) includes the words "for collection", "for deposit", "pay any bank", or like terms signifying a purpose of deposit or collection; or (d) otherwise states that it is for the benefit or use of the indorser or another person. A very large proportion of the indorsements that are used in the business world outside of banking channels, are unrestrictive, a classification that presents no problems. The principal question raised by restrictive indorsements is how they affect indorsees, subsequent transferees, and payors.

A.   INDORSEMENTS THAT PURPORT TO PROHIBIT FURTHER TRANSFER

Under the prior law there was uncertainty about when a restrictive indorsement prevented further negotiation. The Code removes all doubt by providing unequivocally that "*no* restrictive indorsement prevents further transfer or negotiation of the instrument." [3–206(1)] (Emphasis added.) Even an indorsement which expressly prohibits further transfer cannot bar further transfer or negotiation under the Code. There are few practical reasons for a transferor to bar further transfer, and so such indorsements are rare. Under the Code, when they do occur they are given the same effect as unrestrictive indorsements. Thus, the indorsement, "Pay N. Dorsey only," is treated as if it were, "Pay N. Dorsey," or, "Pay to the order of N. Dorsey."

B.   CONDITIONAL INDORSEMENT

Somewhat more prevalent than the indorsement purporting to restrict further transfer, but still not common, is the conditional indorsement which imposes a condition on the right of the indorsee or any later holder to collect. Usually, the purpose of a conditional indorsement is to assure the indorser that some duty *owed to him* will be performed. For example, P, the payee of a note, may indorse it, "Pay X when he delivers 100 shares of Gold Stock to me. (Signed) P," and deliver it to X in return for X's promise to deliver the stock. A conditional indorsement should not be confused with a conditional promise by a maker or a conditional order by a drawer. A condition to a promise or order, if contained in the instrument, prevents the instrument from being negotiable. A conditional indorsement does not. And,

[*116*]

as stated above, like other types of restrictive indorsements, it does not prevent further transfer or negotiation of the instrument. Under the Code, a conditional indorsement is treated in the same way as an indorsement for deposit or collection which is discussed immediately below. [3–206 (1) (2) (3), 3–603 (1) (b)]

C. INDORSEMENT FOR DEPOSIT OR COLLECTION

By far the most important and common restrictive indorsements are those for deposit or collection. Typically, they are expressed, "for deposit," "for collection," or "pay any bank." Each of these indorsements should serve as a warning that a bank or other transferee might hold the instrument, at the outset at least, in trust or as agent for the restrictive indorser rather than as the owner. How such an indorsement otherwise affects persons who come into contact with such instruments depends largely upon the roles they play in the collection process.

If a seller in Boston receives a check or an ordinary draft which is payable to him and is drawn on his customer's bank in Denver, he might conceivably indorse the instrument "for collection," and forward it to his own agent in Denver with instructions to obtain payment and remit the proceeds. However, the seller in Boston usually will indorse the instrument "for deposit," then deposit it in his own bank in Boston, and let the bank attend to collection and to crediting his account with the proceeds. His bank will then indorse the instrument "for collection" or "pay any bank" and forward it through one or more banks to the Denver bank. There will be no actual transfer of funds corresponding to this specific transaction. Rather than transferring actual funds, the Denver bank will credit the presenting bank with the proceeds, this bank will credit the bank from which it received the instrument, and so on until ultimately the Boston bank will credit the seller's account if it has not already done so. In the above case, the Boston bank, the first bank to which the instrument was delivered for collection, is known as the *depositary* bank; the Denver bank, on whom the instrument was drawn, is known as the *payor* bank; and the other banks which participated in the collection process are called *intermediary* banks. [4–105]

1. Depositary Banks and Transferees
   Outside Banking Process

In a consideration of the effect of restrictive indorsements, depositary banks and transferees outside the normal banking process are treated alike. They are governed mainly by Section 3–206(3) which provides that "except for an intermediary bank, any transferee under an indorsement which is conditional or includes the words 'for collection,' 'for deposit,' 'pay any bank,' or like terms * * * *must pay or apply any value given by him for or on the security of the instrument consistently with the indorsement* and to the extent that he does so he becomes a holder for value. In addition, such transferee is a holder in due course if he otherwise complies with the requirements of Section 3–302 on what constitutes a holder in due course." (Emphasis added)

Suppose that P, the payee of a note, indorses it, "for collection," and delivers it to A, his agent, with instructions to obtain payment from M, the maker. Typically, A will present the note to the maker at maturity, obtain payment, and remit the proceeds to P. In this case A becomes a holder, but not a holder for value because he gives no value. Since he is not a holder for value, A is not a holder in due course; thus, if M has any defense against P, he can assert it against A. If A had paid P the amount of the note when he received it, or by mutual agreement they had cancelled some debt owed by P to A, A would have given value, and if he met the other requirements, A would have been a holder in due course. Consequently, A would not have been subject to the defense which M might have had against P, unless A had learned of it prior to giving the value.

Suppose that A, instead of taking the note to M, transfers it to T; can T become a holder in due course? He can to the extent that he pays value for the instrument *consistently with P's restrictive indorsement.* If he actually pays A the amount of the note he becomes a holder for value despite the restrictive indorsement because such payment is contemplated by the indorsement itself. However, he does not pay value consistently with P's restrictive indorsement if he merely credits A *personally* with the amount of the note.

In Blaine, Gould & Short v. Bourne & Co., 11 R.I. 119 (1875) T drew a draft on C, naming himself as payee. After indorsing it in blank, T sold the draft to G. G indorsed it, "Pay A or order on account of G. (Signed) G," and delivered it to A. A then indorsed the draft, "Pay B. (Signed) A," and delivered it to B who obtained payment from C, the drawee, at maturity. B applied the proceeds of the draft on a debt owed to him by A. G sued B to recover the proceeds. G was awarded judgment. The restrictive indorsement gave B as a subsequent indorsee, notice of the fact that A was only an agent to collect and had no authority to apply the proceeds of the draft to pay his own debt. If the above case had been decided under the Code, the result would have been the same. By paying value by satisfying A's personal debt, B was not paying value "consistently with" G's restrictive indorsement.

These principles apply in substantially the same way in determining the rights and duties of the *depositary* bank which receives an instrument under a restrictive indorsement in the course of the normal banking process.

For example, if P, the payee, indorses a check, "for deposit," and delivers it to A, his agent, the depositary bank is charged with knowing that the proceeds must be credited to P's account. If the bank takes the check from A and pays A the amount of the check, or credits A's account or applies it toward satisfaction of A's indebtedness to the bank, the bank is liable to P for conversion because the value it gives is not consistent with P's restrictive indorsement. For the same reason, the bank could not qualify as a holder in due course and, if it sued the drawer, would be subject to any defense that the drawer might have. In contrast, if the bank credits the amount of the check to P's account and allows P to withdraw the proceeds, it could qualify as a holder in due course because in this case it applies the value it gives consistently with P's restrictive indorsement.

2. SPECIAL TREATMENT OF INTERMEDIARY AND PAYOR BANKS

Intermediary banks and payor banks must handle negotiable instruments, especially checks, in vast numbers and by assembly line methods. Their normal operations would be hampered greatly if they were required to stop and consider the effect of each individual indorsement in a chain of in-

[*121*]

dorsements. Consequently, the Code provides that *intermediary and payor banks may ignore a restrictive indorsement of any person other than the bank's immediate transferor or the person presenting the instrument for payment.* (If a payor bank is also a depositary bank, it is classified as a depositary bank only, and is not given any special treatment.)   [3–206(2), 4–205(2)] This special immunity applies to all types of restrictive indorsements but is, of course, most often important in connection with indorsements for deposit or collection.

The need for this protection is demonstrated by the case of Soma v. Handrulis, 277 N.Y. 223, 14 N.E.2d 46 (1938). Plaintiff, payee of a check, indorsed it "for deposit," and was then induced by a defrauder to entrust it to him for "safe-keeping." The defrauder persuaded a third party to indorse the check in blank and deposit it in the latter's account with Globe Bank. Globe Bank indorsed the check for collection and delivered it to the Federal Reserve Bank. The latter obtained payment from West Chester Trust, the drawee bank, and paid Globe Bank, which permitted its depositor to withdraw the proceeds of the check. In holding that on those facts Federal Reserve Bank was liable to the payee, the New York Court of Appeals stated, "The indorsement was restrictive and prohibited further negotiation for any purpose except for collection and deposit in (payee's) account." If the *Soma* case had been decided under the Code, the result would have been different because the Federal Reserve Bank, as an *intermediary* bank, would not have been affected by any indorsement other than that of the Globe Bank, its immediate transferor, and so would not have been liable.

Neither the Globe Bank nor the West Chester Trust were made parties to the action. However, it is clear that under the Code the Globe Bank, as a *depositary* bank, would have been liable to Mrs. Soma; a depositary bank is affected by *all* prior indorsements and cannot become a holder in due course unless it pays in accordance with the terms of a prior restrictive indorsement. [3–206(3)] It also is clear that, under the Code, West Chester Trust, the drawee, would not have been bound by the restrictive indorsement because, as a *payor bank*, it is bound by only the indorsement of the person presenting for payment. [3–206(2)]

Several years after Soma v. Handrulis, in Leonardi v. Chase National Bank, 263 App.Div. 552, 33 N.Y.S.2d 706 (1942) another New York court applied Florida law to reach a result consistent with the Code. The payee deposited a check in a Florida bank after indorsing it for deposit. The depositary bank forwarded the check to defendant intermediary bank "for collection and credit." The defendant bank promptly obtained a final credit (which is equivalent to payment) for the amount of the check from the drawee. Then, learning that the depositary bank had become insolvent, defendant bank used the proceeds of the check to offset a debt owed it by the depositary bank by giving the depositary bank a "final credit" on its books. The payee sued to recover the amount of the check from the defendant intermediary bank, on the theory that defendant had converted the payee's funds to its own use. The court conceded that defendant intermediary bank had received the check as a subagent of the payee and continued as such until "final payment" was made to the depositary bank. However, it held for the defendant intermediary bank stating, "Credit is the exclusive means of payment in ordinary banking practice. 'The cash is not handled' and 'No money passes.' Here the payment to the [depositary] bank was by means of a final solvent credit, as the result of which the agency terminated and the relationship of debtor and creditor ensued between defendant and the [depositary] bank." Under the Code, the result, but not the analysis, would have been the same. As an intermediary bank, the defendant would not have been affected by the plaintiff payee's restrictive indorsement. It would have been free to carry on its dealings with the depositary bank in their usual manner without regard to the depositor's restrictive indorsement.

[124]

Once an instrument is deposited for collection, it normally remains within banking channels until it is finally collected and credited. To deal with the unusual case, the Code provides that after an instrument has been indorsed, "pay any bank," or the like, "only a bank may acquire the rights of a holder (a) until the item has been returned to the customer initiating collection; or (b) until the item has been specially indorsed by a bank to a person who is not a bank." [4–201(2)] Under this provision, if a depositary bank indorses an item, "pay any bank," as is typically the case, and it is later lost or stolen, the finder or thief normally would lack power to negotiate the instrument to anyone else. The above provision makes clear that outside of banking circles, an indorsement, "pay any bank," or the like, is a special indorsement so that the indorsement of a bank, as special indorsee, is necessary for further negotiation.

D. TRUST INDORSEMENTS

Sometimes the purpose of a restrictive indorsement is to benefit the indorser or someone else in some way other than by providing a condition to payment or by providing for collection or deposit. For example, P, the holder of a note, wishing to benefit himself, may indorse it, "Pay T in trust for P," or, wishing to benefit C, may indorse it, "Pay T for the benefit of C." Like other restrictive indorsements this does not prevent further negotiation of the instrument. But since the restrictive indorsee is a fiduciary, such an indorsement raises the question whether a person who takes the instrument from or through such an indorsee can qualify as a holder in due course. This question is answered by Section 3–206(4) which provides

> The *first* taker under an indorsement for the benefit of the indorser or another person * * * must pay or apply any value given by him * * * consistently with the indorsement and to the extent that he does so he becomes a holder for value. In addition such taker is a holder in due course if he otherwise complies with the (usual requirements). A *later* holder for value is neither given notice nor otherwise affected by such restrictive indorsement unless he has knowledge that a fiduciary or other person has negotiated the instrument in any transaction for his own benefit or otherwise in breach of duty." (Emphasis added)

This provision is based on the assumption that the restrictive indorsee in a case of this kind is a fiduciary and, as such, owes a duty to use the instrument and its proceeds for the good of the beneficiary and not for his own advantage. But it also recognizes that trustees frequently and properly sell trust assets and that a purchaser from the trustee may well act in good faith. It requires, however, that a person who deals with the fiduciary, himself, furnish value in a way that is not obviously going to benefit the trustee rather than the beneficiary. The provision also recognizes that after the instrument has been negotiated by the fiduciary, *later purchasers* should not be required to investigate that transaction. Therefore, the duty to act consistently with the restrictive indorsement is limited to the *first* taker. A later taker is not barred from being a holder in due course unless he *knows* when he takes the instrument that the fiduciary negotiated the instrument in breach of his duty.

Consider the following case.

P conveyed land to M. In payment, M made and delivered two 5-year notes for $5,000 each. P indorsed each note, "Pay T in trust for C" and delivered it to T with the understanding that T would collect the notes at maturity and pay the proceeds to C, who was P's son. A month later, T indorsed and delivered both notes to X in payment of a $12,000 debt T owed X. X acted in good faith. A year later, X indorsed and delivered one of the notes to Y in payment of a debt of $6,000 owed by X to Y. At maturity X and Y demanded payment but M refused to pay either note on the ground the warranty of title contained in P's deed had been broken. This was a good defense against X. Even though X acted in good faith, and gave value, as the *first* taker he was not a holder in due course because he did not apply the value in a manner consistent with P's restrictive indorsement. As first taker, X was charged with notice that T negotiated the note in breach of his fiduciary duty. Y, as a *later* holder, was under no duty to apply the value he gave in a manner consistent with P's restrictive indorsement nor was he charged with notice or otherwise affected by the restrictive indorsement unless he *knew* that T had negotiated the note to X in breach of his fiduciary duty. If X, instead of taking the notes in satisfaction of T's own debt, had paid T the value of the notes in cash, he would have paid value in a manner consistent with the restrictive indorsement and could have been a holder in due course.

E. EFFECT OF RESTRICTIVE INDORSE-MENT ON DISCHARGE OF PAYOR

Normally when a party who is liable on a negotiable instrument pays the holder, he is discharged from his liability. There are several exceptions. (See pages 307–309) The only one which is of concern here is provided by Section 3–603(1)(b), which states in substance that unless a payor is either an intermediary bank or a payor bank, one who pays or satisfies the holder of an instrument that has been restrictively indorsed is not discharged from liability on an instrument, unless he pays in a manner consistent with the terms of the restrictive indorsement.

M issues a note to P who indorses "for collection. P," and delivers it to A, P's agent. At maturity A demands payment and M pays A the amount of the note. M's liability is discharged. By paying A cash, M paid in a manner consistent with the terms of the restrictive indorsement.

M's liability would not have been discharged if, instead of actually paying A, M had merely applied the amount of the note to satisfy a debt owed to M by A; for this would not have been consistent with P's restrictive indorsement.

§ 20. Words of Assignment, Waiver, Guarantee, Limitation or Disclaimer

In addition to the ways already considered, the legal consequences of an indorsement may be affected by words of assignment, waiver, guarantee, limitation, or disclaimer of liability. None of these words, however, prevent an indorsement from being effective for the purpose of negotiation, nor do they prevent further negotiation or prevent a transferee from becoming a holder or even a holder in due course. [3–202(4)]

As we have seen, a negotiable instrument may be the physical embodiment of a whole series of dynamic transactions and the original issuance and subsequent transfer and negotiation may effect a whole chain of rights, duties, and liabilities of the various parties concerned. This should become increasingly clear as our discussion continues.

CHAPTER 7

LIABILITY OF PARTIES ON THE INSTRUMENT

§ 1. Various Bases of Liability

Ideally, the holder of a negotiable instrument should be able to see, by mere inspection of it, the chain of persons who are liable to him and the nature of the liability of each. The ideal however is rarely achieved. Some of the persons who come into contact with an instrument sign it, others do not. Some come into contact with an instrument as makers or drawers, others as acceptors or indorsers. Each of these parties assumes a different kind of liability. Moreover, the nature of the various obligations depends on whether or not the person seeking to collect has the rights of a holder in due course. Also, some indorsers incur liability on the instrument as well as on the basis of certain warranties, but other indorsers and those who transfer without indorsement become liable only on their warranties. In addition, parties who obtain acceptance or payment may incur liability on one or more warranties. Furthermore, a negotiable instrument usually is issued or transferred for the purpose of satisfying some underlying obligation the liability on which might or might not be suspended temporarily.

This involved network of rights and liabilities will be delineated in this and following chapters. The present chapter will be concerned primarily with the liability imposed only on those who *sign* an instrument—usually referred to as liability *on* the instrument. [3–401(1)]

§ 2. General Principles Governing Liability on the Instrument

A person who signs an instrument is said to be liable *on* it, as maker, drawer, acceptor, or indorser. The liability incurred by each of these parties differs from the liability of each of the others. Before considering them separately, however, let us consider some general principles which apply to all.

A. PERSON'S SIGNATURE MUST APPEAR ON INSTRUMENT TO INCUR LIABILITY ON IT

The Code expressly provides that, "no person is liable on an instrument unless his signature appears thereon." [3–401(1)] Consistent with this principle, an undisclosed principal, whose liability on a simple contract made on his behalf without disclosing his identity is well recognized, cannot be held liable on a negotiable instrument because his signature does not appear on it. Even when the principal's identity is disclosed orally, he does not incur liability on the instrument if his authorized agent signs only his own name. Nor can a person become liable on an instrument merely by signing a separate writing expressing his willingness to be liable on the instrument.

Although the principle that no person can become liable on a negotiable instrument unless his signature appears on it is sound as a general proposition, it must be applied with caution and with an awareness that it sometimes requires the use of fictions, or at least a little stretching of ordinary language. As shown earlier, there are many ways in which a signature can be applied. And as will be seen in later discussion, the general proposition does not prevent imposing liability on an instrument because an authorized agent signed on behalf of the person held liable [3–403(1)], or because a person who actually did not sign an instrument *is precluded* from denying an unauthorized signature as his own [3–406], or because an unauthorized signature of another person operates as the signature of the unauthorized signer. [3–404(1)]

B. NAME NEED NOT APPEAR TO GIVE PERSON RIGHT TO SUE ON INSTRUMENT

One must not draw from the general proposition that no person is *liable* on an instrument unless his signature appears on it the inference that no one is *entitled to sue* on the instrument unless his signature appears on it. Not only is it not required that a person's *signature* appear on an instrument to entitle him to sue on it; it is not even required that his *name* appear on it. As stated earlier the proper person to sue on an instrument is usually the holder who might be the payee or a special indorsee, whose name appears on it but who has never signed the instrument, or a possessor of a bearer instrument whose name does not appear on it at all.

C. SIGNATURE

Previously considered in discussing the requisites of negotiability was the need to have the instrument signed by the maker or drawer. What was said there regarding what constitutes a signature applies not only to makers and drawers but to acceptors and indorsers as well. (See page 45)

D. DETERMINING CAPACITY IN WHICH PARTY SIGNS

Normally it is clear that the person who signs on the face of an instrument in the lower right hand corner is either the maker or the drawer. It usually is equally certain that a signature on the reverse side is an indorsement and the drawee's signature vertically across the face of a draft is an acceptance. Occasionally a person signs in some unusual place, but his capacity becomes apparent when the instrument is considered as a unit. For example, a signature of John Smith in the lower left hand corner is obviously that of the maker of an instrument which starts "I, John Smith, promise to pay." When for any reason the capacity of the person signing is ambiguous, the problem is governed by Section 3–402 which provides that "unless the instrument clearly indicates that a signature is made in some other capacity, it is an indorsement." Unless it is clear from the instrument that he signed in some other capacity, one who signs a negotiable instrument is an indorser. Parol evidence to the contrary is not admissible. [Comment, 3–402] Sometimes a person whose signature appears on an instrument is not liable in any capacity. For example, a person normally would not be liable on the instrument if he placed "witness" after his name. [Comment, 3–402] Nor would he be liable if he signed below "payment received" for these words show a purpose to give a receipt, not to indorse.

E. SIGNATURE BY AUTHORIZED REPRESENTATIVE

Under the general laws of agency, an agent normally cannot bind his principal without actual or apparent authority to do so. In our present discussion, we may assume that actual authority exists. But even assuming that an agent has authority to bind his principal as maker, drawer, acceptor, or indorser of a negotiable instrument, the legal consequences of his attempt to exercise his authority may vary considerably from case to case depending on how he proceeds.

For example, assume that P. Prince has given A. Axel authority to bind him as maker, drawer, acceptor, or indorser. If A. Axel exercises his authority in the usual way—by signing "P. Prince, by A. Axel, Agent,"—there is no problem. As a matter of law, the principal is liable, the agent is not. Parol evidence to show a contrary understanding is not admissible. But Axel might undertake to exercise his authority by signing in any one of a number of other ways, each of which presents its own problem. Confining our discussion to four relatively simple examples, assume that the name of the principal does not already appear on the instrument and that A. Axel, intending to bind P. Prince and not himself, signs: (1) "P. Prince," (2) "A. Axel," (3) "A. Axel, Agent," or (4) "P. Prince, A. Axel."

If, intending to bind his principal and not himself, A. Axel signs "P. Prince," the legal consequences will be those intended—Prince will be bound and Axel will not. This type of signature, however, may present a problem to the third party or his transferee if he is later required to show the circumstances under which Prince's name was signed.

If the agent signs his name "A. Axel," without explanation, he alone is bound on the instrument

[3–403(2)(a)], even if he intends to bind only his principal, and the party with whom he deals understands his intention. Proof of an oral understanding to the contrary is barred even without the aid of the parol evidence rule. [3–403(2)(a)] The principal is *not* liable on the instrument. This is in accordance with the general rule that no one is liable on an instrument unless his signature appears on it. [3–401(1)] However, if the third party has a valid claim and cannot collect from the agent, he may recover from the principal on the underlying obligation for which the instrument was given.

If an authorized agent, intending to act only for his principal, signs his own name and immediately thereafter indicates his representative capacity, but does not show the name of his principal—for example, "A. Axel, Agent"—he may show in litigation between himself and the person with whom he dealt, or someone having only the latter's rights, that, when he signed, it was understood by the parties that he acted only as agent and was not to be personally liable. [3–403(2)(b)] If he is sued by a later holder in due course, however, the agent is personally liable and may not show that he acted only as agent. Regardless of who is seeking to recover, the principal is not liable on the instrument because his name does not appear on it. A holder who cannot collect from the agent, however, may recover from the principal on his underlying obligation.

If an authorized agent, intending to act only for his principal, shows his principal's name as well as his own but does not indicate that he signs in a representative capacity—for example, "P. Prince, A. Axel"—in litigation between himself and the person with whom he dealt, or someone having only the latter's rights, the agent again may show that when he signed both parties understood that he acted only as agent and was not to be liable personally. [3–403(2)(b)] But if he is sued by a later holder in due course, he is personally liable and may not show that he acted only as agent. The principal, of course, is personally liable because his name was signed to the instrument with his authority.

In any of the above cases, if the agent is required to pay the third party, he is entitled to be indemnified by his principal because he acted with actual authority.

In general, the foregoing discussion of an authorized signing of a negotiable instrument would be equally applicable if, instead of representing P. Prince, an *individual,* A. Axel, the agent, had represented an *organization* which is broadly defined to include a corporation, partnership, government agency, estate, trust, or other legal or commercial entity other than an individual. [1–201(28)(30)] However, the great variety of circumstances in which a legal representative might undertake to exercise his authority by signing a negotiable instrument would seem to dictate caution to anyone responsible for the legal aspects of such matters. This is especially true if one wishes to make certain that a representative who agrees to be liable individually is held to his agreement. As shown above, a representative who wishes to avoid individual liability can easily do so by showing the name of his principal and the representative capacity in which he signs and by inserting the word "by" before his signature. But one who wishes to bind the person or organization represented and also wishes to bind the representative individually cannot always rely on the fact that the representative does not use the word "by" or show his representative capacity. To be safe in these cases it would appear to be good practice to have the representative sign twice; first, showing his representative capacity; and second, before the word "individually." If this practice is followed, whatever disagreement there is in the matter is likely to occur before the signing rather than after a dispute arises and it becomes important to impose liability on the representative.

F.   UNAUTHORIZED SIGNATURES

The Code makes no distinction between the signature made by an agent who is acting innocently but is without actual authority and the signature that is a forgery under the criminal laws. [1–201 (43)] Both kinds of signatures are classified as *unauthorized.* It is basic that an unauthorized signature is *inoperative as the signature of the person or other legal entity whose name is signed* unless the latter *ratifies* the unauthorized act or is *precluded* from denying it. This does not mean that the unauthorized signature has no legal effect. On the contrary, the unauthorized signature *operates as the signature of the unauthorized signer* in favor of any person who in good faith pays the instrument or takes it for value. [3–404(1)] What has been said about an unauthorized signature is true not only when considering whether a person shall be liable on an instrument, the main question now being considered, but also in determining whether there has been an effective negotiation which was discussed in Chapter 6.

The effect of ratifying an unauthorized signature is retroactive so as to (1) impose liability on the ratifying party as if he had signed in the first place and (2) to release the unauthorized signer from liability *on* the instrument. It does not necessarily relieve the latter of civil liability to the ratifying party, nor does it bar criminal action if the unauthorized signing amounts to a forgery. [Comment 3, 3–404]

G.   ALTERATION

Under the Code an alteration might consist of an addition, change or deletion; or it might consist of the completion of an incomplete instrument otherwise than as authorized.   [3–407(1) (b)]

Depending on several variables, an alteration might or might not result in discharging the liability incurred by anyone who had signed as maker, drawer, acceptor or indorser.

If the alteration is (1) by a holder, and (2) fraudulent, and (3) material in that it changes the contract of any party to the instrument, it results in a discharge of any person whose contract is changed by the alteration, unless that party assents or is precluded from asserting the defense. [3–407(2) (a)]

If the alteration does not meet all three of the above conditions, it does not result in discharging the liability of anyone.   The contract may be enforced according to its original terms and if the alteration consists of the completion of an incomplete instrument otherwise than as authorized, it may be enforced at least according to its terms *as authorized*.   [3–407(2) (b)]

Regardless of whether the above three conditions are met, if the instrument is acquired *after the alteration* by a *holder in due course,* he is entitled to enforce it according to its *original* terms if the alteration consists of an addition, change or deletion.   And he can enforce it according to the terms of the instrument *as completed* if the alteration consists of the completion of an incomplete instrument otherwise than as authorized. [3–407(3)] This is so even though the party who signed the instrument never issued it. One who signs an incomplete instrument assumes this risk.

Case 1.   M buys goods from P and delivers P his note for the price payable to P's order. T steals the unindorsed note from P, raises the amount, and sells the note to A. Since T was not the holder, M was not discharged by the alteration. P is entitled to enforce the note against M according to its original tenor.

Case 2.   The holder of a draft that makes no reference to interest, mistakenly thinking that such an instrument bears interest at 6%, in good faith adds "with interest at 6%" following the amount. No one is discharged from liability. The alteration was not fraudulent. The instrument is enforceable, as originally provided, without interest.

Case 3.   M issues a note to P who indorses it "without recourse" and negotiates it to H. H fraudulently deletes "without recourse" from P's indorsement. P is discharged because his contract is changed. M is not.

Case 4.   P negotiates M's note for $1,000 to A who raises it to $10,000 and then negotiates it to H for $9,200. If H is a holder in due course, M and P are liable to H to the extent of $1,000, the original tenor of the note, and A is liable to H for $10,000. If H is not a holder in due course, he is not entitled to recover anything from M or P who were discharged by the holder's (A's) fraudulent alteration which changed their contracts, but A is liable to H for $10,000.

Case 5.   R signs a blank check, locks it in his safe,
and instructs his clerk to complete and cash it
when the payroll is determined.   T steals the
check, fills in the blanks to show himself as payee
and a large sum as payable and cashes the check
at B Bank.   Assuming that B Bank is a holder in
due course, it is entitled to the full amount of the
check as completed.   If not, it is entitled to nothing.

H.   NEGLIGENCE CONTRIBUTING TO UNAUTHORIZED SIGNATURE OR ALTERATION

The foregoing principles that normally furnish
a shield from liability or a basis for recovery on
the ground of *unauthorized signature* or *alteration* are sometimes rendered inoperative by the
fact that the negligence of the person who asserts the wrongdoing substantially contributed to
it.   The broad principle which has governed such
cases for more than a century (see Young v. Grote,
4 Bing. 253, 130 Eng.Rep. 764 (1827)) is stated
in a refined form in Section 3–406 which provides:

> Any person who by his negligence substan-
> tially contributes to a material alteration of
> the instrument or to the making of an un-
> authorized signature is precluded from as-
> serting the alteration or lack of authority
> against a holder in due course or against a
> drawee or other payor who pays the instru-
> ment in good faith and in accordance with
> reasonable commercial standards of the
> drawee's or payor's business.

[*142*]

It should be emphasized that Section 3–406 applies only if there has been *negligence*. If a holder in due course acquires an instrument in which the amount payable has been raised from $500 to $5,000, his recovery will be limited to $500 if the defendant has not been negligent. But under this provision he will be entitled to the full $5,000 if the negligence of the defendant substantially contributed to the alteration. In contrast, it should be noted that if the alteration consists of completing an incomplete instrument (one that is signed while the space for some essential term is completely blank as where the space for the payee's name or for the amount is completely blank) contrary to authority, rather than by merely taking advantage of carelessness which makes it easier to *change* a term already inserted, a holder in due course is entitled to recover on the instrument as completed without regard to whether the party sued has been negligent.

It will be observed that Section 3–406 above protects not only a holder in due course but also a drawee or other payor who pays the instrument in good faith in accordance with reasonable commercial standards of the drawee's or payor's business.

For example, in Foutch v. Alexandria Bank & Trust Co., 177 Tenn. 348, 149 S.W.2d 76 (1941), the plaintiff habitually allowed payees to fill in the amount of checks before he signed them as drawer. On one occasion he signed a check in which the payee had inserted "18.00" well to the right of the dollar sign on one line and then, starting in the middle of the following line, had inserted "Eighteen and no/100" immediately in front of "dollars." After delivery the payee used the same pencil he had used to fill in the original amounts to insert a "4" immediately in front of the "18.00" and "Four Hundred" immediately in front of "Eighteen and no/100." He then cashed the altered check at the drawee bank which charged plaintiff's account. When the plaintiff sued to recover the $400 from the drawee bank, the court held that the plaintiff was precluded by his negligence from asserting the alteration. The court pointed out that the plaintiff's negligence had made it virtually impossible for the bank to detect the alteration.

Section 3–406 extends not only to cases where negligence substantially contributes to a *material alteration* but also to cases where negligence substantially contributes to an *unauthorized signature*. For example, a person who is in the habit of using a signature stamp or an automatic signing device might substantially contribute to a forgery by negligently allowing outsiders to have access to it, or a person might substantially contribute to a forgery by negligently mailing the instrument to the wrong person who has the same name as the intended payee but a different address. (See, for example, Park State Bank v. Arena Court Auction, Inc., 59 Ill.App.2d 235, 207 N.E.2d 158 (1965))

§ 3. Liability of Particular Parties On the Instrument

A. IN GENERAL

A person who signs a negotiable instrument may become liable *on* it as a maker, drawer, acceptor, or indorser. Makers and acceptors are classified as *primary* parties. Drawers and indorsers are classified as *secondary* parties. [3–102(1)(d)] In an effort to simplify the distinction, it is sometimes said that a person who is expected to pay is a primary party whereas one who backs him up is a secondary party. Although this statement contains some truth, it disregards the fact that the person expected to pay an ordinary draft or a check, by far the most common negotiable instrument, is a drawee, who is neither a primary nor a secondary party. In fact, as will be mentioned again later, a drawee, as such, is not a party to the instrument at all. Actually, a primary party—whether maker or acceptor—normally is both expected to pay and legally bound to pay without need for the holder to resort to anyone else first; whereas a secondary party normally is not expected to pay and is not legally bound to pay unless the party expected to pay fails to do so. But even these generalizations are not always sound, as will be seen.

B. MAKER'S LIABILITY

The maker engages that he will pay the instrument according to its original terms or according to the principles already discussed if it is altered. [3–413(1)] (See page 139) Since the maker is primarily liable on the note, unless he has been discharged or has some other defense, he must pay it at maturity. Normally he cannot look to anyone else for reimbursement when required to pay.

C. DRAWER'S LIABILITY

The drawer issues a draft, and like the maker of a note, he is liable only on the instrument and not on the basis of any warranties. Unlike a maker, however, the drawer does not promise to pay, at least not unconditionally; and he does not expect to pay. Instead he orders the drawee to pay. Consider the ordinary check. By issuing it, the drawer in effect says to the bank, "Pay the amount of this check to the holder when he presents it and charge my account." In effect, he says to the payee, "Take this check to the bank and ask for payment and if it does not pay, come back to me and I will." Basically, the drawer has "backup" liability. This is not stated in the draft he signs, which contains no promise but only an order expressed by the word "Pay" addressed to the drawee. In short, the drawer is only secondarily liable. In describing the drawer's secondary liability the Code states, "The drawer engages that upon dishonor of the draft and any necessary notice of dishonor or protest he will pay the amount of the draft to the holder or to any indorser who takes it up." [3–413(2)] What constitutes dishonor and what is required in the way of notice or protest in order to fix the drawer's liability will be discussed later. (See Chapter 8) Typically the holder or his agent presents the draft to the drawee for payment at maturity, the drawee fails to pay, and the holder thereafter mails notice of dishonor to the drawer. Although a drawer, like an indorser, may disclaim secondary liability by indorsing "without recourse," he rarely does so. Just as the maker's primary liability may be increased by any negligence on his part that contributes substantially to an alteration, so may the secondary liability of the drawer be increased. Also the risk of incurring greater liability than he authorized, imposed on the maker when he signs an incomplete instrument, is imposed on a drawer under similar circumstances.

D.   DRAWEE'S LIABILITY

A drawee is not liable on a draft until he *accepts* it. (See page 150 for meaning of acceptance.) [3–409(1)] Therefore so long as he refrains from signing the draft and does not become an *acceptor* he incurs no liability *on it* to the holder as the result of refusing to pay or accept it.

Furthermore, a check or other draft does not *of itself* operate as an assignment of any funds in the hands of the drawee available for its payment. [3–409(1)] This is so even though the drawee holds sufficient funds of the drawer to pay the draft and has made a contract with the drawer binding himself to the drawer to honor the draft when it is presented. Normally the payee is deemed to be only an incidental beneficiary of the contract between the drawer and drawee. Of course, a drawee who fails to honor a proper demand for payment might be held liable to the drawer if the failure violates a duty owed to the drawer on the basis of a contract of deposit or otherwise.

Assume that E owes R $1000 which is overdue.

Case 1. R assigns his right to the $1000 to P. Since a claim for money is freely assignable, P is entitled to collect the $1000 from E upon notifying E of the assignment. E has no choice in the matter; he must pay P.

Case 2. R draws a draft on E for $1000 payable on demand and delivers the draft to P. P presents the draft to E and demands payment. E refuses to pay P. P has no rights against E, even though E may be liable to R on any contract they had between them.

Although a check or draft does not of itself operate as an assignment of the funds in the hands of the drawee available for payment, the intent of the parties to effect an assignment may sometimes be inferred from other facts and, when the inference is clear, such instrument will be treated as a device for carrying out an assignment so as to render the drawee to whom it is addressed liable to the holder as assignee.   [Comment 1, 3–409]

Also, a drawee becomes liable for *conversion* if, having had a draft presented to him for acceptance or for payment, he not only refuses to pay or accept but also refuses to return the instrument despite a demand.   [3–419(1)(a)(b)]   Although such a refusal does not constitute an acceptance, the result is much the same because he thereby becomes liable for the face amount of the draft.   Depending on circumstances, and less frequently, a person named as drawee might become liable to a holder on other bases such as a letter of credit, fraud, promissory estoppel, breach of trust, or on the theory that the holder is a third party creditor beneficiary of the contract between the drawer and drawee.

E.   ACCEPTOR'S LIABILITY

As stated earlier, the *drawee is not liable on a draft until he assents by accepting it* and becoming an acceptor.   A bank's acceptance of a check

is called a *certification*.   (See pages 322–323)
Under the N.I.L. it was possible to accept by
signing the instrument or a separate paper such
as a telegram or a letter.   Because these *extrinsic*
acceptances caused a degree of uncertainty inconsistent with the free transferability of commercial
paper, the Code provides that the acceptance must
appear *on the draft itself*.   [3–410(1)]   *The acceptance may consist of a signature alone*.   It is
customary for an acceptor to sign vertically on
the face of the draft, but a drawee's signature
anywhere else normally is sufficient because usually the only reason he has for signing it is
to accept.   The acceptor may, and usually does,
insert the word "accepted" above his signature.
He may add the date, an important act if the draft
is payable a stated period "after sight."   In the
latter case, if the acceptor fails to insert the date
of his acceptance, the holder may supply the date
in good faith and the inserted date will bind the
acceptor.   [3–410(3)]   Also the acceptor may indicate the place where the draft is payable.   (See
pages 184–185)

As an exception to the general rule that a person does not become liable on an instrument until
he both signs *and delivers* it, a person may become
liable as an acceptor by signing and either delivering the instrument *or notifying* the holder of
his acceptance.   [3–410(1) and Comment 5]

[*150*]

The acceptor's liability on the instrument, like the maker's, is primary, and it also resembles the maker's liability in other ways. [3–413(1)] If the instrument is complete when he accepts it, the acceptor engages that he will pay the draft according to the terms of the draft when he accepted it. Any later alteration will not increase his liability unless he either assents to the alteration or is precluded from asserting it. Similarly, if he signs an incomplete draft, he will be liable on the completed instrument if it is completed within the authority given by him, and he runs the risk of incurring greater liability than he authorized if the instrument is completed in an unauthorized manner and is later acquired by a holder in due course. Note that the acceptor does not necessarily agree to pay the instrument according to the terms as made out by the drawer but rather according to the terms at the time of his acceptance. If between issue and acceptance the instrument has been altered in any respect, the acceptor is liable on the altered instrument. He may have recourse against the presenter and one or more prior parties, however, as will be explained when liability based on warranties is discussed. (See pages 220–224)

Case. 1. R draws a draft for $2,000. P, payee, obtains E's acceptance and negotiates the draft to T. T raises the amount to $5,000. The liability of R, E, and P is discharged. (See page 140)

However, if T negotiates the draft to HDC, E is liable primarily in the sum of $2,000, the tenor of the draft at the time of his acceptance. (R and P are secondarily liable for the same amount. T is liable for $5,000.)

Case 2. R draws a draft on E for $2,000. P raises the amount to $5,000, then induces E to accept. P then negotiates the draft to HDC. E is liable to HDC for $5,000, the tenor of the draft at the time of his acceptance. (R is liable secondarily for $2,000. P is liable for $5,000.)

Case 3. E accepts a draft in which the amount has not been filled in with the understanding that P, the payee, will fill in the proper amount as soon as he learns the price of the goods for which the draft is given. P learns that the amount is $2,000 but fraudulently inserts $5,000. If P sues E, he will collect nothing because E was discharged by the alteration. However, if P negotiates the draft as altered to HDC, HDC is entitled to collect $5,000 from E. (The drawer's secondary liability to HDC is $5,000. P's liability also is $5,000.)

1. ACCEPTANCE VARYING DRAFT

A drawee unwilling to accept according to the terms of a draft as originally drawn may tender an acceptance which varies these terms. It may vary the amount payable, the time of payment, or any other term. Since the variance must be on the instrument itself, it is in a sense an alteration; but since the alteration is not made by a *holder*, it does not result in discharging anyone.

When a drawee proffers an acceptance varying the terms of the draft, two courses are open to the holder. He may refuse the acceptance and treat the draft as dishonored. (See page 186) If he does so, he gives up whatever rights he had against the drawee because the drawee then is entitled to have his varied acceptance cancelled. [3–412(1)] On the other hand, the holder may assent and thereby acquire the obligation of the drawee to the extent of the varied acceptance. If the holder follows the latter course, each drawer and indorser who does not affirmatively assent to the variance is discharged. [3–412(3)] The underlying reason for discharging a drawer or indorser who does not affirmatively assent is that he has agreed to be liable on a certain contract and should not be held liable on a different contract unless he agrees to be. The fact that the new contract may even be beneficial to the drawer or indorser is immaterial in this connection.

F. UNQUALIFIED INDORSER'S SECONDARY LIABILITY

A transferor is one who negotiates or otherwise transfers an instrument to someone else other than by original delivery. A transferor may or may not indorse the instrument. If he transfers an *order* instrument for *value* without any agreement to the contrary, however, the transferee is entitled to his unqualified indorsement.

[3–201(3)]   If the instrument is payable to *bearer* when he receives it and there is no agreement to the contrary when he transfers it, his transferee cannot require him to indorse it.   Of course, a prospective transferee may demand the transferor's indorsement before agreeing to purchase it.   Whether or not he gets it is a matter of bargaining power, not of law.

An unqualified indorser acquires *secondary* liability on the instrument and he also gives several implied warranties.   Qualified indorsers (those who indorse "without recourse") and transferors who do not indorse give implied warranties, *but they incur no secondary liability*.   Liability based on warranties will be considered in Chapter 9. Here we are concerned only with the secondary liability of the unqualified indorser, that is, his liability on the instrument.

The majority of transferors indorse without qualification and so become secondarily liable on the instrument.   The liability of the unqualified indorser, like that of the drawer, does not become fixed unless certain conditions are satisfied.   (See Chapter 8)   He does not say, "I will pay."   Rather he says, "I will pay if the instrument is dishonored and any necessary notice of dishonor is given and any necessary protest is made."   Assuming that these conditions are satisfied, he agrees to be liable according to the tenor of the instrument at the time of his indorsement.   [3–

414(1)] An indorser is not liable for any alteration in the instrument after it leaves his hands
unless he assents to it or is precluded from asserting the alteration. On the other hand, if an
instrument is altered before he transfers it, he is
liable on it according to its altered terms even
though he is totally unaware of the alteration
when he transfers it.

Under the Code, an unqualified indorser's secondary liability runs to the holder of the instrument and any later indorser who takes up the instrument whether or not the later indorser was
obligated to do so. [3–414(1)]

Quite frequently there are several unqualified
indorsers. Since the holder may immediately upon dishonor proceed against any one of them without proceeding against the others, it often becomes important to determine if the one who is
required to pay the holder has any rights against
the others. Such rights depend upon the order of
priority among them. Except when they agree
among themselves to the contrary, unqualified
indorsers are liable to one another in the order
in which they indorse [3–414(2)]; that is, each
indorser is liable to each later indorser. It is presumed that they indorsed in the order in which
their signatures appear on the instrument, reading from the top. [3–414(2)] But parol evidence
is admissible to show that they indorsed in some
other order or that they agreed to be liable in

some order other than that in which they signed. [Comment 4, 3–414]　For example,

> H holds M's note which has been unqualifiedly indorsed by P (payee), A, and B in that order.　At maturity the note is dishonored by M.　H gives due notice to P, A, and B.　H may proceed against any one of the indorsers on the basis of secondary liability.　If H obtains payment from B, B may proceed against A, P, or M.　If B obtains payment from A, A may proceed against P or M. If P pays he must look to M alone.　However, if A and B contracted between themselves that A would be free of liability, as where A indorses for B's accommodation, B acquires no rights against A if B pays H; if A pays H, A is entitled to recover from P or M or from B.

G.　QUALIFIED INDORSER'S LIABILITY

As mentioned earlier, a transferor who wishes to disclaim secondary liability, can do so by affixing a qualified indorsement.　[3–414(1)]　He may signify his intention to sign as a qualified indorser by including the words "without recourse," which usually precede, but may follow, his signature.　Although other words may be used to disclaim secondary liability, they rarely are. Regardless of whether the disclaimer of secondary liability is expressed by the words "without recourse" or by other words, it must appear on the instrument itself; it cannot be proven by parol evidence because the disclaimer varies the terms of the written contract of indorsement.

[Comment 1, 3–414]   Although a qualified indorser incurs no secondary liability, he incurs liability on warranties as do unqualified indorsers and those who transfer an instrument without any indorsement.   With one exception, which will be explained, the warranty liability of a qualified indorser is the same as that of an unqualified indorser and one who transfers without indorsement.   (See page 205)

H.   LIABILITY FOR CONVERSION

For many years the law of torts has recognized that recovery might be had for conversion of intangible property that is evidenced by a document such as a negotiable instrument which gives a large measure of control over the property.   Reference has been made to liability for conversion that might be imposed on a drawee who refuses to return on demand a draft presented for acceptance or payment.   (See page 149)   A maker, drawer, acceptor, or indorser also may be held liable for refusing on demand to pay or *return* an instrument presented for payment.   [3–419(1)(b)]   In addition, any party may be held liable for conversion if he pays an instrument on a forged indorsement.   [3–419(1)(c)]

> M makes and delivers a note to P, for value.   T steals the note from P, forges P's indorsement and then sells the note to I, an innocent purchaser. At maturity, I obtains payment from M who

takes up the note. P is, of course, entitled to recover for conversion from T, the thief, or from I, the innocent purchaser. P is also entitled to recover for conversion from M, who paid the note on P's forged indorsement. Even though M paid in good faith, M's payment is an exercise of dominion and control over the note inconsistent with P's rights as owner. [Comment 3, 3–419]

§ 4. Special Kinds of Liability on the Instrument

The special nature of the liability of one who indorses "without recourse" has been mentioned. Special kinds of liability also may arise when one person signs for the accommodation of another or when he transfers an instrument using an indorsement which contains words of guarantee.

A. ACCOMMODATION AND ACCOMMODATED PARTIES

Normally a person who signs a negotiable instrument does so as part of a transaction in which he has a major interest. In contrast, an *accommodation* party signs an instrument to lend his name to some other party to it. [3–415(1)] The person to whom the accommodation party lends his name is the *accommodated* party.

M offers his note to P to obtain a loan. Not satisfied with M as a credit risk, P tells M that he will make the loan only if M first has A indorse the note. M induces A to indorse the note and then delivers it to P who makes the loan. A is an accommodation indorser. M is an accommodated maker.

[*158*]

An *accommodation* party may sign as maker, acceptor, drawer or indorser. Usually, he signs as indorser or co-maker. However he signs, he becomes liable in that capacity except that he does not become liable to the party accommodated. [3–415(2)(5)] If he signs as a maker or acceptor, he is a primary party and is liable to the holder immediately when the instrument becomes due; he has no right to require the holder to present the instrument to the accommodated party first. [3–415(2)] If he signs as an indorser or drawer he is secondarily liable and is entitled to require presentment, dishonor and notice of dishonor before he pays. (See Chapter 8)

The accommodation party might or might not receive consideration for lending his name. The Code does not require that he receive consideration in order to be bound in the capacity in which he signs. As all parties expect, any consideration furnished by the creditor moves to the accommodated party. In the typical case, where the accommodation party signs before the instrument is delivered, for the purpose of inducing the creditor to extend credit to the accommodated party, the accommodation party's promise is supported by the same consideration that supports the accommodated party's promise. Often, however, the accommodation party signs an instrument after it has been delivered and after the creditor has already furnished the consideration to the accommodated party. For example, the creditor makes a loan to the accommodated party and takes the latter's note, and thereafter the accommodation party signs as an unqualified indorser. When this occurs, the fact that the creditor does not agree to extend the time of the loan or to furnish any other consideration does not shield the accommodation party from liability. All that is required to render the accommodation party liable in the capacity in which he signs is that the creditor shall have taken the instrument for *value* before it is due. [3–415(2)] What is required in order to take an instrument for value is explained more fully when the requisites for being a holder in due course are discussed. (See pages 230–241) It is sufficient here to know that in the above case the creditor gave value when he made the loan because *executed consideration* is always value. It is important to note, however, that an *unperformed promise*, perhaps the most common form of consideration, normally does not constitute value. (See pages 235–236 for exceptions.)

The distinguishing characteristic of the accommodation party is that he is always a *surety*. [Comment 1, 3–415] The accommodated party is his *principal*. Therefore the accommodation and the accommodated parties and those who deal with them as such are governed by general principles of suretyship law. Basically an accommodation party differs from other sureties only in that his liability is on the instrument and he is surety for another party on the instrument. [Comment 1, 3–415] Accordingly, an accommodation party is not liable to the party accommodated and, if he pays the instrument, he has a right to *reimbursement* from the party who is accommodated. [3–415(5)] Also he usually has a right of *exoneration*, and *subrogation*, and, if there are co-signers, he usually has a right of *contribution*. *Exoneration* entitles him to require his principal, the accommodated party, to pay when the instrument falls due even though the accommodation party is a maker or acceptor and the accommodated party is an indorser. Once he has paid the creditor in full, *subrogation* entitles him to take the place of the creditor and to have the creditor's rights against the principal and any security held by the creditor. If there are two or more co-signers, *contribution* entitles him to require the remaining co-signers to pay their share if he pays more than his share. Frequently the accommodation party does no more than sign his name and his various rights are declared by the courts in accordance with well established principles and the probable understanding of the parties. Most other sureties enter written contracts that state many of their rights in some detail.

> Without receiving consideration from P, M makes and delivers a 90–day note payable to P to enable P to purchase a truck from C. P negotiates

the note to C by unqualified indorsement and C delivers the truck to P. As security for the note, P delivers stock to C. After maturity, without first having demanded payment from P, C demands payment from M. M is liable to C on the note. Even though M signed as accommodation maker for P, M is liable in the capacity in which he signed and so has no right to insist on presentment to P first. It makes no difference that M received no consideration from P. To render M liable as maker, it is sufficient that C gave value, which he did by delivering the truck. Since M is a surety, if he makes any payment to C, he is entitled to reimbursement from P. If M pays C in full, M is entitled to be subrogated to C's rights against P as well as to C's rights with respect to the security. This latter right is especially valuable if P is insolvent. If C had first proceeded against P on P's secondary liability, P could not have complained because P had no right to expect M to pay the note; and if P had been required to pay C, he would not have been entitled to reimbursement from M.

B. WORDS OF GUARANTEE IN AN INDORSEMENT

It has been indicated that for purposes of negotiation an indorsement's effectiveness is not altered by the fact that the indorsement contains words of guarantee. (See page 129) However, such words may substantially affect the liability of the indorser.

If an indorser adds to his signature the words "*payment* guaranteed" or other words having the same meaning, he engages that if the instrument is not paid when it falls due, he will pay immediately just as if he were a co-maker. [3–416(1)] Unlike the usual unqualified indorser, one who indorses in this way has no right to insist on either presentment for payment to the maker or drawee or notice of dishonor. [3–416(5)] He is liable to a holder immediately upon maturity without any conditions precedent. If he instead adds the words *"collection* guaranteed," he again waives any requirements that otherwise would have existed with respect to presentment or notice of dishonor, but he adds some conditions to his liability that would not have existed. He does not say, "I will pay." He says, "I will pay if the instrument is not paid when due, provided (1) the holder reduces his claim to judgment and execution is returned unsatisfied, or (2) the maker or acceptor has become insolvent, or (3) it is otherwise apparent that it is useless for the holder to proceed against the maker or acceptor." [3–416(2)] Words of guarantee which do not specify otherwise guarantee *payment*. [3–416(3)]

CHAPTER 8

PRESENTMENT, DISHONOR, NOTICE OF DISHONOR, AND PROTEST

How a negotiable instrument originates, the ways in which it is transferred from person to person and the rights and duties of the parties on the instrument have been described. It will be recalled that unqualified indorsers and drawers are secondary parties. [3–102(1)(d)] (See page 145 As such, they normally are not expected to pay unless the party who is expected to pay (the maker or drawee) fails to do so; and they normally cannot be required to pay unless certain conditions—presentment, dishonor, notice of dishonor, and in some cases, protest—have been satisfied. [3–413(2), 3–414(1), 3–501(1)(a)(b)(c)(2)(a) (b), 3–507(2) and Comment 2, 3–501] In addition to postponing a holder's right to recover from an unqualified indorser or drawer on the basis of secondary liability, a failure or delay in meeting one of these conditions normally has the effect of discharging an unqualified indorser's secondary liability, as well as his liability on the underlying obligation for which he transferred the instrument. [3–502(1)(a), 3–802(1)(b)] (See pages 300–301) In limited circumstances

[*164*]

a holder's delay or failure in making presentment or in giving notice of dishonor might give the drawer the power to discharge his secondary liability by assigning his rights against the drawee. [3–502(1)(b)] (See page 169) In some circumstances a failure or delay in satisfying one of these conditions may give a maker or acceptor the power to discharge his primary liability by making an assignment of his rights against a bank with whom he has deposited funds. [3–502(1)(b)] (See page 173) And a failure to make a required protest may in special circumstances completely discharge the secondary liability of an indorser or drawer. [3–502(2)]

The present chapter will consider the legal consequences of failing to satisfy these conditions, the manner in which they are satisfied, and the special circumstances in which the law excuses a failure or delay in satisfying one of these conditions.

§ 1. Effect of Failing to Satisfy Conditions

A. INDORSERS

A holder normally is not entitled to recover from an *unqualified indorser* unless due presentment has been made to the party expected to pay (the maker, drawee or acceptor), the instrument has been dishonored, the indorser has received due notice of dishonor, and any required protest has been made. In addition, an undue delay with respect to presentment or notice of dishonor or a required protest usually has the effect of *completely discharging* the secondary liability of an unqualified indorser. [3–502(1)(a)]

It should be noted, however, that neither presentment, notice of dishonor nor protest is necessary to charge an unqualified indorser whose indorsement includes *words of guarantee* [3–416 (5)] or an unqualified indorser who indorses *after maturity*. [3–501(4)] Consequently, the liability of such parties is not affected by a failure to present, give notice, or make protest. On the opposite extreme, the *qualified indorser*—one who indorses "without recourse"—is liable only on his warranties and is not liable secondarily. For this reason his liability cannot be affected by a failure or delay with respect to presentment, notice, or protest.

1. Reason for Discharging Secondary Liability of Indorser—Recoupment

If following dishonor an indorser pays the holder, the indorser becomes the owner of the instrument and is entitled to *recoup*—that is, recover what he has paid—from the maker if the instrument is a note or from the drawer or acceptor if the instrument is a draft. In addition, an indorser who pays has a right to recoup from any unqualified indorser prior to himself who has received due notice of dishonor. Each successive indorser who is required to pay is entitled to recoup from the maker, drawer, or acceptor or any prior unqualified indorser who has received due notice of dishonor.

At maturity M delivers a note to P, and by a series of unqualified indorsements, the note is negotiated by P to X to Y to Z. Z duly presents it to M for payment. If the note is dishonored by M, Z has an immediate right to sue M, but this right is likely to have little value because a maker normally pays his notes at maturity if he is able to do so. Fortunately for Z, he is not limited to an action against M. If Z has given due notice of dishonor to Y, X, and P, he is entitled to recover the amount of the note from any of them. If Y pays Z, Y in turn becomes the owner of the note and is entitled to recoup from X who in turn is entitled to recoup from P, whose only rights are against M, the person with whom he dealt.

The right of recoupment obviously can be very valuable. Frequently a valuable right of recoupment can be rendered valueless, however, by a delay in presenting an instrument or in giving notice of dishonor. In collecting money, time frequently is of the essence because payment is made on a "first come, first served" basis. A man who is solvent and willing to pay one day may be insolvent or unwilling to pay the next. There is always the risk that a debtor will waste his fortune, lose it by bad luck, transfer it in fraud of his creditors, or abscond. Undue delay in presenting usually increases the risk that the party expected to pay will not do so. Undue delay in giving notice of dishonor usually increases the risk that any indorser who pays the holder will be unable to recoup what he pays from either the party expected to pay or from a prior indorser.

The law does not permit a holder to saddle this risk unfairly on a prior indorser. Therefore, a holder who, without excuse, delays unduly in presenting an instrument or in giving notice of dishonor is deprived of his right to recover from an indorser on his secondary liability. Since the right of recoupment is given to each successive indorser who may be required to pay, each successive indorser has a similar interest in due presentment and notice of dishonor so that his right of recoupment will not be unduly jeopardized. The law protects his right of recoupment by *completely* discharging him from his secondary liability if there is an undue delay *even when he cannot show that he suffered any loss as the result of the delay*. Later in this chapter the meaning of *protest* and how protest aids in enforcing the indorser's right of recoupment will be explained. Normally, it is not required, but when it is, a failure to make it on time completely discharges an unqualified indorser even though he cannot show that he suffered any loss as the result of the failure. [3–502(2)]

B. DRAWERS

As stated earlier, a drawer normally cannot be required to pay an instrument until certain conditions—presentment, dishonor, and notice of dishonor—have been satisfied.

A holder's failure to satisfy these conditions, however, does not, of itself, result in the immediate discharge of the secondary liability of a drawer as it does in the case of the secondary liability of the unqualified indorser. To understand how a failure to satisfy these conditions might bear on the discharge of the liability of a drawer and why it is not given the same effect that it has on the liability of an unqualified indorser it is necessary to keep in mind the difference between the unqualified indorser's and the drawer's relationship to the instrument.

Normally, regardless of whether he receives an instrument as a payee or as a transferee, an unqualified indorser pays fair value for it. When he later negotiates the instrument by his unqualified indorsement, he is unlikely to receive much more than he paid for it; and in many cases he receives less. Consequently, even if he is completely discharged from liability because a holder fails to make due presentment or to give due notice of dishonor, the unqualified indorser does not receive a windfall. He is merely protected from

[*169*]

the possibility that he might not be able to avoid a loss by recouping from some prior party.

The relationship of the drawer to a draft is quite different. It usually costs the drawer virtually nothing to execute and deliver a draft. All he needs is a printed form and a pen. Yet he normally receives consideration in roughly the amount of the draft when he issues it to the payee. Whether he can possibly suffer any loss as the result of a holder's failure to make due presentment or to give due notice of dishonor depends mainly on: a) the arrangements the drawer has made with the drawee, and b) the solvency of the drawee. If the drawee is a total stranger who owes nothing to the drawer the drawer cannot possibly lose anything merely because the holder fails to present the draft for payment or acceptance or, following dishonor, fails to give the drawer due notice of dishonor. If the drawee is indebted to the drawer however, or if the drawer has deposited funds with the drawee for the purpose of paying the draft when it is presented, the failure to make due presentment or to give due notice of dishonor may or may not cause the drawer a loss.

If the drawer suffers no loss as the result of the holder's failure to make due presentment or to give due notice of dishonor, discharging him completely as the result of the failure would grant him a windfall to the extent of whatever he re-

[*170*]

ceived for issuing the draft. This would be unfair to the holder. But it would be unfair to the drawer to saddle him with a loss if loss did result from the holder's failure to make due presentment or to give due notice of dishonor. With the various possibilities in mind, the framers of the Code determined to give the drawer a right to obtain a discharge from liability, but only to the extent necessary to enable him to avoid any losses he might otherwise suffer as the result of the holder's failure to make due presentment or to give due notice of dishonor. The extent of this right and the manner of exercising it are provided in Section 3–502(1)(b) which states:

> Where without excuse any necessary presentment or notice of dishonor is delayed beyond the time when it is due * * * any drawer * * * who because the drawee * * * becomes insolvent during the delay is deprived of funds maintained with the drawee * * * to cover the instrument may discharge his liability by written assignment to the holder of his rights against the drawee * * * in respect of such funds, but such drawer * * * is not otherwise discharged.

The following examples illustrate how a failure to make proper presentment or to give due notice of dishonor affects a drawer's liability under the Code.

Case 1.   On April 1st, R signs and delivers to P, payee, a draft for $5,000 payable on July 1st, drawn on

[*171*]

E. On May 1st P indorses "P" and delivers the draft to H for value. H fails to present the draft to E for payment until August 1st at which time E flatly refuses to pay although he admits that R has deposited $5,000 with him to meet the draft when it fell due and that he, E, is completely solvent and capable of paying the draft. H promptly notifies R of E's refusal and demands payment from R. R refuses to pay, contending that he has been discharged by H's delay in presenting the draft to E for payment. H is entitled to recover from R the full amount of the draft. A drawer is not discharged from his secondary liability automatically upon a holder's failure to make due presentment or to give due notice of dishonor. Moreover, since E did not become insolvent during H's delay in making presentment, R cannot obtain his discharge by making an assignment to H of his rights against E with respect to the funds on deposit. In short, R will have to pay H and then proceed against E for breach of the contract of deposit. In contrast, as shown earlier, P, who indorsed without qualification, is completely and automatically discharged from his secondary liability even though P suffered no loss as the result of the delay in presentment.

Case 2. On May 1st R places $10,000 in the hands of E to meet a draft for that sum. On May 15th R issues the draft to P. The draft is payable on June 1st. On this latter date, E is solvent and able to pay the draft, but P does not present the draft for payment until October 1st at which time E is insolvent and able to pay creditors only thirty cents on a dollar. Although R is not automatically discharged by the delay in present-

[*172*]

ment, he can obtain a discharge by giving P a written assignment of his claim for $10,000 against E. Since P is responsible for the unfortunate situation, he is required to suffer the loss and the inconvenience of following E's insolvency proceeding.

When protest is required, a failure to make it completely discharges a drawer just as it completely discharges an unqualified indorser. [3–502(2)]

C. DRAWEES

Since a drawee as such is not liable on a draft but only on his contract with the drawer, his position is quite different from that of either an unqualified indorser or a drawer; and his liability is not affected at all by a failure to present or to give due notice of dishonor in the manner required to activate or retain the liability of these parties.

D. MAKERS AND ACCEPTORS

Since makers and acceptors are liable *primarily* rather than *secondarily*, they normally are required to pay at maturity and have no right of recoupment against anyone else if they are required to pay. Therefore, the liability of a maker or acceptor normally is not affected by a holder's failure to make due presentment or to give due notice of dishonor.

Sometimes, however, a maker or acceptor deposits funds and arranges for someone else to make the actual payment on his behalf. When he does, the position of the maker or acceptor is quite similar to that of the drawer who deposits funds with a drawee to pay a draft. If the depositary refuses to pay as agreed, the maker or acceptor has a right of recoupment from the depositary. If the depositary happens to be a *bank* —but not otherwise—the Code seeks to protect the maker's or acceptor's right of recoupment against any loss that might result from the bank's becoming insolvent during the holder's delay in making presentment or in giving notice. It does this in the same way it protects the drawer's right of recoupment in similar circumstances—by granting the maker or acceptor a discharge from liability upon his making a written assignment to the holder of his rights against the payor bank with respect to such funds. [3–502(1)(b)] The liability of a maker or acceptor is not affected by the holder's failure to make protest.

§ 2. Satisfying Requirements

In most cases the handling of matters relating to presentment, notice of dishonor and protest is left to banks whose specialized personnel are familiar with the requirements and have established routines for satisfying them. There remain, however, a substantial number of businesses who find it worthwhile to handle these matters themselves.

A. PRESENTMENT

Unless presentment is excused, there can be no dishonor of an instrument which is not duly presented; and if there is no dishonor, there is no right to proceed against drawers and indorsers on their secondary liability.

A presentment may be made either for the purpose of obtaining *acceptance* of a draft or check or for the purpose of obtaining *payment* of any kind of instrument. As will be explained, the principles that determine in which cases presentment is required differ in some respects for the two types of presentment. (See pages 178–181) But the legal effect of an unexcused failure or delay in making a necessary presentment is the same for both; and the legal requirements for making an effective presentment are substantially the same for both.

1. WHAT CONSTITUTES EFFECTIVE PRESENTMENT

Basically, presentment for acceptance is a *demand* for acceptance and presentment for payment is a *demand* for payment. [3–504(1)] To be effective as a presentment, however, the demand may have to satisfy certain requirements. What these requirements are depends in large part on what, if anything, is requested at the time by the person upon whom the demand is made. (See page 177)   According to Official Comment 1 to Section 3–504, if nothing more is requested by the person upon whom the demand is made, any demand upon the party to pay, no matter where or how made, is an effective presentment. Of course, it must be made by or on behalf of the holder and it must be made upon the maker, acceptor, drawee, or other payor. Presentment may be, and frequently is, made through a clearing house.   [3–504(2)(b)]   It may be made by mail in which case it is effective when the letter is received.   [3–504(2)(a)]   Although Comment 1, mentioned above, seems to imply that presentment may be made over the telephone, there is a case to the contrary.   (See Kirby v. Bergfield, 186 Neb. 242, 182 N.W.2d 205 (1970))   Even assuming that an effective presentment can be made by telephone, however, it is usually desirable in case of dishonor by telephone to make a second demand by another means rather than rely on the telephone conversation.   Normally, presentment is made at the place of business or residence of the party who is expected to pay or accept, but unless some other place is provided in the instrument or objection is raised immediately, the Code allows the holder to make an effective presentment wherever he can find the payor or someone authorized to act for him.   [Comment 1, 3–504]

To balance the liberal attitude concerning what might suffice as a presentment in the first instance, Section 3–505(1) gives the party on whom presentment is made the power to require

1. exhibition of the instrument;
2. reasonable identification of the person making presentment;
3. evidence of authority if presentment is made for another;
4. production of the instrument at a place specified in it or, if none is specified, at any reasonable place; and
5. a signed receipt on the instrument for any partial or full payment and its surrender upon full payment.

If the party on whom presentment is made requires any of these things, the presentment is ineffective unless the presenting party complies within a reasonable time. [3–505(2)] If the instrument is a draft accepted or a note made payable at a bank in the United States, the instrument must be presented at such bank even though the party on whom presentment is made does not require it. [3–504(4)] If the instrument has two or more makers, acceptors, or drawees, an effective demand may be made on any one of them. [3–504(3)(a)]

2. TIME OF PRESENTMENT

The time of presentment involves the hour of the day and the day. The first presents few problems as presentment normally must be made at a reasonable hour, and if made at a bank must be made during its banking day.   [3–503(4)]   Determining the *day* of presentment is the most critical problem faced by a holder intending to satisfy the requirements regarding presentment. This decision may depend on whether the presentment is made to obtain payment or to obtain acceptance, the nature of the instrument, the position of the secondary party whose liability the holder wishes to fix, and other factors.

a.   Presentment for Acceptance

There are only three situations in which presentment for acceptance is required to fix or retain the secondary liability of indorsers or drawers. The *first* occurs when the draft itself provides that it is to be presented for acceptance.   The *second* occurs when the draft is made payable elsewhere than at the drawee's residence or place of business.   The *third* occurs when the date of payment depends upon presentment for acceptance, as when a draft is payable a stated period after sight.   [3–501(1)(a)]

In these three situations the day when presentment for acceptance must be made depends on whether it is payable (1) at or a fixed period after a stated date, (2) after sight, or (3) on demand.   If payable at or a fixed period after a stated date, such presentment must be made on or before the date it is payable.   [3–503(1) (a)]   If payable after sight, it must be presented for acceptance *or negotiated* within a reasonable time after date or issue, whichever is later. [3–503(1) (b)] If payable on demand, a necessary presentment for acceptance must be made within a reasonable time after the secondary party whose liability is under consideration became liable on the instrument. [3–503(1)(e)] Normally a drawer becomes liable when he issues a draft, and an indorser becomes liable when he indorses and delivers it.

Even though presentment for acceptance is not required, a holder may present a draft for acceptance. [3–501(1) (a)] Unless it is payable at a stated date, however, a drawee's refusal to accept a draft which the holder is not required to present for acceptance is not a dishonor. If a draft is payable at a stated date, optional presentment for acceptance must be made within the same time as if presentment for acceptance is required—i. e., on or before the date stated.

b. Presentment for Payment

If an instrument *shows the date on which it is payable*, presentment for payment is due on that date. [3–503(1) (c)] This means that a primary party can be required to pay on that date and that a refusal to pay by a maker, acceptor or drawee following a due demand for payment on that date constitutes a dishonor. It also means that presentment on that date is necessary to fix or retain the liability of parties who are entitled to insist on presentment. An instrument is deemed to show the date on which it is payable if it states that it is payable: (1) on a specific date, (2) a fixed period after a specific date, or (3) a fixed period after sight and the acceptance indicates the date of acceptance. In the two latter situations, the time for presentment for payment is determined by excluding the day from which the time is to begin and including the date of payment. For example, if an instrument is dated June 1st and is payable "twenty days after date," it becomes due on June 21st. (If it is not paid on that date the holder is entitled to sue on the following day. [3–122(1)(a)]) This principle applies also when calculating the time for making presentment for acceptance. In fact, this method of calculation is used in determining time throughout the law of contracts and is not limited to the law of negotiable instruments. [Comment 1, 3–503] If a presentment falls on a day which is not a full business day for the person making the presentment or which is not a full business day for the person who is expected to pay or accept, presentment is due on the next following day that is a full business day for both parties. [3–503(3)]

The proper time for presenting a *demand* instrument for payment depends on the purpose for which presentment is made. If the purpose is to *render a refusal to pay a dishonor* so as to entitle the holder to sue a secondary party immediately, the presentment may be made upon its date, or if no date is stated, on the date of issue. [3–122(1) (b)] If the purpose is to *retain the liability of a secondary party,* presentment is timely if it is made within a reasonable time after the secondary party became liable on the instrument. [3–503(1) (e)] To determine whether an *indorser* is discharged because of a delay in presenting a demand instrument for payment, a reasonable time is measured from the time he negotiates the instrument. To determine whether a presentment is effective with respect to a *drawer,* a reasonable time is measured from the time of issue. To determine whether a *maker* or *acceptor* with funds on deposit in a bank may obtain a discharge by assigning his rights to the holder, presentment for payment must be made within a reasonable time after issue, in the case of a maker, and within a reasonable time after acceptance, in the case of an acceptor. [3–503(1)(e)]

c. Reasonable Time for Presentment

If the issue is raised in a case in which presentment must be made "within a reasonable time," the party seeking to recover has the burden of proving that the demand for payment or acceptance was made within a reasonable time. What constitutes a reasonable time to present is determined by the nature of the instrument, relevant trade and banking usage, and the facts of the particular case.   [3–503(2)]   In deciding this question, courts may consider a variety of circumstances such as the distances involved, communications and transportation facilities available, whether the instrument is intended to serve as continuing security, and perhaps of most importance, whether the instrument bears interest. It is impossible to reconcile the numerous cases dealing with this problem.

In the case of an ordinary uncertified check drawn and payable within the United States, it is *presumed* that a reasonable length of time in which to present for payment or initiate bank collection is seven days after indorsement to determine whether an *indorser's* liability is discharged, or thirty days after date or issue, whichever is later, to determine whether a *drawer* may discharge his liability by making an assignment of his rights against the bank.   [3–503(2)]   *These presumptions are not conclusive.*   They may be rebutted by competent evidence material to the question of reasonableness in the case under consideration. For example, if a check is drawn for a large sum and the drawer, drawee, and payee all are situated in the same city, a court is likely to consider it to be unreasonable to delay thirty days before presenting the check for payment.

If an instrument that is otherwise payable at a definite time contains an acceleration clause, and the event accelerating the time for payment occurs, presentment for payment is due within a reasonable time thereafter. [3–503(1)(d)] In addition to the factors that would normally be taken into consideration in determining a reasonable time, it would be necessary here to take into account the knowledge of the fact of acceleration which the holder, or other person charged with responsibility for making the presentment, might or might not have.

d. Presentment by Collecting Bank

In general, banks are governed by the principles described above. There is one important exception. Usually, if an instrument shows the date on which it is payable, presentment for payment must be made *on that date*. [3–503(1)(c)] However, in the case of an instrument that is *not* payable by, through or at a bank, a collecting bank normally can make a proper presentment for payment of such an instrument by sending notice that it holds such item for collection in time to be received *on or before* the day when presentment is due. [4–210(1)]

In Batchelder v. Granite Trust Co., 339 Mass. 20, 157 N.E.2d 540 (1959), it was held that presentment was sufficient to retain an indorser's secondary liability on a note when the bank, ten days before the note fell due, mailed notice to the maker that it held the note and then retained the note until it was due. If a proper request—for example, exhibition of the instrument or evidence of authority to present (see page 177) —is made by the party expected to accept or pay, however, the bank must comply with the request by the end of the bank's next banking day after it learns of the request. [4–210(1)]

e.   Domiciled instrument

Often the maker of a note or the acceptor of a draft makes it payable at a particular place or bank. Such notes or drafts are referred to as *domiciled* instruments. Sometimes the place of payment is indicated only for convenience. At other times it is intended to prevent the holder of an instrument bearing a favorable interest rate and *payable at a stated time* from taking advantage of the favorable interest rate by extending the time simply by not presenting it for payment until shortly before the statute of limitations has run. (See Hawkland, Commercial Paper and Bank Deposits and Collections (1967) at pages 69–70) Domiciled instruments are effective for this purpose because a tender of payment to the holder of any instrument when or after it is due discharges the person making the tender to the extent of all subsequent liability for interest, costs and attorney's fees [3–604(1)]; and the fact that the maker or acceptor of an instrument payable *otherwise than on demand* is able and ready to

[*184*]

pay at every place of payment specified in the instrument when it is due, is equivalent to tender. [3–604(3)]

Since the maker of a *demand* instrument must make an *actual* tender of full payment in order to obtain a discharge to the extent of subsequent interest, costs and attorney's fees, he cannot enjoy the above major advantage that accrues to one issuing a domiciled instrument that is payable at a *definite* time. It appears, however, that he can effectively offer the payee the principal advantage of a demand instrument—the right to demand payment at any time—without himself incurring the risk of being required to pay interest until shortly before the statute of limitations has run out. He can accomplish this by issuing a domiciled instrument for some fixed period satisfactory to himself and including a provision giving the holder the right to accelerate payment by demanding payment at any earlier time.

Under the Code, the terms of the draft are held not to be varied by an acceptance that provides for payment at a bank or place in the United States unless the acceptance provides that the draft is to be paid *only* at such bank or place. [3–412(2)] Whether a note or acceptance stating that it is payable at a bank is equivalent to a draft drawn on the bank payable when it falls due out of any funds of the maker or acceptor in current account or otherwise available for such payment depends on which of two alternative provisions of the Code is adopted.   [3–121]

B.   DISHONOR

1.   WHAT CONSTITUTES

In general, an instrument is dishonored if a *necessary* or *optional* presentment is duly made and due acceptance or payment is refused or cannot be obtained within the time prescribed.   [3–507(1)(a)]

Presentment for *payment* is always *necessary* unless excused.   [3–501(1)(b)(c)]   As stated above, presentment for *acceptance* is *necessary* in only three situations.   (See pages 178–179).   If presentment for *acceptance* is not *necessary,* it is *optional* if, but only if, the draft is payable *at a stated date.*   [3–501(1)(a)]   Presentment for *acceptance* of a *demand* draft is never *optional* although it may be *necessary* in one of the three circumstances referred to above.   Therefore, if presentment for acceptance of a demand draft is not necessary, a refusal to accept it does not constitute a dishonor.   For example, a bank's refusal to certify an ordinary check for a holder who would prefer the bank's liability to cash does not constitute a dishonor.   Consequently, the holder would not, by giving notice of such refusal, acquire an immediate right to recover from either a drawer or an unqualified indorser on the basis of secondary liability.

If a party upon whom a proper demand for acceptance or payment has been made flatly refuses to comply or refuses to comply unless the presenting party does more than legally required, the dishonor is clear. Dishonor is equally clear if the drawee of a draft announces that the drawer has insufficient funds on deposit or has stopped payment. In contrast, dishonor does not occur if the party on whom the demand is made refuses to comply until the holder has satisfied some legal requirement. For example, as previously mentioned, the party to whom presentment is made may insist that the holder exhibit the instrument, that he produce it at a place specified in it, or that a necessary indorsement be obtained. [Comment 2, 3–510]

Similarly, it does not constitute dishonor if the person on whom a demand for *payment* has been made defers payment pending a reasonable examination to determine whether the instrument is properly payable, as long as payment is made before the close of business on the day the demand is made. [3–506(2)] A person upon whom a demand for *acceptance* has been made may, without dishonor, defer acceptance until the close of the next business day following presentment. [3–506(1)]

In any case in which a necessary presentment is excused (see pages 196–197), dishonor occurs if the instrument is not duly accepted or paid. [3–507(1)(b)]

The foregoing principles are modified in some respects where the presentment is made by or on behalf of a bank.

C. NOTICE OF DISHONOR

If, following dishonor, due notice of dishonor is not given, the effect is the same as if there had been undue delay in making presentment. However, if a necessary notice is given, the holder has an immediate right to recover from the party to whom it is given.

1. METHOD OF GIVING NOTICE

Notice of dishonor may be given in any reasonable manner. [3–508(3)] For example, it may be given orally face to face or over the telephone, by mail, by telegraph, or through a clearing house. However, the person giving notice should remember when choosing a means of communication that he may be required to prove in court that he has given notice. Need for proof is one reason why notice of dishonor usually is given in writing and why, if it is given orally, it usually is confirmed in writing. It is noteworthy that a written notice of dishonor is effective when sent even though it it not received by the addressee. [3–508(4)]

Accordingly notice sent by ordinary mail is given as soon as a properly addressed letter bearing sufficient postage and containing the notice is deposited in a mail box, chute, or other receptacle maintained by the Post Office for mailing letters.

No special words must be used to give notice of dishonor. Sending the dishonored instrument with a stamp, ticket, or writing, stating that acceptance or payment has been refused is sufficient. Accordingly a certificate of protest or a notice of debit with respect to the instrument is sufficient. [3–508(3)] Although the notice is intended to convey the idea that the party giving notice is asserting his rights against the party given notice, this need not be expressly stated as it is clearly implied by the notice. Any words that identify the instrument and state that it has been dishonored are sufficient. [3–508(3)]

2.   PERSONS GIVEN NOTICE

Notice of dishonor may be given to any person who may be liable on the instrument. [3–508(1)] Notice to one partner is notice to every other partner. [3–508(5)] Notice to joint parties who are not partners must be given to each of them unless one is authorized to receive such notice for the others. When a party is in insolvency proceedings instituted after the issue of the instrument, notice may be given either to him or to the representative of his estate, for example, a trustee in bankruptcy or an assignee for the benefit of creditors. [3–508(6)] When a person entitled to notice is dead or incompetent, notice may be sent to his last known address or given to his personal representative. [3–508(7)]

3. PERSONS GIVING NOTICE

Notice of dishonor may be given by or on behalf of the holder or any party who has received notice or can be compelled to pay the instrument. In addition, an agent or bank in whose hands the instrument is dishonored may give notice to the principal or customer or to another agent or bank from which the instrument was received. [3–508(1)]

4. SEQUENCE IN WHICH NOTICE MAY BE GIVEN

Since notice of dishonor is intended to facilitate the recoupment by each party required to pay, it need not be given in any special order. Often a holder gives notice of dishonor only to his immediate transferor, assuming that each successive party receiving notice will in turn give notice to his transferor. If the holder's transferor pays, this procedure is sufficient for the holder. But since it may be impossible to collect from his immediate transferor, it is advisable for the holder to give notice to all the prior indorsers he can

[*190*]

locate so that if he cannot recoup from one he can from another. When duly given, notice of dishonor operates for the benefit of all parties who have rights on the instrument against the person notified. [3–508(8)]

5. TIME ALLOWED FOR GIVING NOTICE

When given by the holder at dishonor to his transferee, notice usually must be given before midnight of the third business day after dishonor. When given by any prior holder, it must be given before midnight of the third business day after that party receives notice of dishonor. [3–508 (2)] However, a bank is required to give notice before its midnight deadline, which is midnight of the banking day following the banking day on which the bank receives the item or notice of dishonor. [3–508(2), 4–104(1)(h)]

D. PROTEST

The term *protest* has several meanings. Often it refers to the entire procedure of presenting, giving notice of dishonor, and protesting. Sometimes it refers only to the making of protest.

Used in the technical sense, protest refers to a certificate of dishonor made under the hand and seal of a United States consul or vice consul, a notary public or another person authorized to certify dishonor under the law of the place where it occurs. [3–509(1)] In practice, protest is almost always made by a notary public. Although it need not be in any special form, it "must identify the instrument and certify either that due presentment has been made or the reason why it is excused and that the instrument has been dishonored by nonacceptance or nonpayment." [3–509(2)]

Under the prior law, the notary public was required to have actual knowledge of the essential facts which he certified. Under the Code it is sufficient if the protest is made on information satisfactory to him. [3–509(1)] Typically, satisfactory information might consist of information furnished by the party making presentment, the admission of the dishonoring party, or the fact that the instrument was not paid when it was presented a second time. [Comment 4, 3–509] It is assumed that there usually is no sound motive for making a false protest; consequently, the basis on which protest is made is rarely questioned. [Comment 4, 3–509]

1. WHEN PROTEST IS REQUIRED

Protest is required only when there has been a dishonor of a draft which appears on its face to be either drawn or payable outside of the states, territories, dependencies and possessions of the United States, the District of Columbia and the Commonwealth of Puerto Rico. [3–501(3)] Such a draft is commonly referred to as a *foreign bill*.

An unexcused failure to protest such an instrument following dishonor completely discharges the drawer as well as all indorsers whether or not they have incurred any loss from the failure. [3–502(2)] This result contrasts with the legal effect of the failure to make due presentment or to give due notice of dishonor which completely discharges indorsers but gives a drawer, at most, a right to obtain a discharge by making an assignment of his rights against the drawee. Even though a dishonored instrument is not a foreign bill and protest is not required, it may be, and very frequently is, protested because of the advantages of protest in proving dishonor.

2. TIME FOR MAKING PROTEST

Any necessary protest is due within the same time that notice of dishonor is due. [3–509(4)] (See page 191) Any protest that is not necessary may be made at any time before it is offered in evidence. [Comment 7, 3–509]

3. PROTEST AS EVIDENCE

Protest, as a requirement, is intended to protect the right of recoupment of drawers and indorsers of foreign bills. Since foreign bills are made in one country and payable in another, proving dishonor of such instruments may be difficult. Protest reduces this difficulty substantially because a certificate of protest is admissible as evidence

[*193*]

and creates a rebuttable presumption of dishonor. This is one reason why it is customary to protest even those instruments which are not required to be protested. Also, it is common practice to include in the certificate of protest a certification that notice of dishonor has been given. [Comment 6, 3–509] The inclusion of this provision in the certificate of protest creates a rebuttable presumption that notice of dishonor has been given as stated. [3–510(a)]

4. FORWARDING PROTEST

It is not necessary in order to satisfy the requirement of protest to forward a copy of the protest to persons who are entitled to insist on protest. Since it serves as a notice of dishonor, however, it is customary, when protest is made, to send a copy of the certificate of protest to all persons who are entitled to notice of dishonor. This is so regardless of whether or not protest was required. The original certificate of protest usually is attached to the dishonored instrument and goes with the instrument to each person who pays and takes up the instrument.

5. OTHER TYPES OF EVIDENCE

Although a certificate of protest has been the most frequently offered evidence of dishonor and notice of dishonor, there are other types of evidence which may be admitted. For example, oral testimony by the party presenting the instrument and giving the notice may be admitted. Likewise, entries made in the regular course of business sometimes may be admitted. Before the Code, protest was the only type of evidence which had the advantage of creating a rebuttable presumption in favor of the facts it purported to establish. Under the Code, there is also a rebuttable presumption of any dishonor or notice of dishonor which is shown in (1) a purported stamp or writing of the drawee, payor bank, or presenting bank on the instrument or accompanying it which states that acceptance or payment has been refused for reasons consistent with dishonor; or (2) any book or record of the drawee, payor bank, or collecting bank kept in the usual course of business which shows dishonor even though there is no evidence to indicate who made the entry. [3–510(b)(c)]

§ 3. Excusing Omission or Delay in Presentment, Notice or Protest

In some cases, making proper presentment, giving due notice, and making proper protest would be an empty formality contributing nothing to the persons intended to benefit by them. In other cases, whatever advantage might accrue from complying with these requirements is more than outweighed by the disadvantage to the person of whom compliance normally is required. Consequently, the law makes allowance by excusing either a delay or omission in a number of circumstances as described in Section 3–511 of the Code which provides:

(1) Delay in presentment, protest or notice of dishonor is excused when the party is without notice that it is due or when the delay is caused by circumstances beyond his control and he exercises reasonable diligence after the cause of the delay ceases to operate.

(2) Presentment or notice or protest as the case may be is entirely excused when

    (a) the party to be charged has waived it expressly or by implication either before or after it is due; or

    (b) such party has himself dishonored the instrument or has countermanded payment or otherwise has no reason to expect or right to require that the instrument be accepted or paid; or

    (c) by reasonable diligence the presentment or protest cannot be made or the notice given.

(3) Presentment is also entirely excused when

    (a) the maker, acceptor or drawee of any instrument except a documentary draft is dead or in insolvency proceedings instituted after the issue of the instrument; or

    (b) acceptance or payment is refused but not for want of proper presentment.

(4) Where a draft has been dishonored by nonacceptance a later presentment for payment and any notice of dishonor and protest for nonpayment are excused unless in the meantime the instrument has been accepted.

(5) A waiver of protest is also a waiver of presentment and of notice of dishonor even though protest is not required.

(6) Where a waiver of presentment or notice of protest is embodied in the instrument itself it is binding upon all parties; but where it is written above the signature of an indorser it binds him only.

Presentment for acceptance or payment also is completely excused if (1) the place of acceptance or payment is specified in the instrument and neither the party to accept or pay nor anyone authorized to act for him is accessible at such place or (2) the place of payment is *not* specified and neither the party to accept or pay nor anyone authorized to act for him is accessible at his place of business or residence. [3–504(2)(c)]

§ 4. Effect of Excusing Omission or Delay

An excuse may extend to one or more conditions and may affect the liability of one or more parties. Regardless of which conditions and whose liabilities are affected, the legal effect of excusing an omission or delay is the same as if each condition excused had been met within the time normally allowed.

CHAPTER 9

LIABILITY BASED ON WARRANTIES

Whether or not a person signs an instrument, he may become liable on the basis of certain warranties. These warranties fall into two categories: (1) those imposed on persons who *transfer* instruments and (2) those imposed on persons who *obtain payment or acceptance.*

§ 1. Transferors' Warranties

In the absence of a contrary agreement, any person who transfers an instrument and receives consideration gives five separate implied warranties relating to (1) title, (2) signatures, (3) alterations, (4) defenses, and (5) insolvency proceedings. [3–417(2)] These warranties arise regardless of whether the transfer is merely by assignment or is by negotiation, with or without indorsement. With one minor exception which will be mentioned (see page 205), they are the same for all transferors. Transferors by indorsement, qualified as well as unqualified, give these warranties *not only to their immediate transferees but also to any subsequent holders who take the instrument in good faith.* Unless he is a depositor for collection or a collecting bank, however, one who transfers an instrument without indorsement gives these warranties only to his immediate transferee.   [3–417(2), 4–207(3)]

Confusion is sometimes caused by the fact that in addition to giving the five transferors' warranties mentioned above, transferors give the same three *presenters'* warranties that are given by those who obtain payment or acceptance.   (See pages 223–224)   Although, as will become clear from later discussion, there are several important differences between the two classes of warranties, it should be sufficient here to mention the basic difference: presenters' warranties run only to those who pay or accept whereas transferors' warranties run only to the transferor's immediate transferee and later holders.

A.   WHY HOLDER MAY PREFER TO SUE TRANSFEROR ON WARRANTY

Because transferors of negotiable instruments usually indorse without qualification, secondary liability normally furnishes a sufficient basis for recovering from a transferor when the party who is expected to pay does not.   But if the holder's right to recover on the basis of secondary liability is barred because the instrument was transferred without an indorsement or by a qualified indorsement or if the secondary liability of an unqualified indorser is discharged by the holder's failure to satisfy the requirements with respect to presentment, dishonor, notice of dishonor, or protest, the holder often may still avoid or minimize his loss by suing a prior party on one or more of the transferors' warranties. Even though the defendant indorsed without qualification and his secondary liability has not been discharged, it may be desirable for the holder to sue on the basis of a breach of warranty, rather than on secondary liability, because his right to sue for breach of warranty arises immediately on discovering the breach though the time for payment and possible dishonor has not arrived. In cases where the aggrieved party is entitled to sue on an underlying obligation, he may sometimes prefer to proceed on the basis of the breach of warranty because it is easier to prove. Finally, proceeding on the basis of breach of warranty allows the aggrieved party to rescind rather than seek money damages.

B.   WARRANTY OF TITLE

The first warranty given by the transferor for consideration is that "he has good title to the instrument or is authorized to obtain payment or acceptance on behalf of one who has a good title and that the transfer is otherwise rightful."   [3–417(2)(a)]   This warranty is intended to protect the transferee against the risk that the transferor had neither title nor proper authority and that as a result: (1) the true owner, who might be either the person for whom the transferor purported to act or some other person, might assert his claim and bring an action to recover the instrument or its value; (2) the transferee's own lack of title might be asserted against him as a defense when he demands payment; (3) the transferee will be liable for breach of the same warranty if he later sells the instrument; or (4) if the transferee or some later party obtains payment or acceptance from the party who is expected to pay, he may be held liable for a breach of the *presenters'* warranty of title which will be considered shortly. (See pages 212–215)

A transferor might breach the warranty of title in any of several ways. The signature of the payee or some other party in the chain of title might have been forged by the transferor or another. A finder, thief, or unauthorized agent, might sell an instrument that is payable to someone else who has not indorsed it. In cases such as these, the transferor is not a holder or an owner, and neither is his transferee. The warranty is obviously broken.

In some cases, however, the warranty is broken even though the transferor is actually the holder. Thus, an instrument that is payable to bearer or to the order of the transferor might have been found or stolen by him or acquired by him as agent and transferred without authority of the owner. In cases of this kind, although the transferor is a holder because the instrument runs to him, he

[*201*]

breaks the warranty of title because he is not the owner and does not have authority from the owner. In these cases, if the transferee acquires the instrument as a holder in due course, however, the latter gets good title because a holder in due course gets good title by negotiation from even a finder, a thief, or an unauthorized agent. Nonetheless, the warranty of title is broken. (See page 97)

When a breach of this warranty results from a forgery in the chain of title, there can be no later holder or holder in due course unless the person whose signature is forged reacquires the instrument. Normally, therefore, if there is a forgery in the chain of title, this warranty is broken not only by the forger but also by any later transferor.

> M delivers his note to P, payee, as payment of a debt. T steals the note, forges P's blank unqualified indorsement, and sells the note to A. A sells the note to B without indorsing. B indorses "without recourse" and sells the note to C. C indorses without qualification and sells the note to H. At maturity M refuses to pay H. Since the note runs to P, who never indorsed, T, A, B, and C broke the transferor's warranty of title. As an unqualified indorser, C is liable to H secondarily as well as on the warranty. The same is true of T whose forged indorsement operates as if he had signed his own name. As a qualified indorser, B is not liable secondarily but, as an indorser, his warranty liability runs through to H.

As a transferor without indorsement, A is not liable secondarily, and his liability on the warranty runs only to his immediate transferee, B, not to C or H.

C. WARRANTY SIGNATURES ARE GENUINE OR AUTHORIZED

The second warranty given by a transferor for consideration is that "all signatures are genuine or authorized." [3–417(2)(b)] If a signature of a payee or an indorsee in the chain of title is unauthorized, there is a breach of this warranty as well as a breach of the warranty of title. If the signature of a maker, drawer, drawee, acceptor, or indorsee not in the chain of title is unauthorized, however, there is a breach of this warranty but no breach of the warranty of title.

The most obvious purpose of this warranty is to protect the transferee against the risk that he will not be able to collect because some person who appears to be liable on the instrument is not. The warranty also protects the transferee against the further risk that he will be liable on the same warranty if he transfers the instrument. Also, depending on the facts, if he or his transferee acquires payment or acceptance after learning that the signature of the maker or drawer is unauthorized, he might be held liable for breach of the presenters' warranty that he has no such knowledge. (See pages 215–220)

[*203*]

P forges M's signature as maker of a note payable in one year to the order of P. P negotiates the note to A for consideration. A negotiates the note to H for consideration. Five months before maturity, H learns of the forgery. There was no breach of the warranty of title, but H is entitled to recover from A or P for breach of the transferors' warranty that all signatures are genuine or authorized.

D.   WARRANTY AGAINST MATERIAL ALTERATION

A person who buys a negotiable instrument usually assumes that he is entitled to recover according to the tenor of the instrument at the time of his purchase from the various parties whose signatures appear on the instrument at that time. If the instrument has been materially altered, however, the liability of the parties who signed before the alteration usually is limited to the tenor of the instrument before it was altered, and sometimes such liability is completely discharged. Primarily to protect transferees against losses that result in this way, each transferor who receives consideration warrants that "the instrument has not been materially altered." [3–417(2)(c)] This warranty also helps protect against the risks that the transferee will be held liable for breach of the same warranty if he transfers the instrument or that he will be held liable for breach of the *presenters'* warranty against material alteration if he or a subsequent party obtains payment or acceptance.

> M makes a note for $9,000 payable to the order of P. P skilfully raises the amount to $29,000. P then negotiates the note to A. A negotiates the note to HDC. The transferors' warranty against alteration was broken by P and A. HDC is entitled to collect $9,000 from M and the balance of the $29,000 from P or A; or HDC may rescind his contract with A and recover whatever consideration he paid A. Of course, P and A might be liable *secondarily* for the full $29,000.

E. WARRANTY REGARDING DEFENSES

This is the only warranty that differs depending on the nature of the transfer. Any transferor *other than a qualified indorser* warrants *absolutely* that "no defense of any party is good against him." [3–417(2)(d)'] If the indorsement is "without recourse," the qualified indorser's warranty is merely that he has *no actual knowledge* of any defense of any party good against him. [3–417(3), 1–201(25)] To fill the gap left by the less than absolute liability of the qualified indorser, it is not unusual for the transferee who takes by a qualified indorsement to insist that the indorser give an express warranty regarding defenses generally or regarding some matter about which the transferee is particularly concerned. For example, the qualified indorser might be required to warrant absolutely that there are no defenses or that the maker or some prior indorser is not an infant.

> R, an adjudicated incompetent, draws a draft on E, payable to the order of P, on demand. By a qualified indorsement, P negotiates the draft to A. By an unqualified indorsement, A negotiates the draft to H. When H demands payment, R properly refuses on the ground of incompetency. Regardless of his knowledge of the defense, A, as an unqualified indorser, is liable to H for breach of the transferors' warranty against defenses. P, as a qualified indorser, is liable for breach of this warranty only if he had actual knowledge of the incompetency when he negotiated the note. If he broke the warranty, P is liable to H as well as A. If P had not indorsed, he would have been liable on the warranty regardless of his knowledge, but his warranty would have run only to his immediate transferee, A. (See page 198.)

F.   WARRANTY OF NO KNOWLEDGE OF INSOLVENCY PROCEEDINGS

A transferor does not give any warranty that the party expected to pay or anyone else is a good credit risk or that he is solvent in the commercial sense. The transferee normally is expected to check these things for himself before he buys. However, a transferor for consideration does warrant that "he has *no knowledge* of any insolvency proceedings instituted with respect to the *maker or acceptor or the drawer of an unaccepted instrument.*"   [3–417(2)(e)]   (Emphasis added) This warranty prevents a holder who is aware that such proceedings have been commenced from passing his almost certain loss to his transferee.

> R draws a draft on E, payable to the order of P. P negotiates the draft to A. Aware that P is insolvent, but unaware that insolvency proceedings have been instituted against P, A sells and delivers the draft to H. A broke no warranty. Even assuming that A had known that insolvency proceedings had been instituted against P, A would not have broken this warranty because P was the *payee*, not a maker, acceptor, or drawer.

G. HOLDER IN DUE COURSE AND TRANSFEROR'S WARRANTIES

The transferor's warranties extend to all transferees, including even a holder in due course in a case where breach of the warranty does not destroy any rights the holder in due course otherwise would enjoy. For example, a holder in due course of a stolen bearer instrument may rescind the transfer for breach of the warranty of title even though a holder in due course is not subject to a claim or defense based on nondelivery. Likewise, he can rescind for breach of the warranty against alteration, even though the alteration is the wrongful completion of an incomplete instrument and such completion does not impair his right to collect on the instrument as completed. Also, he can rescind for breach of the warranty against defenses although the defense is lack of consideration or some other defense which cannot be asserted against a holder in due course.   Giving the holder in due course the advantage of these warranties protects him from being harassed by these or other defenses and from being required to prove his status as a holder in due course in a lawsuit not of his own choosing. [Comment 9, 3–417]

§ 2. Presenters' Warranties

Anyone who pays or accepts a negotiable instrument is likely to do so on the basis of one or more assumptions. For example, a maker or acceptor who pays is likely to assume that the person obtaining payment is entitled to do so, that all of the signatures on the instrument are genuine, that the instrument has not been altered, that any documents delivered at the time of payment or acceptance are genuine and that he has no valid defense against the claim for payment. A drawee who pays or accepts is likely to make similar assumptions and to assume also that the draft is not an overdraft and does not otherwise exceed the bounds of his agreement with the drawer and that the drawer has not issued any stop payment order. An unqualified indorser or a drawer who pays assumes what other payors assume and, in addition, that the instrument has been dishonored and that the other conditions to his own liability have been met. If a person pays or accepts because he is mistaken about any one of these or other matters, the law in some cases allows him to get his money back or rescind his acceptance, but in other cases it does not. This area of the law is very complicated, and courts, legislators and writers have had much difficulty in trying to develop and describe the governing legal principles.

The problem is not new. A leading case, and the starting point for most of the discussion of the law in this area, is Price v. Neal, 3 Burr. 1354, 97 Eng.Rep. 871, which came before Lord Mansfield in 1762. It involved two drafts. The drawee paid one after first accepting it, and he paid the other without having accepted it. Some time later he sought to recover both payments on the ground that the drawer's signature had been forged. Lord Mansfield decided that the drawee-acceptor could not recover either payment. In reaching this conclusion he said: "The plaintiff cannot recover the money unless it be against conscience in the defendant to retain it. * * * But it can never be thought unconscientious in the defendant to retain this money, when he has once received it upon a bill of exchange indorsed to him for a fair and valuable consideration, which he had bona fide paid, without the least privity or suspicion of any forgery."

For various reasons, American courts generally have followed and expanded the doctrine of Price v. Neal in similar or analogous cases involving mistaken payment or acceptance of commercial paper. For example, in Central Bank & Trust Co. v. G. F. C., 297 F.2d 126 (5th Cir. 1961), a bank sued to recover a payment it had made to the payee of a check that had overdrawn the drawer's account with the bank. The court denied the bank any right to recover the payment. Although the court did not impute negligence or other fault to the bank, it stated that in most cases of this kind the holder has no way of knowing of the paying party's mistake whereas the paying party can make such mistakes only if it is lax. The court indicated, however, that the basic reason for denying recovery in this and similar cases is that in the modern complicated business world, allowing recovery would often cause serious delay, uncertainty, and confusion, affecting not only the parties directly involved but many others as well.

A. THE DOCTRINE OF FINALITY

On the assumption that it is usually better to end the transaction on the instrument when it is paid or accepted rather than set aside a whole series of transactions when a mistake or wrongdoing is later discovered, the Code starts by adopting the broad principles established by Price

v. Neal and cases having the same general thrust. It does so by providing that "payment or acceptance of any instrument is final in favor of *a holder in due course, or a person who has in good faith changed his position in reliance * * *"* (Emphasis added) [3–418 and Comment 1] Notice that the benefit of the doctrine of finality under the Code extends only to a holder in due course or one who has in good faith changed his position in reliance on payment or acceptance. A person who does not fall into one of these two categories is governed by general principles of restitution and so can almost always be required to give up any benefits received as the result of a material mistake. In short, only holders in due course and those who change their position in reliance on payment or acceptance get the benefit of the general rule that payment or acceptance is final even when made as the result of a material mistake. Even as to these favored parties, however, the general rule is subject to several exceptions. Aside from minor variations required by the special circumstances relating to bank deposits and collections, these exceptions are embodied in three implied warranties which relate to (1) the title of the presenting party, (2) the signature of the issuing party, and (3) material alteration. Normally, one who wishes to set aside a payment or an acceptance given to a holder in due course or to one who changed his position in good faith reliance must proceed on the basis of one of these three warranties which usually are given by *persons who obtain payment or acceptance and by prior transferors.*

> R draws a draft on E who is not indebted to him. P, payee, obtains the draft by fraud and negotiates the draft to H who is not a holder in due course because he knows the draft is overdue. Mistakenly believing that he (E) is indebted to R, E pays H. H deposits the proceeds in his savings account. When E discovers his mistake, he is entitled to recover the payment from H. Even though none of the presenters' warranties is broken, the doctrine of finality of payment does not apply because H is neither a holder in due course nor a good faith relier who changed his position as required by Section 3–418. According to ordinary principles of restitution, E is entitled to recover the payment which he made in good faith as the result of a material mistake. Since none of the presenters' warranties was broken, if H had been either a holder in due course or one who changed his position in good faith reliance on the payment, the doctrine of finality embodied in Section 3–418 would have applied and E would not have been entitled to recover the payment.

B. WARRANTY OF TITLE

The first warranty given by a person who obtains payment or acceptance and by any prior transferor is that "he has a good title to the instrument or is authorized to obtain payment or acceptance on behalf of one who has a good title."

[3–417(1)(a)] This warranty is intended to protect one who pays to or accepts for the wrong party.

This warranty is most likely to be important when payment is obtained by one who is not a holder.

> M issues a note payable to P's order. T steals the note, forges P's indorsement, and sells the note to A. Thinking A is the holder, M pays A. (A is not the holder because the note runs to P.) Assuming that P is not precluded from asserting the unauthorized signature, M, having paid on the forged indorsement, is liable to P for conversion. [3–419(1)(c)] (See pages 157–158) M is entitled to recoup his loss from A on the basis of A's breach of the presenters' warranty of title. A had neither title nor proper authority to obtain payment. If A is unavailable or without funds, M may recoup his loss from T on the basis of T's breach of the presenters' warranty of title, which is given by prior transferors (See page 223).

Also, this warranty may be helpful to a drawee who is induced to accept a draft presented by someone who lacks title. The warranty allows him to rescind his acceptance, thus avoiding liability to the presenting party and simultaneously avoiding the risk of becoming liable to some later party who purchases the instrument in reliance on the acceptance. If the instrument does fall into the hands of a holder in due course before the acceptor can rescind his acceptance, he will be required to pay; but, in this case, the warranty of title gives him the right to recover his loss by suing the party who obtained the acceptance.

Occasionally the warranty of title may be broken even though the party who obtains payment or acceptance is in fact the *holder* of the instrument. For example, although a finder or a thief of a bearer instrument has possession and is a holder, he nonetheless lacks title. This warranty normally is not important in these circumstances, however, because a person usually can discharge his liability on an instrument by paying the holder whether or not he has title. (See pages 304–309)

It is interesting to consider this warranty in the light of the doctrine of Price v. Neal. Under that doctrine, payment to or acceptance for one acting in good faith is treated as equal to an admission of the genuineness of the *drawer's* signature; consequently, the drawee may not thereafter complain that the *drawer's* signature has been forged. In contrast, the warranty of title enables the paying or accepting party to relief whenever the presenting party lacks title because an indorsement of the *payee or some other party in the chain of title* has been forged. This difference in treatment is said to be justified by the fact that normally a drawee can avoid loss when the *drawer's* signature is forged simply by comparing the signature on the instrument with one it has on hand, whereas a party making payment or acceptance normally has no reasonable opportunity to make a similar comparison to determine the genuineness of an *indorser's* signature. [Comment 3, 3–417]

Many scholars doubt the validity of this distinction especially in the modern business world where there is really no practical way of checking all signatures of makers or drawers consistently with the need for speed. At present, a sounder reason might be that it tends to let the loss remain where it first falls among innocent parties rather than upsetting a series of transactions with all of the waste of time and effort that involves.

C. WARRANTY AGAINST KNOWLEDGE SIGNATURE OF MAKER OR DRAWER IS UNAUTHORIZED

Those who obtain payment or acceptance and prior transferors do not warrant *absolutely* that the signature of the person named as the issuing party is genuine or authorized. At most, they warrant that they have *no knowledge* that the "signature of the maker or drawer is unauthorized." [3–417(1)(b)] "Knowledge," for this purpose means "actual" knowledge. [1–201 (25)]

To understand the special nature and effect of this second presenters' warranty it should be noted that it relates only to the signature of the *maker* or *drawer*—the parties who normally *issue* an instrument.   The only other signature that might concern a person who is paying or accepting is that of an indorser in the chain of title, but the authenticity of the signature of an indorser in the chain of title is already covered by the warranty of title discussed above.

> M makes a 60-day note and delivers it to P, the payee, for goods sold.   A week later, P offers to sell the note to A but A says he will buy the note only if N first indorses it.   P asks N to indorse.   N refuses.   P forges N's indorsement.   P then indorses the note and delivers it to A for value.   A negotiates the note to B for value.   At maturity, B obtains payment from M.   At the time B knows that N's signature has been forged. B has broken no warranty.   N is neither a maker nor drawer so the warranty relating to their signatures is not broken.   N is not in the chain of title so the warranty of title is not broken.   Also, M suffers no damage because he was discharged by his payment in good faith to B, the holder.

By providing by implication that the warranty is not broken by one who obtains payment from a drawee or acceptor *without knowledge* that the drawer's signature has been forged, the Code in effect adopts the holdings regarding both of the drafts in the case of Price v. Neal.   The Code

goes beyond these holdings, however, by imply-
ing also that one who obtains payment from a
maker, drawer, or indorser or acceptance from
a drawee without knowledge that the signature
of the maker or drawer has been forged does not
break this warranty.

In contrast, when a person obtains payment or
acceptance *with knowledge* that the signature of
the maker or drawer has been forged, this warranty usually is broken. There are two exceptions, and both are limited to cases where a holder
in due course obtains *payment* while acting in
good faith.

The first exception is that this warranty is not
given or broken when a holder in due course obtains payment from a *maker or drawer in good
faith while knowing that the paying party's signature is forged.* [3–417(1)(b)(i)] It is reasoned that a maker or drawer should know his
own signature, and if not, he should bear whatever
loss or inconvenience results from his mistake,
rather than thrust it on a holder in due course
who has obtained payment in good faith. However, this exception is recognized regardless of
whether the payor is negligent.

One must not assume that this exception is
broader than it actually is. First, a person cannot
be a holder in due course if he knows when he
acquires an instrument that the signature of the

maker or drawer is unauthorized. Also, even assuming that a person acquires an instrument as a holder in due course, he does not act in good faith if he knows when he obtains payment that the payor is not legally obligated to make it. Knowledge that the signature of the maker or drawer is unauthorized does not negate his good faith, however, if the holder in due course has good reason to believe that the maker or drawer is legally obligated to pay him, as would be true if the holder in due course thinks that the negligence of the maker or drawer substantially contributed to the unauthorized signature. (See pages 142–145)

The second exception is made if the holder in due course takes a draft after it has been accepted *or* obtains acceptance without knowledge that the drawer's signature has been forged, but later learns of the forgery and obtains payment from the acceptor in good faith. [3–417(1) (b) (iii)] In this situation, it is sufficient to establish the good faith of the holder that he has relied on the acceptance because in this case he rightly feels that the acceptor should pay. If the acceptor had refused to accept when it was presented by a prior party, the holder in due course probably would not have purchased the instrument. If the acceptor had refused to accept when the draft was presented by the holder in due course, the latter would have been on notice of the unauthorized signature sooner and would have been in a better position to pursue his transferor or some prior party. This second exception goes further than the holding of Price v. Neal, in which case it appears, not only that the defendant was a holder in due course by our modern standards, but also that he obtained payment *without knowledge* of the forgeries.

> P forges R's signature on a draft and negotiates it to HDC. Before maturity, HDC, unaware of the forgery, obtains E's acceptance. HDC then learns of the forgery. Nonetheless, he honestly believes that he is entitled to be paid and obtains payment from E. E is not entitled to recover the payment from HDC. A holder in due course who obtains an *acceptance* in good faith, being unaware that the drawer's signature is unauthorized, does not give or break the warranty of no knowledge if later, having learned of the forgery, acting in good faith, he obtains *payment* from the acceptor.

In contrast, whenever a holder in due course *obtains an acceptance* with actual knowledge that the drawer's signature has been forged, he gives and breaks the warranty. His good faith, if it exists, does not help him. Furthermore, if he later obtains payment from the acceptor on the basis of such an acceptance, he again breaks this warranty.

> P forges R's signature to a draft. P negotiates the draft to HDC. HDC then learns of the forgery. Nonetheless, HDC obtains E's acceptance.

At maturity, HDC obtains payment from E. Even assuming that HDC obtained the payment in good faith, E is entitled to recover it. HDC broke the warranty that he had no knowledge that R's signature was unauthorized when he obtained the acceptance, and later when he obtained payment. Also, HDC would have broken the warranty if, without having obtained acceptance, he obtained payment from E knowing that R's signature had been forged.

D. WARRANTY AGAINST MATERIAL ALTERATIONS

Finally, a party who presents an instrument for payment or acceptance and any prior transferor give an *absolute* warranty—that is, one which *does not depend upon knowledge*—"that the instrument has not been materially altered." [3–417(1)(c)] Again there are two exceptions, both of which parallel the exceptions relating to the second warranty and apply only in cases where a *holder in due course obtains payment in good faith*.

The first exception is that a holder in due course who obtains payment in good faith does not give this warranty to a *maker* or *drawer*. [3–417(1) (c) (i and ii)] A maker or drawer who pays an altered instrument is as likely to be at fault as when paying an instrument on which his signature is unauthorized; but, once again, the exception applies regardless of fault.

Of course, good faith again poses a problem. On the one extreme, if the holder in due course himself made the alteration, his bad faith in obtaining payment is clear and so he gives and breaks the warranty. On the opposite extreme, if a holder in due course is totally unaware of the alteration when he obtains payment, his good faith is clear and so he would neither give nor break the warranty. Knowledge of the alteration at the time of obtaining payment might or might not negate good faith. Normally it does. It does not, however, if the holder in due course has good reason to think that the maker or drawer is legally or morally bound to make the payment in question. For example, since parties to an instrument remain liable to a holder in due course according to the original tenor of an instrument which has been altered by deletion, addition, or change, he does not show lack of good faith or give the warranty when he obtains this limited payment while aware of the alteration. Similarly, he does not show lack of good faith or give the warranty despite knowledge of the alteration if he obtains payment from the maker or drawer according to the terms of the altered instrument, if he has reason to think that the maker's or drawer's negligence has substantially contributed to the alteration or if he knows that the alteration consists of wrongfully completing an incomplete instrument. In such cases, a holder in due course has a right to

[*221*]

payment according to the terms of the altered instrument. (See pages 139–142)

The second exception is recognized when a holder in due course, acting in good faith, obtains payment from an *acceptor* who had accepted the instrument *before* it was acquired by the holder in due course. This exception is recognized whether the alteration occurred before or after the acceptance. [3–417(1)(c)(iii)(iv)] If the alteration occurred before the acceptance, it is recognized even though the acceptance expressly states that the instrument will be paid as originally drawn.

It seems clear that a holder in due course who purchases an instrument which already has been accepted acts in good faith and so does not give this warranty if he obtains payment from the acceptor while unaware of the alteration. Even though he is aware of the alteration when obtaining payment, he may act in good faith if he has good reason to think that the alteration was made *before* the instrument was accepted. In this case, he buys the instrument relying on the assumption that the acceptor is liable according to its terms as altered, and the acceptor is in part responsible for this assumption. A holder in due course does not act in good faith, however, and hence he gives and breaks this warranty if he obtains full payment according to the altered terms knowing that the alteration was made *after* the acceptance. In this case he has no basis for assuming that the acceptor is liable except according to the terms of the instrument at the time of his acceptance.

If the holder in due course, himself, *obtains the acceptance,* he gives the warranty just like anyone else, and the acceptor can hold him liable if the instrument has been altered before it is presented. This is so whether or not the holder in due course knows of the alteration when he obtains acceptance. Similarly if the holder in due course, having obtained acceptance of an altered instrument, later obtains payment, he gives and breaks this warranty just like anyone else.

It should be emphasized that normally the only warranties given by a person who obtains payment or acceptance relate to title, the signature of the issuing party, and alterations. For example, no warranties are given to protect a drawee who pays an overdraft or who pays in disregard of a stop payment order. Of course, the presenting party might give an *express* warranty with respect to any matter normally not covered.

E.   PRESENTERS' WARRANTIES GIVEN ALSO BY PRIOR TRANSFERORS

As mentioned earlier, the three presenters' warranties that have been discussed are given not only by those who obtain acceptance or payment but also by prior transferors. [3–417(1)] (See pages 199)

> M issues a note to P. P fraudulently raises the amount and negotiates the note to A. A negotiates the note to HDC. At maturity, HDC acting in good faith obtains payment from M. Since HDC obtained payment from the maker in good faith, he did not make or break the presenters' warranty against material alteration. [3–417(1) (c)(i)] Although A is a prior transferor, M cannot recover from A for breach of A's *transferors'* warranty against material alteration. The reason is that transferors' warranties run only to the transferor's immediate *transferee* and any subsequent *holder* who takes the instrument in good faith; and M is neither. As a prior transferor, however, A is liable to M on the basis of the *presenters'* warranty against material alteration unless he, A, is also a holder in due course who acted in good faith. [3–417(1)(c)(i)] If M cannot recover from either HDC or A, M can recover for breach of the presenters' warranty against alteration from P, a prior transferor who is clearly not a holder in due course who acted in good faith.

F. TRANSFEREES OF HOLDER IN DUE COURSE

The special advantage given holders in due course concerning warranties relating to the signature of the issuing party and alterations extends also to their transferees under the "shelter" provision of the Code. [3–201(1)] (See pages 258–260)

> M issues a note to P. P alters the note to increase the sum payable and then negotiates it to HDC. HDC negotiates the note to T who is not a holder in due course in his own right because he knows the note is overdue. T, acting in good faith and unaware of the alteration, obtains payment from M. T has not given or broken the warranty against material alteration because he has the *rights* of a holder in due course who does not give this warranty when he obtains payment from a maker while acting in good faith.

§ 3. Principles Applicable to Both Transferors' and Presenters' Warranties

There are a number of generalizations that can be made without distinguishing between warranties made by transferors and those made by presenters.

To begin, there can be no relief on the basis of a breach of either type of warranty without good faith reliance. For example, if a person purchases an instrument knowing that the amount has been raised, he cannot obtain relief on the basis of the *transferors'* warranty against alteration and a person who pays an instrument knowing that it has been altered cannot obtain relief on the basis of the *presenters'* warranty against alteration. Also, breach of either class of warranty normally gives the injured party the right to elect between rescinding the transaction and taking back whatever he parted with or letting the transaction stand and suing for damages.

Regardless of whether a transferors' or a presenters' warranty is broken, if the aggrieved party elects to recover damages he is limited to actual damages that are reasonably foreseeable by the party who broke the warranty. The general object is to put the aggrieved party in the position that he would have been in monetarily if there had been no breach. For example, if a transferor's warranty is broken by a transferor without indorsement (who incurs no secondary liability) the transferee can usually recover the difference between the value of the instrument as it was and as it would have been if there had been no breach. If the signature of the maker, acceptor, or drawer, or an unqualified indorser in the line of title, is forged, this may be the face amount of the instrument. But if no one else is liable on the instrument and the person whose name has been forged was insolvent when payment was due the amount of recovery normally would be limited to what might have been recovered from that person if he had actually signed. Also, any incidental or consequential damages that are reasonably foreseeable may be recovered. This would include the reasonable costs of litigation to which the aggrieved party is necessarily subjected as the result of the breach of warranty. Regardless of which type of warranty is involved, if a person is acting as a selling broker, the extent of his liability for breach of warranty depends on whether he discloses this fact. If he does, he warrants only his good faith and authority; if he does not, he is liable on either a transferors' or presenters' warranty just as if he were acting as principal. [3–417(4)] As is true of warranties generally either transferors' or presenters' warranties can be eliminated by express agreement. If a transfer is made by indorsement, however, a disclaimer of liability must be made in the indorsement; otherwise proof of the disclaimer would violate the parol evidence rule. Finally, by indorsement or otherwise a transferor or presenter may add one or more express warranties. For example, a transferor may warrant that a primary party is solvent.

CHAPTER 10

HOLDERS IN DUE COURSE

§ 1. Importance

Although the elements essential to liability are present, a defendant may possibly avoid liability by proving one or more defenses. The range of defenses which might be asserted effectively depends largely on whether or not the plaintiff has the rights of a holder in due course. If he has, he holds the instrument free of most defenses of prior parties. [3–305(2)] (See pages 273–288) He also holds the instrument free of any prior party's right to claim the instrument itself even if it was obtained by fraud, theft, or other illegal means from that person. [3–305(1)] (See pages 288–289.) He enjoys freedom from liability based on warranties under some circumstances in which others would be held liable. (See pages 215–223.) He has the advantage of being able to transfer his special rights and privileges to others. (See pages 258–260) These and other advantages are mentioned in various scattered sections of the Code. Earlier the requirements of a holder in due course were described in broad terms. Because of their vital importance in many cases, they will now be described more fully.

§ 2. Requirements

The basic requirements are stated in Section 3–302(1) of the Code which provides:

> A holder in due course is a holder who takes the instrument
>
> (a) for value; and
>
> (b) in good faith; and
>
> (c) without notice that it is overdue or has been dishonored or of any defense against or claim to it on the part of any person.

Section 3–302(1) should be considered carefully and remembered because when it is necessary to determine whether a party is a holder in due course, it is the logical starting point. In many cases, however, it is necessary to proceed further to find the answer. (For a discussion of a few special situations in which a holder is not a holder in due course even though he satisfies the requirements of Section 3–302(1) set forth above, see pages 260–261.)

§ 3. Instrument

The "instrument" referred to in Section 3–302 (1) is a "negotiable instrument." [3–102(1)(e)] Although, as was explained earlier (see page 68), an instrument that fails to be negotiable only because it is not payable to bearer or to order is governed by Article 3 in other respects, *there can*

*be no holder in due course of such an instrument
or of any other instrument that is not a negotiable
instrument as defined by Section 3–104(1).*

§ 4. Holder

An easily forgotten truism is that *one cannot be
a holder in due course unless one is a holder.* As
explained earlier, a *holder* is a person who is in
possession of an instrument that *runs* to him; and
a bearer instrument runs to whoever is in possession of it, whereas an order instrument runs to
the payee if it has never been indorsed, and to
the last indorsee if it has.   (See pages 94–95)

§ 5. Value

The Code contains two overlapping but clearly
different definitions of value.   A general definition, contained in Article 1 defines value broadly
as including, among other things, "any consideration sufficient to support a simple contract."   [1–
201(44)]   Article 3, which governs commercial
paper, defines value much more narrowly.   This
definition will be explained shortly.   Here it is
sufficient to recognize that *throughout our discussion of commercial paper, value is used only
in this narrow sense.*   (See pages 231–241)

In the law of commercial paper, *consideration*
has the same meaning that it has in the law of
simple contracts.   Its meaning is quite different

from the meaning of value in the sense in which it is used in the law of commercial paper. Equally important, in the law of commercial paper each of these terms has a special legal significance of its own.

The primary legal significance of value is that unless a holder has taken an instrument for value, he cannot be a holder in due course. [3–302(1) (a)] Value is therefore an essential element in establishing this highly desirable *status*. The primary legal significance of consideration is that lack or failure of consideration is a *defense* which can be asserted by a defendant who is sued on an ordinary contract, on an instrument that is not negotiable, or on an instrument that is negotiable, by a plaintiff who lacks the rights of a holder in due course. [3–306(c), 3–408] Both concepts have less important legal significance in other areas of commercial paper. For example, unless the plaintiff or some prior party has given *value* before an instrument is overdue, there is normally no right to recover from an accommodation party [3–415(2)]; and a transferors' warranties are given only by a transferor who receives *consideration*. [3–417(2)] The meaning of each term, however, remains the same in the various contexts in which it is used.

The starting point for determining the meaning of value in the narrow sense in which it is used in the law of commercial paper is Section 3–303 which provides:

> A holder takes the instrument for value
>> (a) to the extent that the agreed *consideration has been performed* or that he acquires a security interest in or a lien on the instrument otherwise than by legal process; or
>>
>> (b) when he takes the instrument in payment of or as security for an antecedent claim against any person whether or not the claim is due; or
>>
>> (c) when he gives a negotiable instrument for it or makes an irrevocable commitment to a third person.   (Emphasis added.)

An examination of the foregoing provision of the Code shows that although the legal significance of value and consideration are distinctly different, to a certain extent the key to the meaning of value is consideration.

Since the Code does not define consideration, it usually will be necessary for the courts to refer to cases decided in their own jurisdictions to determine its meaning and, consequently, the meaning of value. Consideration has been defined by the courts and writers in various ways. A reasonably workable definition is that "consideration consists of doing or *promising* to do what one is not already legally bound to do, or refraining or *promising* to refrain from doing what one has a legal right to do, in return for a promise." A somewhat shorter definition might be "giving up or *promising* to give up a right, power, or privilege, in return for a promise."

A. EXECUTORY PROMISE NORMALLY NOT VALUE

Both foregoing definitions recognize that *consideration* might consist of a *promise*, even though the promise remains executory, that is, unperformed. Referring to Section 3–303, and particularly the phrase "to the extent that the agreed consideration *has been performed*," it will be seen that normally an executory promise cannot constitute *value*.

. The foregoing general principles relating to value and consideration are illustrated by the following case:

> M issues a note for $1,000 to P as a gift. Since P gives up nothing in return for M's promise in the note, M receives no consideration and can assert this as a defense if sued by P or any later party who lacks the rights of a holder in due course. Next, assume that P negotiates the note to X in return for X's promise to pay $900. Since X was not previously legally bound to pay $900, his promise to do so is consideration for the obligation of P as transferor. However, as long as X's promise is unperformed, X has not given value and so is not a holder in due course. Consequent-

ly, if X sues M, he can be defeated by M's defense, lack of consideration. Assume that X negotiates the note to Z who pays $900 cash. Since his consideration has been completely executed, Z has given value, and if he meets the other requirements, he is a holder in due course. As such, he is entitled to recover from M at maturity because M's defense—lack of consideration—is not good against a holder in due course.

B.   NOTICE OF CLAIM OR DEFENSE WHILE PROMISE IS EXECUTORY

If an instrument is negotiated to a party in return for his promise, that party does not become a holder for value immediately. However, by fulfilling his promise, he can become a holder for value and consequently a holder in due course. If he learns of a defense or claim before he has fully carried out his promise, he can become a holder in due course only to the extent that his promise has been carried out when he learns of the defense or claim.   [3–303(a)]   For example,

P induces M by fraud to deliver a note for $1000. Before maturity P negotiates the note to H, who acts in good faith, in return for H's promise to pay $1000 in four equal monthly instalments. After paying three instalments, H learns of P's fraud. If H nonetheless pays P the remaining $250, he will be entitled to recover at most only $750 from M at maturity because H can be a holder in due course only to that extent. If H had agreed to pay only $750 as the total consideration for the instrument in three equal instalments and paid the $750 before learning of P's fraud, H might have become a holder in due course to the fullest possible extent and as such entitled to recover the full $1000 from M.

C. EXECUTORY PROMISE AS VALUE

The basic reason for not recognizing a holder as a holder in due course, except to the extent that his promise has been performed before he learns of a defense or claim, is that to the extent that his promise is executory a holder who learns of a defense or claim normally can avoid his loss by simply refusing to carry out his promise. If he is unable to avoid loss in this way, it becomes necessary to accord him the status of a holder in due course to protect him although his promise given in return for the instrument is still executory. The Code expressly recognizes this in two situations. [3–303(c)]

The first situation arises when a holder acquires an instrument in return for an executory promise that constitutes an irrevocable commitment by the holder to a third party. For example, suppose that a bank credits a depositor's account with the amount of a check and then, while unaware of a defense on the deposited check, certifies a check drawn by the depositor for the balance of the account. In this case the bank is held to have given value for the deposited check even though it does not pay the certified check until after it has learned of a defense on the deposited check. See Freeport Bank v. Viemeister, 227 App.Div. 457, 238 N.Y.Supp. 169 (1929).

The second situation occurs if a holder issues his own negotiable instrument in return for the instrument on which he seeks payment; that is, there is an exchange of negotiable instruments. For example, suppose a bank gives its own draft in return for the note of a third party, and after learning of a defense on the note, it pays the draft to a transferee who is a holder in due course. In this case justice obviously requires that the bank should not be denied the status of holder in due course merely because it learned of a defense before making a payment it was bound to make. See First National Bank of Waukesha v. Motors Acceptance Corp., 15 Wis. 2d 44, 112 N.W.2d 381 (1961). The Code goes beyond this, however, and provides that a person becomes a holder for value of an instrument for which he issues his own negotiable instrument even though he is never called upon to pay a holder in due course. It is reasoned that the possibility of the instrument falling into the hands of a holder in due course furnishes a sufficient basis for giving him this protection. [Comment 6, 3–303]

D. BANK CREDIT AS VALUE

In the typical case in which a bank receives one or more negotiable instruments for deposit in a customer's account, the bank immediately credits the customer's account, but the depositor acquires no right to draw against the items and the bank need not permit him to do so until the item is collected. As might be expected, the bank does not become a holder for value merely by crediting the depositor's account. If the depositor is permitted to draw against a deposited item before it is collected, however, the bank immediately becomes a holder for value concerning that item. [4–208(1)(a)] Consequently, if it becomes necessary for the bank to sue on the item, the bank normally enjoys the status of holder in due course unless it had learned of a defense or claim before allowing the withdrawal. This is true even though the deposit is made under a restrictive indorsement such as "for deposit only" and the deposit slip expressly states that the bank is acting only as agent for collection. It is reasoned that the provision is for the protection of the bank and that the bank may waive the protection. First National Bank v. Margulies, 35 Misc.2d 332, 232 N.Y.S.2d 274 (1962).

When a bank credits a depositor with a series of deposits and permits a number of withdrawals over a period of time, it is not always easy to determine whether the depositor has been permitted to withdraw funds credited on the basis of a particular item before the bank learns of a claim or defense on the item.   In tracing the deposits to withdrawals, the Code applies the rule of "first in, first out" or "fifo" as it is sometimes called.   [4–208(2), 4–209]   For example,

> D's account in X Bank starts with a zero balance. On three successive days, D deposits in his account checks for $100 each by A, B, and C in that order. X Bank immediately credits D's account as each check is deposited.   After D withdraws $200, X Bank learns that the checks of B and C are subject to defenses.   If X Bank subsequently permits D to withdraw the remaining $100, it will nonetheless be treated as having given value for B's check before receiving notice because the deposit based on this check was withdrawn when D obtained the $200.   However, since the deposit of C's check occurred last, it is presumed to have been withdrawn last.   Consequently, the bank is deemed not to have given value for C's check until after it received notice of C's defense.   Therefore, in an action against C the bank could not enjoy the status of a holder in due course.

In contrast with the typical case involving the deposit of one or more negotiable instruments as described above, a bank may acquire a negotiable instrument under circumstances that give the depositor or transferor a *right* to draw against it and impose on the bank a *duty* to allow this. Whether this right and the corresponding duty

[*238*]

arise from an express contract between the parties or from rules governing the collection process, the bank is considered as having given value immediately when the right arises and before any withdrawal against the item has been made. [4–208(1)(b)] Thus another exception occurs to the general rule that an executory promise does not constitute value.

E. TAKING INSTRUMENT AS PAYMENT OR SECURITY FOR ANTECEDENT DEBT AS VALUE

An executory promise is the only form of *consideration* which normally does not constitute *value*. Conversely, the Code recognizes at least one situation in which a holder who has not furnished consideration in the usual sense still is treated as having given value. This exception occurs if a debtor, not legally bound to do so, negotiates to his creditor *as security* an instrument issued by a third party and does not require the creditor to extend the time for payment of the debt or to give up anything else in return for the instrument given as security.

This exception is provided by Section 3–303 (b), which states that a holder takes an instrument for value "when he takes the instrument *in payment* of or *as security* for an antecedent claim against any person whether or not the claim is due." (Emphasis added.) If the instrument is taken in *payment* for a debt there clearly is consideration because the creditor gives up his right to the original debt. If he takes it merely as *security* and gives up no rights, he furnishes no consideration. He is treated as giving *value*, however, and so may qualify as a holder in due course. [3–303(b)]

> P holds a draft accepted by A. P negotiates the draft to X, as security for a debt owed by P to X. X does not agree to extend the time for payment or incur any other detriment in return for the draft. When P fails to pay the secured debt, X sues A as acceptor. A asserts a defense that is good only against one who is not a holder in due course. Judgment for X. Although X did not incur a detriment and so did not furnish *consideration* for the draft, he gave *value* by taking the draft as security for an antecedent debt. Assuming that X met the other requirements, X is a holder in due course and not subject to A's defense.

A person acquiring a lien against a negotiable instrument by virtue of *legal process* and not by voluntary action of the owner of the instrument is not considered to have given value. [3–303 (a)]

Suppose a creditor receives a check of a third party from his debtor with the understanding that he will attempt to collect the proceeds and will apply the funds, if any, upon the transferor's debt. In Wilson Supply Co. v. West Artesia, 505

S.W.2d 312 (Tex.Civ.App.1974) it was held that the creditor did not pay value because the check was not received *in payment*. The dissent argued that the check was taken both in payment of and as security for an antecedent claim under Section 3–303(b).

§ 6. Good Faith

Since at least as early as Miller v. Race, 1 Burr. 452, 97 Eng.Rep. 398 (1758), the courts, and more recently, the legislatures, have been trying to develop a definition of good faith that is satisfactory to all concerned. That they have not been wholly successful is attributable mainly to disagreement over the extent to which the test of *good faith* should be subjective, depending only on what is found to be the state of the holder's mind, or *objective*, depending on other facts. As seen above, the requirement that a holder give *value* is totally objective, having nothing to do with the holder's state of mind when he takes the instrument. As will be seen, the requirement of taking *without notice* sometimes depends on the holder's state of mind and sometimes on extrinsic circumstances; thus it is both subjective and objective.

The 1952 Edition of the Code required "good faith," "including observance of reasonable commercial standards of any business in which the holder may be engaged." This latter requirement was deleted from later editions because it seemed to imply an objective rather than a subjective test of good faith. The test of good faith as it is now stated in the Code is entirely subjective. The Code provides that good faith means "honesty in fact in the conduct or transaction concerned." [1–201(19)] Taken literally, this does not require either diligence or prudence. (See Riley v. First State Bank, 469 S.W.2d 812 (Tex.Civ.App. 1971)) A gullible person might be found to have acted in good faith in circumstances where a shrewd person would not.

Under the prevailing subjective test, a holder is not necessarily barred from being a holder in due course merely because he receives the instrument from a total stranger or for substantially less than its face value, or because in some way he has failed to observe reasonable standards of the business community. Nor is the requisite good faith negated by the fact that *after* he takes the instrument in circumstances establishing good faith and the other requisites of being a holder in due course, he learns facts that make him suspicious. Manufacturers & Traders Trust Co. v. Murphy, 369 F.Supp. 11 (W.D.Pa.1974).

It is said that the subjective test promotes the policy of encouraging the free transferability of commercial paper. In some cases, however, it has appeared to run counter to the general policy of protecting consumers from unfair or deceptive practices; and some courts and legislatures have reacted against it.   (See pages 262–271)

§ 7. Without Notice

Even though a holder acquires an instrument for value and in actual good faith, he does not qualify as a holder in due course unless he also takes the instrument "without notice" of any of three things: (1) that it is overdue, (2) that it has been dishonored, or (3) that there is a defense against it or a claim to it by any person. [3–302(1)(c)]

Any one of these three things should serve as a danger signal to a person who is contemplating taking an instrument for value.   It should warn him that he may be buying a lawsuit and that he should not expect to occupy the favored position of holder in due course.

Of course, a person should be barred from being a holder in due course by *actual* notice of any of these things.   If he sees the danger signal but chooses to disregard it, he must take the consequences.

But actual notice is not always necessary to bar a person from being a holder in due course. This is clearly established by Section 1–201(25) which provides that a person has "notice" of a fact when "(a) he has *actual knowledge* of it;

or (b) he has *received* a notice or notification of it; or (c) from all the facts or circumstances known to him at the time in question he *has reason to know* that it exists." (Emphasis added) It is also established by Section 1–201(26) which provides that "a person *'receives'* a notice or notification when (a) it comes to his attention; or (b) it is duly delivered * * * at any * * * place held out by him as the place for receipt of such communications." (Emphasis added)

To bar a purchaser from becoming a holder in due course, however, notice must be received at such time and in such manner as to give a reasonable opportunity to act on it. [3–304(6)] If notice is given to an organization, it is effective when it is brought to the attention of the person conducting the transaction or when it would have been brought to his attention with the exercise of due diligence, whichever is sooner. [1–201 (27)] For example, a notice received by a bank president a minute before a teller cashes a check is not likely to be effective to bar it from being a holder in due course. [Comment 12, 3–304] But if the president acts swiftly and succeeds in bringing the notice to the teller's attention before he cashes the check, the bank is charged with notice and cannot be a holder in due course of the check.

Although a public filing or recording is often binding notice of a prior claim to a property interest so as to bar a later purchaser or lienor of goods or real property, such recording is not effective to charge a purchaser of a negotiable instrument with notice so as to bar him from becoming a holder in due course.

Suppose that notice is received but is forgotten before the instrument is purchased. Can the purchaser be a holder in due course? Prior to the Code, courts were divided. (See Graham v. White-Phillips Co., 296 U.S. 27, 56 S.Ct. 21, 80 L.Ed. 20 (1935)) The Code avoids taking sides by providing that "the time and circumstances under which a notice or notification may cease to be effective are not determined by this Act." [1–201(25)]

Because the requirement of good faith is so often confused with the requirement of taking without notice, perhaps it should be emphasized that these are two separate requirements. No degree of good faith makes it possible for one who fails to meet the notice requirement to qualify as a holder in due course and good faith is not established by showing that a person received an instrument without notice. Of course, these two requirements are closely related so that the conclusion that a holder has failed to satisfy one of these requirements is often bolstered by evidence that he failed to meet the other.

A.   NOTICE INSTRUMENT IS OVERDUE

The fact that an instrument is overdue is not, of itself, sufficient to bar a person from being a holder in due course. He must be *charged with notice* of the fact.   [3–302(1)(c)]

Since a person is charged with notice of what he *has reason to know,* [1–201(25)(c)] he is charged with notice of what the instrument itself provides and the date on which he acquires the instrument. If an instrument provides that it is payable on July 1, 1975, the purchaser has reason to know that it is overdue if he takes it on July 2, 1975. This is so even though he can prove that he did not bother to inquire or to examine the instrument to find out when it was due and, in fact, believed that it was not overdue.

Demand instruments present a difficult problem. A person is charged with having notice that a demand instrument is overdue if he has reason to know that he is taking it after demand has been made or more than a reasonable time after its issue.   [3–304(3)(c)]   In the case of *checks* drawn and payable within the states and territories of the United States and the District of Columbia, a reasonable time is presumed to be thirty days.   [3–304(3)(c)]   This presumption is rebuttable and can be overcome by evidence that a longer or shorter period is reasonable.

The Code offers no guidance for determining a reasonable time in the case of demand notes and ordinary demand drafts beyond the general rule that "What is a reasonable time for taking any action depends on the nature, purpose, and circumstances of such action." [1–204(2)] The cases are difficult to reconcile if one considers *only* the time periods. Britton, Bills & Notes § 120 (2d ed. 1961). For example, in one case it was held that twenty days was an unreasonable length of time after the issue of a demand note, but in another case it was held that four years was a reasonable time for a similar instrument. In the latter case the court was impressed by the fact that the note was purchased as an investment by one brother from another. Gershman v. Adelman, 103 N.J.Law 284, 135 A. 688 (1927). In an earlier case, it was held that a demand note was not overdue 18 months after its date, primarily because the note was kept alive by continuous payments of monthly interest. McLean v. Bryer, 24 R.I. 599, 54 A. 373 (1903).

The instrument's nature and purpose is significant in determining a "reasonable time after its issue," as shown by the tendency to hold that a reasonable length of time after issue is shorter for a check which bears no interest and does not normally circulate than for a demand draft or note that bears interest and frequently circulates or a certified check that occasionally circulates.

Similarly, a reasonable period of time for an interest-bearing certificate of deposit, which commonly is held as an investment, is usually longer than for other kinds of instruments.

When an instrument contains an acceleration clause and the event stipulated occurs, the instrument immediately becomes overdue. This does not, however, prevent the then holder from negotiating the instrument to another. The Code provides that one who purchases such an instrument before the time provided for payment has notice that the instrument is overdue if he has reason to know that the event accelerating the instrument has occurred, but otherwise not. [3–304(3)(b)]

Instruments payable in instalments, particularly instalment notes, are quite common. This manner of payment does not interfere with negotiability. When such an instrument contains an acceleration clause, knowledge of a default in the payment of one instalment clearly constitutes notice that the instrument is overdue. Even when such an instrument does not contain an acceleration clause, a person who knows of a default in the payment of any instalment is charged with notice that the instrument is overdue. In fact, he is charged with such notice whenever he has reason to know that any part of the *principal* is overdue. [3–304(3)(a)]

Similarly, when instruments issued in a series are payable at different times, a purchaser who has reason to know that one of the instruments is overdue is charged with notice that all are overdue even though they contain no acceleration clause and the instrument he purchases has not yet matured according to its terms. [3–304(3)(a)] In contrast, the Code provides that a person can become a holder in due course even though he knows that there has been a default in the payment of *interest* on an instrument. [3–304(4) (f)] This difference in treatment is explained by the fact that interest payments frequently are delayed. [Comment 6, 3–304]

B. NOTICE INSTRUMENT HAS BEEN DISHONORED

In most cases, a dishonor occurs when a demand for payment or acceptance is properly made upon the party expected to pay, and payment or acceptance is refused or cannot be obtained within the time allowed. [3–507(1)(a)] (See pages 186–188) In the case of bank collections, an instrument is dishonored if it is seasonably returned by the midnight deadline. [3–507(1)(a), 4–301] A dishonor also occurs if presentment is excused and the instrument is not duly accepted or paid. [3–507(1)(b)]

Very often, particularly when presented for payment through ordinary banking channels, a dishonored instrument bears a stamp or other notation such as "not sufficient funds," "no account," or "payment stopped." Regardless of actual knowledge, anyone purchasing such an instrument is charged with knowing that the instrument has been dishonored.

Sometimes a dishonored instrument bears no evidence of dishonor, and the person selling such an instrument does not always reveal the dishonor. In these cases, whether or not a person is charged with notice of the dishonor so as to be barred from being a holder in due course depends upon whether or not the trier of fact concludes from other evidence that he had actual knowledge, had received notice, or had reason to know of the dishonor. [1–201(25)] (See pages 243–244)

C. NOTICE OF DEFENSE AGAINST INSTRUMENT OR CLAIM TO IT

A purchaser cannot be a holder in due course if he takes an instrument with notice that any person has a defense against it or a claim to it.

In general, a *defense* is asserted negatively as a shield to protect one against being subjected to liability whereas a *claim* is asserted affirmatively as a sword to impose liability on someone else. In the context of the present discussion, a defense might be based on virtually any matter that would furnish a basis for a defense to an action on a simple contract as well as any of the bases that are unique to commercial paper; whereas a claim to the instrument might be asserted by anyone who contends that he has an adverse property interest in it.   Thus a claim might be asserted by one who contends that he is the legal or equitable owner or that he has a lien against it.   Perhaps the most obvious kind of claim is that which is asserted against a thief or other converter.   But the most common kind of claim is that which is asserted by one who is induced to issue or transfer an instrument in a transaction that is voidable in whole or in part because it was induced by fraud, duress, mistake or similar means, or because of incapacity or illegality or for any other reason. Sometimes a claim arises from circumstances that render attempts to transfer void as when they are made by adjudicated incompetents or when they are induced by fraud in the factum that occurs despite the exercise of due care.

Usually, the special facts that give rise to a defense give rise to a corresponding claim and vice versa.   Thus, in a common case, a person who is induced to issue or transfer an instrument by fraud might act negatively and assert the defense of fraud as a shield if he is sued on the instrument or he might act affirmatively and assert a claim as a sword to recover the instrument or to impose liability for conversion.   In some cases a defense arises without a corresponding claim as where a party issues or transfers an instrument without receiving consideration.   Sometimes a claim arises without any corresponding defense; for example, a purchaser of an instrument who pays but is denied delivery has a claim against the seller but he has no need for a defense because he has no liability on the instrument.

In most cases it is obvious whether a party is or is not charged with notice of a claim or defense, but there are a few matters that merit special attention.

1. DISCHARGE

A person has notice of a claim or defense if he has notice that *all* parties have been discharged, but is not barred from being a holder in due course merely because he knows that less than all of the parties have been discharged. [3–304(1)(b), 3–602]

> M is induced by fraud to deliver a note to P. P negotiates the note to X. X negotiates the note to Y. Y negotiates the note to H but before doing so strikes out the signatures of X and P thereby discharging them from liability. Here H is charged with notice that P and X are discharged from liability. Since the liability of M and Y has not been discharged, however, H may still be a holder in due course so as to cut off M's defense of fraud.

2. COUNTERCLAIMS AND SET-OFFS

Athough a counterclaim or set-off is in one sense defensive, it does not constitute a defense so as to bar one who has notice of it from being a holder in due course.

> M is induced by fraud to deliver a note for $1000 to P who owes M $400. P negotiates the note to H who knows that P owes M $400 but is unaware of the fraud. H can be a holder in due course and thus free of both the defense of fraud and the counterclaim for $400.

3. NOTICE PROMISE OF PRIOR PARTY IS UNPERFORMED

It is common for a negotiable instrument to be issued or negotiated in return for consideration in the form of a promise. If the promise is broken, this usually gives rise to a claim or defense between the two immediate parties; therefore notice of the breach normally bars a person from being a holder in due course. But a purchaser is not charged with notice of a defense or claim merely because he knows that the instrument was issued or negotiated in return for an executory promise or was accompanied by a separate agreement if he has no notice of a breach. [3–304(4)(b)]

4. INSTRUMENT AS NOTICE OF DEFENSE OR CLAIM

Usually a person will not purchase an instrument until he has examined it. It seems reasonable, therefore, to charge him with having notice of any defenses or claims which are apparent from an examination of the instrument itself. [3–304 (1)(a)] Some cases are clear. For example, a bungling forgery or an obvious alteration which raises the amount payable, should make a purchaser suspicious and serve as notice. Just how cautious or suspicious a purchaser must be remains a question.

Prior to the Code even though a purchaser received a *complete* instrument he was barred from being a holder in due course if he knew that originally it was blank concerning some material matter. The Code provides that a purchaser is not charged with notice of a defense or claim merely because he knows that an incomplete instrument has been completed unless he also has notice of an improper completion. [3–304(4)(d)] Under this provision it is possible for a purchaser to be a holder in due course even though a blank is filled out in his presence if he has no reason to know that the completion is improper. [Comment 10, 3–304] For example, in Sun Oil Co. v. Redd Auto Sales, Inc., 339 Mass. 384, 159 N.E.2d 111 (1959), it was held that the plaintiff seller was not prevented from being a holder in due course of a check because its agent received the check from its customer, a gas station operator, knowing that the check had been signed in blank by the defendant, an accommodation party, and that the operator had filled in the plaintiff's name as payee and the amount in the agent's presence according to a common practice among the parties.

The most obvious type of irregularity is an alteration of the amount payable, but an irregularity also might be a change of date, of the payee's name, or of some other material term. The fact that an instrument is antedated or postdated is not, however, such irregularity as to charge a purchaser with notice of a defense or claim [3–304(4)(a)]; neither is the fact that early in 1975 an instrument contains an obvious change in the date from January 2, 1974, to January 2, 1975. [Comment 2, 3–304] A person who purchases a negotiable instrument is charged with observing what appears on the reverse side of the instrument as well as the face. Consequently, he is expected to heed any irregularities with respect to indorsements. Hence, a person who receives an instrument which has been indorsed on the reverse side, "In payment for poker losses (Signed) J. Smith" would be charged with knowing of a defense in most states even though he did not read the indorsement or know that gambling transactions are illegal.

But the fact that an indorsement is qualified, or for accommodation or restrictive, or contains words of guarantee or assignment, is not sufficient of itself to charge a person with notice of a defense or claim.

5.   FIDUCIARIES

Although a person is not charged with notice of a defense or claim merely because he has notice that a person negotiating an instrument is or was a fiduciary [3–304(4)(e)], he is charged with such notice if he knows that a fiduciary had negotiated the instrument in payment of or as security for his own debt or otherwise in breach of duty. [3–304(2)] As mentioned earlier, if an instrument is restrictively indorsed for the benefit of the indorser or another, the person who takes the instrument from the restrictive indorsee can be a holder for value, and a holder in due course, only to the extent he applies any value given by him consistently with the restrictive indorsement. (See pages 125–128) But a later holder is not affected by the restrictive indorsement unless, as indicated above, he knows the fiduciary has broken his duty. [3–206(4)]

§ 8. Notice of One Defense or Claim Subjects Holder to All

The principle that a purchaser cannot be a holder in due course if he takes an instrument with notice of any defense against it or claim to it by any person [3–302(1)(c)] applies even though the defense or claim of which he has notice does not affect the defense or claim ultimately asserted against him.

M is induced by *fraud* to deliver a note to P. P negotiates the note to X. X is induced by *duress* to negotiate the note to Y. Before maturity Y negotiates the note to H for value. H is aware of the duress but unaware of the fraud. Since duress is a defense, H is not a holder in due course. If H sues M, P's fraud is a good defense even though H was unaware of the fraud when he purchased the note. Similarly, if H had been aware of the fraud but was not aware of the duress, he would not have been a holder in due course and consequently would have been required to return the note to X if X had asserted a claim to it on the basis of the duress.

§ 9. Payee as Holder in Due Course

Under the Code, a payee, like any other holder, can be a holder in due course so long as he meets the usual requirements. This is so regardless of whether he takes the instrument by issue (first delivery) from the maker or drawer or from a third party (remitter). [Comment 2, 3–302] In fact, in most cases where he acts in good faith and gives *executed* consideration (value) the payee is a holder in due course because normally he cannot be charged with notice that the instrument is overdue or has been dishonored or is subject to any claim or defense. If the issuing party happens to have a defense of which the payee is not aware— for example, material mutual mistake—the existence of the defense does not prevent the payee from being a holder in due course. But recognizing the payee as a holder in due course would do

him no good because even a holder in due course
is subject to any defense of the party with whom
he deals.   (See pages 272–273)   About the only
case in which it makes any difference whether a
payee is a holder in due course is that in which
he does not deal directly with the maker or drawer but instead obtains the instrument from a remitter who obtained it from the maker or drawer.
In this case, if the payee qualifies as a holder in
due course, he takes the instrument free of any
defense based on the remitter's wrongdoing; otherwise not.

> X orders goods from P on credit, but P refuses
> to sell to X on this basis.   Therefore, X induces
> his bank to sell to him, on credit, a draft drawn
> by the bank on itself naming P as payee.   X
> then forwards the draft to P.   If P ships the
> goods, acts in good faith, and meets the require-
> ment with respect to notice, he is a holder in due
> course.   Consequently, if P demands payment from
> the bank and the latter refuses payment on the
> ground that X induced it to issue the draft by
> fraud, this defense will not be effective against
> P.   The result and analysis would be the same if
> it is assumed that the bank sent the draft direct-
> ly to P.   [Comment 2, 3–302]

§ 10. Taking Through Holder in Due Course— The Shelter Provision

Although it is important to keep in mind the
requirements for being a holder in due course it
is almost as important to remember that under

the *Shelter Provision* of Section 3–201(1), the "transfer of an instrument vests in the transferee such rights as the transferor had therein." By virtue of this broad principle (which applies to most other forms of property as well), even though a person does not satisfy the requirements for being a holder in due course, he is entitled to enjoy all of the benefits of that status if he can prove that someone prior to himself in the chain of ownership was a holder in due course. The primary significance of the Shelter Provision and the basis for its name is the fact that it enables one who is not a holder in due course to share the shelter from claims and defenses enjoyed by a holder in due course through or from whom he acquired the instrument.

> M is induced by P's fraud to execute and deliver a note. P negotiates the note to H under circumstances making H a holder in due course. After maturity, H negotiates the note to T who knows it is overdue. T is entitled to recover the amount of the note from M. Even though T is not a holder in due course because he knew the note was overdue when he received it, he is free of M's defense because he has all of the rights of H who was a holder in due course.

Giving the transferee who is not a holder in due course the rights of his transferor who is has the effect of increasing the market for instruments held by holders in due course. But this rule does not apply to improve the position of a transferee who has been a party to any fraud or illegality affecting the instrument or who as a prior holder had notice of a claim or defense. For example, a payee who has induced the maker to issue a note by fraud cannot wash the paper clean by running it through a holder in due course and then purchasing it. And, of course, one to whom a holder in due course transfers an instrument as security, acquires no greater interest in the instrument than the amount due on the obligation secured.

> HDC holds a note made by M for $15,000. HDC borrows $10,000 from L and negotiates the note for $15,000 to L as security for the loan. The interest of L in the note made by M never exceeds the amount due on the $10,000 loan.

§ 11.   Transactions that Cannot Give Rise to Holder in Due Course

Even though he satisfies the usual requirements previously described, a person cannot become a holder in due course of an instrument: "(a) by purchase of it at judicial sale or by taking it under legal process; or (b) by acquiring it in taking over an estate; or (c) by purchasing it as part of a bulk transaction not in the regular course of business of the transferor." [3–302 (3)] In these situations it is normally understood that the transferee merely is acquiring the rights of the prior holder and there is no substantial interest in facilitating commercial transactions, which is the underlying reason for giving holders in due course their special advantages. Of course, in accordance with the Shelter Provision discussed in the preceding paragraph, if the prior holder has the rights of a holder in due course, the transferee under one of the above transactions acquires the same rights. [3–201 (1)]

§ 12. Assignee with Principal Advantage of Holder in Due Course

In order to make it possible for the assignee of rights that arise from a contract that is not negotiable to acquire the principal advantage that normally is reserved for a holder in due course, Section 9–206(1) provides:

> *Subject to any statute or decision which establishes a different rule for buyers or lessees of consumer goods,* an agreement by a buyer or lessee that he will not assert against an assignee any claim or defense which he may have against the seller or lessor is enforceable by an assignee who takes his assignment for value, in good faith and without notice of a claim or defense, except as to defenses of a type which may be asserted against a holder in due course of a negotiable instrument. (Emphasis added.)

The italicized portion of Section 9–206(1) above preserves for buyers and lessees of consumer goods the benefits of decisions rendered and statutes enacted in many states to protect such persons against the risk of losing defenses they had against persons with whom they dealt in the underlying business transaction, either by expressly waiving in the original contract the right to assert such defenses against assignees, as provided by Section 9–206(1), or by executing negotiable instruments which might later be acquired by holders in due course.   (See pages 264–271)

§ 13. Special Treatment of Consumers

As explained above, there are two basic methods by which a transferee can acquire contract rights free from defenses that were good against his transferor or some prior party.   First, he might acquire a negotiable instrument as a holder in due course.   Second, he might take an assignment of a non-negotiable contract in which the obligor has agreed not to assert defenses or claims against an assignee.   The existence of these means has greatly facilitated a vast amount of credit which in turn has contributed greatly to the economy.   Businessmen, lured by freedom from possible defenses, have received such paper in payment for goods or services, by purchasing it, and by taking it as security for loans.

In normal commercial settings, these devices for cutting off defenses have been at least benign and at best beneficial.   When applied, however, by two professionals with a non-professional in the middle, these devices often result in grave injustice, especially when the non-professional is uninformed, unsophisticated, and economically disadvantaged, as he too frequently is.

The unfairness has been most striking in cases in which a consumer—who may be defined generally as one who purchases or leases goods or services primarily for personal, family or home use—executes a negotiable instrument, most frequently an instalment note, or a contract waiving defenses against an assignee, but does not receive what he bargained for. When he refuses to make further payments, he is sued by the person to whom the seller's rights have been transferred, usually a financial institution, and then learns that the non-performance of the seller with whom he contracted is not a good defense against its transferee. As applied in these and similar cases, the devices for cutting off defenses have been among the natural targets of the consumer movement and have been under attack by some courts, some legislatures, the Federal Trade Commission, scholars, and others who have joined in a loose alliance to limit the effect of such devices. The diverse forms these attacks have taken will be mentioned briefly.

A.   THE COURTS

In most cases in which courts have refused to give effect to the devices intended to limit the defenses of a consumer sued by financial institutions, the decisions have been based on the terms of Section 3–302, which defines a holder in due course, or the terms of Section 9–206 which declares the legal boundaries of consumer agreements to refrain from asserting defenses against assignees.

One might reasonably suppose that since the financial institution is in a close relationship with the dealer, it is most likely to be denied protection from defenses on the ground that it had notice of a defense, which constitutes a bar to such protection under both Section 3–302 and Section 9–206. This is especially so since Section 1–201 (25) charges a person with notice of a defense if, "from all of the facts and circumstances known to him * * * he has reason to know that it exists." But very few cases that have ruled against financial institutions have done so on this basis. Instead, in the bulk of such decisions, the courts have expressly or impliedly relied on one or both of two related bases: (1) lack of good faith, and (2) the unity of the dealer and the financial institution—and they usually have supported these bases by one or more arguments.

1. LACK OF GOOD FAITH

In reviving seemingly lost defenses that consumers have asserted against financial institutions to whom consumer notes and contracts have been transferred, many courts have relied on the fact that neither Section 3–302 nor Section 9–206 offers the advantage of cutting off defenses to one who does not take the instrument in good faith in the sense of honesty in fact. [1–201 (19)] Among the reasons that courts have expressly or impliedly given for holding that a financial institution has not met the good faith requirement are the following: it acted in collusion with the dealer to defraud the consumer; it had reason to be suspicious because it was familiar with the dealer's practices or the practices in the dealer's industry, or because the price at which the dealer was willing to sell was extremely low; its failure to inquire seemed to be motivated by a fear of learning the truth; its speed in purchasing the paper suggested a primary purpose to cut off the consumer's defenses, rather than a normal business purpose; its legal separation from the dealer was only a guise intended to cut off the consumer's defenses; or it failed to observe the reasonable commercial standards of its business—a test expressly included in the Section 3–302(1)(a) requirement of good faith in the 1952 Official Text of the Code but omitted from all later Official Texts.

2.   UNITY OF DEALER AND FINANCIAL INSTITUTION

Many courts that have refused to enforce devices intended to cut off consumer defenses have relied on the fact that Section 3–305(2), which declares what defenses are good against a holder in due course, makes it clear that even a holder in due course does not take an instrument free from defenses of the person with whom he deals; and they also have relied on the implication of Section 9–206 that the assignor and the assignee must be acting separately. Freedom from defenses does not extend under either of these sections to cases in which the court finds that the dealer and the financial institution were acting together as a single entity. Among the reasons expressly or impliedly given by courts for finding a financial institution to be in unity with a dealer so as to subject it to consumer defenses that otherwise would be barred are the following: it participated in the underlying transaction by furnishing forms, investigating credit, approving the consumer, counseling the dealer and in similar ways; it dealt directly with the consumer; it was only an agent for the dealer; it had a substantial voice in controlling the underlying transaction; it was but a part of the same corporate family, holding a controlling interest in the dealer's stock or vice versa; it was named in the original printed forms; it, along with the dealer, was named as a "seller" in the contract signed by the consumer; and its speed in acquiring the consumer paper indicated that there was in fact but one transaction, with the consumer on one side and the dealer and financial institution on the other.

3.   SUPPORTING ARGUMENTS

In most cases in which a court has denied a financial institution freedom from defenses on the ground of lack of good faith or unity of action with the dealer, despite the presence of a defense-defeating device, the court has bolstered its decision with one or more of the following arguments: a financial institution that participates closely in the original transaction is not within the class of persons intended to benefit from the holder in due course concept; a financial institution that furnishes forms and procedures designed to put the consumer in a straitjacket should not be permitted to benefit from such conduct; the free flow of credit basis for the holder in due course concept has no application to consumer financing which normally involves only the consumer, a dealer and a finance company; the holder in due course concept was designed to facilitate the free flow of commercial paper among legitimate businesses and was not intended to permit a transferee to insulate himself from fraudulent practices by feigning ignorance; stricter standards for those who wish to take commercial paper free from defenses encourages them to police dealers more carefully and to ferret out the dealers who are dishonest or financially unstable; in the light of the totality of the transaction, it would be unconscionable to deny the consumer his defenses; the Code itself by Section 2–302 encourages the courts to refuse to carry out unconscionable provisions in sales transactions; and the Code encourages a general policy of protecting consumers by providing in Section 9–206(1) that waiver of defense clauses are "subject to any statute or decision which establishes a different rule for buyers or lessees of consumer goods."

B. THE LEGISLATURES

The difficulty courts have had in trying to strike a proper balance between the policy of promoting the free transfer of commercial paper and the policy of protecting the consumer who buys on credit has led legislatures in many states to deal with the matter by statutes which limit the operation of devices intended to bar consumers from asserting defenses. Some statutes have focused their attacks almost entirely on devices intended to cut off defenses of consumers while others, such as the Uniform Commercial

Credit Code, have dealt with these and numerous other aspects of consumer credit as well.

Most such statutes that have been adopted or proposed have defined a consumer transaction as one wherein goods or services intended primarily for personal, family, or household use, are sold or leased; or in some similar way. They have then limited defense-defeating devices in one or more of the following ways: by forbidding the use of negotiable notes in consumer credit transactions; by flatly providing that notes given in consumer credit transactions are not negotiable; by denying holder in due course status to one who knowingly purchases consumer paper; by requiring that consumer notes be so designated and then providing that such a note cannot be negotiable; by voiding agreements by consumers to waive defenses against transferees; and by providing that the transferee of a consumer note or contract is subject to any defense of which he receives notice within a stated period (typically one month) after the consumer receives notice of the transfer, notwithstanding any agreement by the consumer to the contrary. In addition, some statutes contain special provisions re-affirming the courts' power to refuse to enforce unconscionable provisions against consumers.

C.   FEDERAL TRADE COMMISSION

To combat the injustice that often results from cutting off claims and defenses of consumers, the FTC in several cases has held on an ad hoc basis that it is an unfair or deceptive act or practice in violation of Section 5(a) of the Federal Trade Commission Act for a merchant to take a negotiable instrument from a consumer without first warning the consumer that it might be negotiated to a holder in due course so as to cut off defenses or claims that might arise from the transaction. See, e. g. Certified Building Products, Docket 8875 (1973). Feeling that this ad hoc disclosure approach is not wholly adequate, the FTC for several years has been investigating the desirability of adopting a trade regulation rule to deal with the problem. Under "Revised Proposed Rule Protecting Consumers' Rights in Credit Transactions," promulgated January 5, 1973, and expected to be adopted soon, the FTC would require, among other things, that a seller of consumer goods furnish a buyer with a written statement explaining his rights and see that any consumer note, or check post-dated more than ten days, or instalment contract, received by him, contains an adequate notice that any transferee is subject to any claim or defense the consumer has against the seller. The Rule would also bar any agreement that purported to deprive the con-

[270]

sumer of his freedom to assert any of his rights, remedies, claims or defenses, and in other ways protect consumers against the loss of their claims and defenses.

As the above sketch shows, there is a definite trend toward preserving consumers' defenses despite the holder in due course doctrine and the provisions of Section 9–206 which was intended to make it possible for an assignee to enjoy the same freedom from defenses usually reserved for a holder in due course. But not all courts and legislatures have followed the trend; and those that have done so have approached the problem in many different ways. Consequently, it is likely to be years before significant and reliable generalizations can be made on the subject. Meanwhile, anyone concerned with a case in which it might be contended that a consumer is barred from asserting a defense against a seller's transferee might be well advised to assume, until he has researched the latest cases and statutes, that there is at least a possibility that his case will not be governed by the usual principles of the law of commercial paper and contracts relating to the cutting off of defenses.

CHAPTER 11

DEFENSES AND CLAIMS

Although the principal advantage of being a holder in due course is freedom from defenses and claims, it is important to recognize that this immunity has its limits. The present chapter considers the various defenses and claims and the extent to which they may be asserted effectively against those who have the rights of a holder in due course and those who do not. (For the distinction between a defense and a claim see pages 250–252)

§ 1. Defenses Effective Against Holder in Due Course

For purposes of analysis, it is convenient to group defenses which can be asserted against a holder in due course into two general categories. First, there are defenses which arise from the transaction by which he acquires the instrument or at some later time. Second, there are defenses which arise before he acquires the instrument.

A. DEFENSES ARISING AT TIME OF TRANSFER OR LATER

The need for good faith and other requirements for becoming a holder in due course minimize the

likelihood of a defense arising at the time of negotiation to a holder in due course. Occasionally,
however, a defense arises at that time. For example, as part of the transaction of transfer, the
holder in due course may agree to cancel his transferor's obligation by striking out his signature;
or unknown to the holder in due course, a transaction may be voidable on the ground of illegality;
or the parties may be acting on the basis of a
mutual material mistake. Also, defenses may
arise after he acquires an instrument. For example, an obligor might pay the holder in due
course; the latter might renounce his rights in a
separate writing without giving up the instrument; the transferor or a prior party might obtain a discharge in bankruptcy; or a secondary
party might be discharged by the holder's failure
to make a proper presentment or to give due notice of dishonor. *Regardless of the nature of the
defense arising when he receives the instrument
or later, a holder in due course is subject to the
defense just as if he were not a holder in due
course.*

B. DEFENSES ARISING BEFORE NEGO-
TIATION TO HOLDER IN DUE
COURSE

Many defenses, including those already mentioned, may arise *before* the time the instrument
is negotiated to a holder in due course. The prin-

cipal advantage of being a holder in due course is that most of these defenses are cut off when he acquires it. The defenses which arise prior to the time the instrument is negotiated to a holder in due course sometimes are classified as *real* and *personal*. Real defenses are good against holders in due course, as well as against persons who are not, and personal defenses are good only against those who do not have the rights of a holder in due course. Although the Code does not use the terms real and personal as applied to defenses, many courts and lawyers continue to do so.

The defenses available to a prior party to the instrument and not cut off when the instrument is negotiated to a holder in due course are set forth in Section 3–305(2) of the Code which provides:

> To the extent that a holder is a holder in due course he takes the instrument free from * * * all defenses of any party to the instrument with whom the holder has not dealt except
> (a) infancy, to the extent that it is a defense to a simple contract; and
> (b) such other incapacity, or duress, or illegality of the transaction, as renders the obligation of the party a nullity; and
> (c) such misrepresentation as has induced the party to sign the instrument with neither knowledge nor reasonable opportunity to obtain knowledge of its character or its essential terms; and

(d) discharge in insolvency proceedings; and

(e) any other discharge of which the holder has notice when he takes the instrument.

1.   INFANCY

Infancy is a defense against a holder in due course to the same extent that it is a defense to an action on a simple contract under the state law governing the transaction.   With very few exceptions—for example, contracts of enlistment, marriage, and those specially provided by statute—the contracts of an infant are voidable entitling the infant to disaffirm or rescind his contract even though he has received and enjoyed the benefits. In most states the same applies to contracts for necessaries;   but if an infant rescinds a contract for necessaries received, he is nonetheless bound to pay their fair value on the theory of quasi contract.   Consequently, in the great majority of transactions an infant who incurs liability on a negotiable instrument may avoid this liability in whole or in part even against a holder in due course.

2.   OTHER INCAPACITY

Incapacity also may be recognized if at the time the transaction occurred the defendant was insane, intoxicated or a corporation acting outside the powers given by its charter, and in a few other special circumstances. Unlike infancy, which enables a defendant to avoid liability against a holder in due course even though his liability is merely *voidable,* parties limited by other types of incapacity are shielded from such liability only if the governing state law declares that such incapacity renders transactions *void.* Since incapacity other than adjudicated incompetency normally renders transactions *voidable* and not void, incapacity other than infancy and adjudicated incompetency usually does not constitute a valid defense against holders in due course.

3.   DURESS

Duress occurs when one person, by the exercise of wrongful pressure, induces another to become fearful and to do something he otherwise would not do. The wrongful pressure may consist of physical violence, but usually it consists of threats. A threat to start a civil action usually is not considered to be wrongful. The threat to have someone prosecuted for a crime, though not wrongful in itself, is considered to be wrongful when made to induce someone to enter a contract. Normally duress merely renders a contract voidable and so is not a good defense against one having the rights of a holder in due course. In its very extreme form, however, as where one party points a loaded gun at another or physically compels him to manifest his assent to contract, duress renders a transaction void. Such duress would be a good defense even against one having the rights of a holder in due course. Actually, duress of this kind is rare.

4. ILLEGALITY

In general, a transaction is illegal if it is contrary to public policy as provided by statute or as declared by the courts. A negotiable instrument may be issued or negotiated in a transaction which is illegal because it involves gambling, usury, bribery, concealing a crime, promoting immorality, restraining trade; because it occurs on Sunday; or for many other reasons. Generally, the defense of illegality is not good against a holder in due course even though the instrument in question was issued or negotiated in direct violation of a statute or was given for a consideration held to be against public policy. However, if the courts of a state hold, either on the basis of statutory construction or otherwise, that a particular transaction is *void,* a party who issues, accepts, or negotiates an instrument as part of the transaction can effectively defend on the ground of illegality even against a holder in due course.

5. FRAUD

The Code recognizes that a person might be induced to sign a negotiable instrument by either of two quite different kinds of fraud. The first kind, sometimes called *fraud in the inducement* or *fraud in the procurement,* occurs when the defrauded person is fully aware of the character and essential terms of the instrument he signs but is induced to want to sign by deception with respect to some other matter. For example, a person might be induced to sign and deliver his check for $1,000 in payment for a stone which the seller payee has fraudulently represented to be a diamond. The second kind of fraud, sometimes called *fraud in the factum* or *fraud in the essence,* occurs when the defrauded person is induced to sign an instrument by deception with respect to its *character or terms.* For example, he might be induced to sign a note for $10,000 relying on a false representation that it is only a receipt or that the amount is only $1,000. Fraud of the *first* kind is *not* a defense against a holder in due course. The *second* kind of fraud *might or might not* be a good defense, depending on whether the defrauded party can prove that *he had no reasonable opportunity to learn the true character or terms of the instrument.* If he can prove this, fraud regarding the character or terms of the instrument is a good defense even against a holder in due course; otherwise not. To determine whether the deceived party had a reasonable opportunity to avoid the deception, a court may consider any relevant factors, including the age, mental and physical condition, education and experience of the defrauded party and, if he was victimized because he trusted the other party, his reasons for the trust.   For example, a person deceived by clever sleight of hand by an honest-appearing defrauder or who was deceived because he trusted a theretofore trustworthy son, would have a better chance of asserting the fraud successfully against a holder in due course than one who was deceived because he trusted a stranger who acted suspiciously.

6.   DISCHARGE IN INSOLVENCY PROCEEDINGS

The main purposes of bankruptcy and other insolvency proceedings—to restore the debtor's motivation and to give society the benefit of his services—would be frustrated if debtors could not be completely discharged from their liability on negotiable instruments.   Consequently, if a debt that is evidenced by a negotiable instrument is discharged in an insolvency proceeding, the discharge is a good defense even against a holder in due course, regardless of notice.   [3–305 (2) (d)]

7.   DISCHARGE OF WHICH HOLDER IN DUE COURSE HAS NOTICE

As stated earlier (page 252, a holder is not barred from being a holder in due course by having notice when he takes an instrument that one or more parties to it have been discharged, unless he has notice that *all* of the parties to it have been discharged.   If the holder in due course takes an instrument with notice that any party to it has been discharged, however, that discharge is a good defense against him.   If he does not have such notice, the discharge usually is not a good defense.   There are a few exceptions based on statutes that supersede Article 3.   For example, as mentioned above, a discharge in an insolvency proceeding usually is a good defense against a holder in due course regardless of whether he has notice of it when he takes the instrument.

All of the classes of defenses that have been described above as not being cut off when the instrument is acquired by a holder in due course are mentioned in Section 3–305(2).   In addition to the defenses set forth in Section 3–305(2) there are several other defenses that may not be cut off when the instrument is acquired by a holder in due course.

8.   MATERIAL ALTERATION

The first of these defenses is material alteration which was discussed earlier.   (See page 140) A material alteration in the nature of unauthorized completion of an incomplete instrument is not, as seen earlier, a defense against a holder in due course.   (See page 140)   But a material alteration in the nature of a deletion, change, or addition to a completed instrument normally can be asserted against a holder in due course who is entitled to enforce the instrument only according to its original tenor. (See page 140)   If the negligence of the person who is asserting the alteration as a defense substantially contributed to the alteration, however, he is precluded from asserting the alteration against a holder in due course. [3–406]   (See pages 142–144)

9.   UNAUTHORIZED SIGNATURE INCLUDING FORGERY

Thus far, the discussion of defenses that might be effective against a holder in due course has been limited to defenses that might be asserted by a party to the instrument; that is, someone who is liable on the theory that he signed the instrument. But when a holder in due course sues a person on the theory that he signed the instrument, that person can defend by proving even against the holder in due course that his signature was unauthorized unless, of course, he is precluded from proving it by the fact that his negligence substantially contributed to the unauthorized signature. [3–406]   Observe that this problem will rarely arise if the unauthorized signature is that of an indorser in the chain of title. The reason is that if there is an unauthorized signature in the chain of title there normally can be no later holder in due course, because there can be no later *holder* unless the instrument is later

acquired by the person whose signature was unauthorized.

§ 2.   Defenses Against One who Lacks the Rights of a Holder in Due Course

One who lacks the rights of a holder in due
course is subject to any defense of the party with
whom he dealt or of any prior party.   Thus, he
is subject to all of the defenses that are good
against a holder in due course and all of the other
defenses that might be asserted in an action on a
simple contract [3–306(b)], including lack or failure of consideration, non-delivery (where parties
agreed that delivery would be required), incapacity, illegality, fraud, duress, undue influence,
material mistake, and many others.   In general,
these defenses are established by the same evidence when asserted by a person who is sued on
a negotiable instrument as when asserted by one
who is sued on a simple contract.

Even though consideration rarely presents a
serious problem, it merits brief discussion.   In
general, "want or failure of consideration is a defense as against any person not having the rights
of a holder in due course."   [3–408]   Although
consideration is used in the same sense as in the
law of simple contracts, in the law of commercial
paper there are several special situations wherein
consideration is not required to render a promise
enforceable.

Thus, Section 3–408 provides that "no consideration is necessary for an instrument or obligation thereon given in payment of or as security for an antecedent obligation of any kind." Under this provision, if a person signs an instrument intending that it be used as security for an antecedent obligation, whether his own or a third party's, he is liable in the capacity in which he signs even though the creditor does not furnish any consideration by extending the time of payment or by incurring any other detriment in return. [Comment 2, 3–408] According to Comment 2 of Section 3–408, this provision, "is intended also to mean that an instrument given for more or less than the amount of a liquidated obligation does not fail by reason of the common law rule that an obligation for a lesser liquidated amount cannot be consideration for the surrender of a greater." This reading of Section 3–408 has not been accepted by everyone. It is clear, however, that consideration is not required to render a cancellation or renunciation of liability on an instrument binding. (See pages 316–318) Also, if an accommodation party signs an instrument after value has been given for it, he becomes liable in the capacity in which he signs, to the holder at the time or to any later holder, even though the holder incurs no legal detriment in return for the signing. [Comment 3, 3–415]

In addition to these special cases wherein the Code renders promises enforceable even though not supported by consideration, the Code follows the law of simple contracts by recognizing that no consideration is necessary if the doctrine of promissory estoppel or some other equivalent of consideration obviates the need for it.   [1–103] Also, a seal on a negotiable instrument has its normal effects so long as they are consistent with the provisions of Article 3.   [Comment, 3–113] Since there is nothing in Article 3 to the contrary, instruments under seal are governed by any state law by which a seal either creates a presumption of consideration or gives rise to a longer statute of limitations.

The nondelivery of an instrument—even one that is incomplete—is not a defense against a holder in due course, nor is the fact that an instrument was delivered for a special purpose or is subject to some condition which has not been satisfied.   Any of these defenses, however, is good against one who lacks the rights of a holder in due course.   [3–306(c)]   This is so regardless of whether the defense is asserted by a maker, drawer, acceptor, or indorser.

A.   OUTSIDE AGREEMENT

A person sued on a negotiable instrument might assert a defense based on an outside writing.   A negotiable instrument might be but one of several writings that are executed as part of the same transaction. An outside writing might contain terms intended to control the rights and duties that arise from the instrument. Often these terms are not consistent with the normal effect of the instrument and limit the duties of the party signing the instrument. If the negotiable instrument is later acquired by a holder in due course, he and his transferees will not be adversely affected by any term of the outside writing unless he had notice of the term when he took the instrument. But if the instrument is never acquired by a holder in due course, any transferee holds the instrument subject to the terms of the outside writing executed as part of the same transaction that gave rise to the instrument whether he knew of the outside writing or not. For example, if a contemporaneous outside agreement provides that a negotiable instrument is to be discharged without need for payment on the occurrence of some specified event, one lacking the rights of a holder in due course would be bound by this.

It should be noted that the parol evidence rule does not bar a defendant from proving a contemporaneous outside agreement even though it is inconsistent with the terms of the negotiable instrument, because the rule does not apply at all unless the instrument in question is intended to be the complete and final embodiment of the agreement of the parties and it is assumed in this case that the parties intended otherwise. Furthermore, it is a basic rule that writings executed as part of the same agreement must be read together in determining the rights and duties of the parties. Perhaps it is also noteworthy that the outside writing does not interfere with the negotiability of the instrument because negotiability is determined by the terms of the instrument itself and not by anything said or written outside the instrument.

In addition to being subject to many other possible defenses, one who lacks the rights of a holder in due course is subject to the defense of *discharge* regardless of the basis for the discharge or his lack of knowledge when he acquires the instrument. This applies to all forms of discharge, including those which might operate as a discharge on a simple contract. For example, if a negotiable instrument is issued in return for the payee's promise to render personal services, the payee's death prior to performance would discharge the maker's or drawer's obligation just as it would discharge an obligation on a simple contract. Because of its importance and pervasive nature, the subject of discharge will be discussed separately in Chapter 12 where a number of bases for discharge peculiar to the law of negotiable instruments will be considered.

B. DEFENSE THAT THIRD PARTY HAS CLAIM—JUS TERTII

Sometimes a party sued on a negotiable instrument has no defense of his own but knows that some party prior to the plaintiff has a claim that would entitle him to recover the instrument from the plaintiff. This is sometimes referred to as *jus tertii*, meaning right of a third party. If the defendant could assert the right of the third party as a defense against the plaintiff, it might obviate the necessity for the third party to bring an action. But, even assuming plaintiff is not a holder in due course, the general rule is that the defendant is not entitled to assert the third party's claim as a defense. Exceptions are recognized, however, when (1) the defense is that the plaintiff or someone through whom he holds the instrument acquired it by theft, (2) the payment or satisfaction of plaintiff would be inconsistent with the terms of a restrictive indorsement, or (3) the third party himself defends the action for the defendant. [3–306(d)]

> M delivers his note to P. H fraudulently induces P to negotiate the note to him. M refuses to pay H on the ground that H obtained the note from P by fraud. H sues M. Judgment for H. Although P had a claim for fraud which entitled him to recover the note from H, or to defend on the ground of fraud if H sued him as an indorser, M is not entitled to assert this defense against H

[*287*]

even though H clearly is not a holder in due course. It would have been otherwise if P had defended the action for M, or if the note had been indorsed in blank by P and stolen by H, or if P had indorsed the note on condition that H first deliver some stock to him (one kind of restrictive indorsement) and the stock had not been delivered, for in this case payment would have been inconsistent with the terms of the restrictive indorsement.

§ 3. Claims Asserted Against Holder in Due Course

When an instrument is acquired by a holder in due course, any previous claim against it is cut off. [3–305(1)] This is so even though the holder in due course acquired the instrument from a finder or thief who never became the owner of the instrument and who had the power to transfer ownership only because the instrument was payable to bearer.

Furthermore, the holder in due course is protected against not only the claims that might have been asserted against his transferor or any prior party but also against any claim that the *immediate* transferor of the holder in due course might normally have asserted. For example, if an infant or an adjudicated incompetent negotiates an instrument under such circumstances that the transferee becomes a holder in due course, the latter holds the instrument completely free of any claim of the infant or incompetent. This is so even though infancy or an adjudication of incompetency are *defenses* which are good even against a holder in due course. (See, e. g., Snyder v. Town Hill Motors, Inc., 193 Pa.Super. 578, 165 A.2d 293 (1960)) Similarly, if the holder in due course acquires an instrument in a transaction based on a material mutual mistake, the transferor normally could assert the mistake as a defense if sued by the holder in due course, but could not recover the instrument on the ground of mistake.

The only *claims* that can be asserted effectively against a holder in due course are those which arise after he becomes a holder. For example, if a holder in due course contracts to sell an instrument, but fails to deliver it, the buyer has a claim which he can effectively assert against the holder in due course.

§ 4. Claims Asserted Against Person Lacking Rights of Holder in Due Course

Unless the party having a claim to an instrument loses his claim because of delay or other inequitable conduct or has sacrificed his claim in some other way, he is entitled to recover the instrument from anyone who acquires it until it reaches the hands of a holder in due course. [3–306(a), 3–305(1)]

§ 5. Procedure

In the law of commercial paper, especially the area concerned with defenses and claims, procedure bears a close relationship to substantive law and merits at least brief consideration.

A. PLAINTIFF

The proper party to sue on a negotiable instrument normally is the holder who is usually the owner. His status as holder usually is sufficiently established by proof that he is in possession of an instrument that runs to him.

The holder usually is the owner or is acting for the owner. If an instrument is lost, destroyed, or stolen, however, the owner lacks possession and is not the holder. As owner he alone usually is entitled to payment. Recognizing this, the Code permits one claiming to be the owner under such circumstances to recover from anyone who is liable on the instrument, with necessary safeguards.

Since he does not have possession of the instrument, however, he does not enjoy the usual procedural advantages accorded a holder. To recover it is necessary for him to allege and prove that he is the owner, the terms of the instrument, the facts that prevent the production of the instrument and facts establishing defendant's liability.   [3–804]

Also, to protect the defendant who is required to pay without actually receiving the instrument against the risk that he may later have to pay a holder in due course or someone else having rights superior to the plaintiff's, the court may in its discretion require the plaintiff to furnish security sufficient to indemnify the defendant against loss that results from his being required to pay a second time. [3–804] The likelihood of the court requiring security depends on a variety of factors such as the length of time elapsed if the plaintiff claims the instrument was lost or stolen and the degree of proof if he claims it was destroyed. [Comment, 3–804]

B. BURDEN OF PROOF

Normally a plaintiff has the burden of proving the facts on which his right to recover is based and the defendant has the burden of proving any defenses on which he relies to avoid the liability which normally flows from the facts proven by the plaintiff. Generally the burden of proof is the same when someone sues on a negotiable instrument. An exception is recognized with respect to consideration. Ordinarily a person suing on a simple contract must allege and prove consideration. In an action on a negotiable instrument, lack of consideration is a matter of defense. [3–408] If the defendant contends that he received no consideration, he has the burden of proving this as an affirmative defense. Nicholas v. Zimmerman, 307 N.E.2d 900 (Ind.App. 1974). Of course, lack or failure of consideration is not a good defense against a holder in due course.

C. SIGNATURES

Any one who sues on a negotiable instrument relies on one or more signatures. For example, a holder suing a maker relies on the maker's signature and any intervening indorsements necessary to establish his status as holder. A defendant is held to have admitted any signature which he does not expressly deny in his pleading. [3–307(1)] The defendant is required to deny the signature in his pleading if he wants to raise the issue so that the plaintiff is assured of a fair warning and has an opportunity before the trial itself to gather evidence that the signature is genuine. Also, not requiring proof unless the signature is specifically denied in defendant's pleading saves much time and expense; for signatures on negotiable instruments are almost always genuine. Nonetheless, signatures sometimes are denied and plaintiffs then have the burden of proving them. [3–307(1)(a)]

Even assuming that a signature is denied, however, the person relying on it has the advantage of a rebuttable presumption which requires the trier of the facts to find that the signature is genuine or authorized unless evidence is introduced to support a contrary finding. [1–201(31), 3–307(1)(b)] The presumption arises not only because forged or unauthorized signatures are uncommon but also because evidence relevant to the issue is more likely to be accessible to the person denying the signature. Because this second basis would not apply if a purported signer has died or has become incompetent, the presumption is not recognized in such cases. [3–307(1)(b)]

D. ESTABLISHING DEFENSES

When the signatures relied on by the plaintiff have been admitted or established, the mere production of the instrument normally entitles the holder to recover on it unless the defendant sustains the burden of establishing all of the essential elements of a valid defense. [3–307(2)] In Telpner v. Hogan, 17 Ill.App.3d 152, 308 N. E.2d 7 (1974), it was held that the burden of proving the defense of payment was not sustained by proving that defendant had delivered to an attorney checks in the amount of notes sued on without proving also that the attorney was duly authorized to receive payment or that the money reached the hands of the holder of the notes.

E.   ESTABLISHING STATUS AS HOLDER IN DUE COURSE

If the defendant does not establish a defense, the holder normally is entitled to recover whether or not he is a holder in due course. (See, e. g., Blake v. Coates, 292 Ala. 351, 294 So.2d 433 (1974)). Once a defense is established, however, anyone asserting the rights of a holder in due course to avoid the effect of the defense has the burden of proving that he, or someone through whom he holds, is in all respects a holder in due course. [3–307(3)]

F.   THIRD PARTIES

Often a party who loses an action on a negotiable instrument has a right of recourse against some prior party, who in turn may have recourse against a party prior to him, and so on. When a right of recourse exists, it is possible to have the matter settled in several lawsuits. Usually, however, it is more efficient to settle the various issues and determine the various liabilities in a single lawsuit. For the purpose of supplementing existing state and federal statutes relating to procedures for interpleader and joinder of parties and to help provide for more efficient disposal of multi-party litigation, Section 3–803 provides:

> Where a defendant is sued for breach of an obligation for which a third person is answer-

able over under this Article he may give the third person written notice of the litigation and the person notified may then give similar notice to any other person who is answerable over to him under this Article. If the notice states that the person notified may come in and defend and that if the person notified does not do so he will in any action against him by the person giving the notice be bound by any determination of fact common to the two litigations, then unless after reasonable receipt of the notice the person notified does come in and defend he is so bound.

(For some procedural aids relating to proof of presentment, dishonor, notice of dishonor and protest, see pages 191–195)

CHAPTER 12

DISCHARGE

Chapter 7, entitled "Liability of the Parties on the Instrument," is concerned mainly with the *imposition and nature of the duties* acquired by a person who signs and issues or transfers a negotiable instrument—liability *on* the instrument. The main concern of the present chapter is *how these duties are discharged*—that is, terminated or brought to an end. Before proceeding with discharge of liability *on* the instrument however, it is fitting to consider briefly the circumstances under which the issue or transfer of an instrument might result in the discharge of the *underlying obligation* for which the instrument is issued or transferred.

§ 1. Discharge of Underlying Obligation by Issue or Transfer

It is easy to overlook the fact that an instrument usually is issued or transferred for the purpose of discharging some *underlying obligation*, such as the duty to pay off a loan or to pay for goods, services, or rent. Normally, this underlying obligation is contractual and can be discharged like any other contractual obligation. Thus, it might be discharged by a breach of contract, rescission, release, merger, accord and satisfaction, novation, judgment, intervening impossibility of performance, change of law, and in several other ways. We are concerned here only with determining the circumstances under which the underlying obligation is discharged by the issue or transfer of a negotiable instrument.

One who issues or transfers an instrument to satisfy an underlying obligation is likely to think that the delivery of the instrument immediately and completely discharges him from further liability on the underlying obligation. There are a few situations wherein this assumption is justified, but usually it is not.

The general rule is that the effect of the issue or transfer of an instrument is merely to *suspend* the right of the creditor to sue on the underlying obligation. [3–802(1)(b)] If the instrument is payable *on demand*, the right to sue normally is suspended until it is *presented for payment*. If the instrument is payable at *a definite time*, the right to sue is suspended until the instrument is *due*.

> S sells and delivers goods to B with no express agreement as to the time of payment. Later, S takes B's 90-day note for the price as payment. A few days later, S changes his mind, tenders a return of the note to B and demands immediate payment. B refuses. S promptly sues for breach of the sales contract. Judgment for B. When

> S took B's note, the right to sue on the under-
> lying contract was automatically suspended un-
> til the note became due.

If an instrument is *paid*, the underlying obligation is *discharged*; but if it is *dishonored*, the
creditor can bring an action either on the instrument *or* on the underlying obligation. [3–
802(1)(b)]

> S takes B's check as payment for goods sold and
> delivered. The check is duly presented for pay-
> ment at the drawee bank, but is dishonored by
> non-payment. S has a choice. He may sue B
> on his secondary liability as drawer of the check
> or he may sue B on the underlying obligation and
> pursue the remedies available to a seller of goods
> under Article 2.

There are basically two exceptions to the general rule that the issue or transfer of an instrument merely suspends the right to sue on the underlying obligation. The first exception is recognized when it is found that the obligee expressly
or impliedly agreed to take the instrument as
absolute payment. [3–802(1)(a)] The second
exception is recognized when the obligee receives
an instrument on which a *bank* is drawer, maker,
or acceptor and *there is no recourse on the instrument against the underlying obligor*. [3–
802(1)(a)] When an obligee receives an instrument in either of these two special circumstances,
the liability of the obligor on the underlying obligation is immediately discharged. Perhaps it

should be emphasized that neither of these exceptions is recognized very often. It is not common for a creditor to take even a negotiable instrument with the understanding that the debtor's underlying obligation is absolutely discharged. And even when a debtor tenders an instrument on which a bank is maker, drawer or acceptor, the creditor usually will insist on the debtor's indorsement, in which case the right to sue on the underlying obligation is merely suspended as if no bank had become liable.

Case 1. A owes B $1,000. B demands payment. A states that his only asset is a bearer demand note for $3,000 made by C who is known by A and B to be in financial difficulty. B agrees expressly to take the note without A's indorsement as absolute payment of the debt of $1,000. The note is dishonored and proves to be completely worthless. B cannot recover from A on the note or on the underlying obligation. The result would have been the same even if B had not *expressly* agreed to take the note as absolute payment because such an understanding would have been clearly *implied*.

Case 2. C renders services to D. Without indorsing, D delivers to C in payment a certified check drawn by X payable to C. The check is dishonored because, totally unknown to D, the bank is insolvent. C promptly notifies D of the dishonor. C has no rights against D either on the check or on the underlying obligation. A bank is acceptor and there is no right of recourse on the instrument against D, the underlying obligor, who neither drew nor indorsed the check. The result would have been the same if the facts remained the same except that the instrument involved was a cashier's check, an official check or a bank draft. The result would be otherwise, however, regardless of which of the above instruments were used, if C had induced D to indorse, for in this case there would have been recourse on the instrument against D, the underlying obligor, on his irregular or anomalous indorsement.

Even though the underlying obligation usually is merely suspended and not discharged by the *issuance or transfer* of a negotiable instrument, it is fundamental that *the underlying obligation is totally discharged whenever the obligee's obligation on the instrument is discharged.* [3–802(1) (b)] For this reason, it usually is sufficient to focus attention on the obligee's liability on the instrument, knowing that when this is discharged so also is his liability on the underlying obligation.

T owes L $500 for rent. In payment, T, on May 5, 1974, negotiates to L by an unqualified indorsement, a note for $500 made by X and payable to the order of T on June 1, 1974. On July 1, 1974, L for the first time demands payment from X, but the note is dishonored because X is short of funds. L sues T on the *underlying obligation*. L cannot recover from T. As explained in Chapter 8, L's unjustified failure to make a timely presentment when the note became due discharged T, as indorser, from liability on the note even though T cannot show that he suffered any loss as the result of the delay. When T's secondary liability on the note was discharged so was his liability on the underlying obligation.

The obligations that might be incurred on the basis of warranties were discussed in Chapter 9. It will be recalled that even though the secondary liability of an unqualified indorser on the instrument might be discharged by a failure to make proper presentment or to give him due notice of dishonor, he might still be liable on the basis of one or more of the transferors' warranties. This is so even though the underlying obligation of an unqualified indorser was discharged by the discharge of his liability on the instrument.

B owes S $5,000. B delivers S in payment a cashier's check for $5,000 on which the payee's name has been indorsed in blank by a forger who sold it to B. B did not indorse. The bank refuses payment because of the forgery of the payee's signature. S sues B. Since B did not indorse the check, he is not liable *on* it. Neither is he liable on the underlying obligation because a bank is drawer and there is no recourse on the check against B. However, as explained in Chapter 9, a transferor of an instrument for consideration warrants that he has title to it. B is liable for breach of this warranty because the instrument is still owned by the original payee whose signature was forged.

The foregoing discussion relates to the question of the time of the discharge of the *underlying obligation* for which an instrument is issued or transferred. The remainder of the Chapter relates to the discharge from liability *on the instrument itself*.

§ 2.　Discharge of Liability on Instrument—Basic Propositions

To facilitate an understanding of the law governing the discharge from liability on the instrument, one should recognize four general propositions that pervade the subject and are often sources of confusion. The first is that the "instrument," itself, is not discharged. Rather it is the *liability* of one or more persons on the instrument that is discharged. This is commonly expressed by stating that one or more *persons* have been discharged. Second, the liability of various parties may be discharged at different times. Third, a party's liability may be discharged with respect to one or more persons while remaining with respect to one or more others. Finally, discharge of liability on an instrument is not always final; liability that has been discharged, can sometimes be revived.

§ 3.　Discharge as a Defense

In discussing defenses, it was explained that even a holder in due course is subject to the defense of discharge if (a) he knew of it when he acquired the instrument, (b) it was a discharge in an insolvency proceeding, or (c) it arose at the time that he acquired the instrument or later. It was also explained that one who lacks the rights of a holder in due course is subject to the defense of discharge regardless of its nature, his knowledge of it, or the time that it arose. (See page 286)

§ 4. Bases for Discharge of Liability on Instrument—In General

Putting to one side the limited exemptions that are given to a holder in due course, a person who is sued on a negotiable instrument may assert effectively a defense of discharge that is based on (1) any agreement or act that would discharge a simple contract for the payment of money [3–601(2)] (for examples, see page 282), or (2) any provision of Article 3. Some of these latter bases of discharge have been discussed sufficiently already. For example, it has been seen that a fraudulent and material alteration by a holder discharges the liability of all parties whose contracts on the instrument are changed by the alteration (see pages 139–141); that an acceptance which changes the terms of a draft with the consent of the holder discharges the liability of the drawer and indorsers (see pages 152–153); and that an unexcused delay or failure in making a necessary presentment or in giving a required notice of dishonor discharges the secondary liability of unqualified indorsers (see pages 165–166).   There remain to be considered in this Chapter some other bases for discharge provided by Article 3 which have been mentioned already but require further discussion and some bases which have not yet been mentioned.

§ 5.   Payment or Satisfaction

By far the most common way of obtaining a discharge from liability on an instrument is by payment or satisfaction.   As was mentioned earlier, however, it is fundamental that one can obtain a discharge from liability in this way only by rendering payment or satisfaction to the *proper person*.   Normally the proper person is the *holder*.   A holder, it will be recalled, is any person who is in possession of an instrument that runs to him.   Sometimes a proper person to pay is not, strictly speaking, the holder but someone who legally stands in his position.   For example, such person might be an agent, or other representative of the holder or his estate, or it might be a transferee from the holder who, under the Shelter Provision of Section 3–201(1) has acquired the holder's rights.

Case 1.   X has possession of a note on which the indorsement of P, the payee, is forged.   At maturity X obtains payment from M, the maker.   M is not discharged from his liability as maker because *X was not the holder.* M is liable to P for conversion. [3–419(1)(c)] (see page 157) M's remedy is to proceed against X and prior transferors, including the forger, on the presenters' warranty of title.

Case 2. H is holder of a time note. At maturity H obtains payment from M, the maker, *but does not deliver the note to M.* Subsequently, H negotiates the note to X who has notice that the note is overdue but has no notice that it has been paid. X is not entitled to obtain payment from M. When M paid H his liability was discharged because he *paid the holder* even though he did not obtain possession of the instrument. The discharge can be asserted against X even though he is a holder and had no notice of the discharge. The defense of discharge would not have been valid if M had paid H before the note was due and X had been a holder in due course without notice of the discharge.

Case 3. H is holder of a note made by M. H negotiates this note to X for value after maturity. H then persuades M to pay him the amount of the note by fraudulently promising to deliver the note to him later. Although X is not a holder in due course, he is entitled to recover from M. X acquired whatever rights H, as holder, had at the time of the transfer. [3–201(1)] The defense of discharge by payment is not valid because M *did not pay the holder and so remained liable as maker.*

A. PAYMENT TO OWNER WHO IS
NOT HOLDER

Since a holder is a person who has possession of an instrument that runs to him, an owner might not be a holder because (1) although he has possession, the instrument does not run to him or (2) although the instrument runs to him, he lacks possession, or (3) the instrument does not run to him and he lacks possession. In none of these situations would paying the *owner*, of itself, discharge the payor's liability *on* the instrument.

In situation (1) where the owner non-holder has possession, if the payor pays but does not acquire possession of the instrument and it does not show on its face that it is overdue, the payor runs the risk that it might later be acquired by a holder in due course against whom the payment is not a good defense. But payment to the owner non-holder creates no such risk to the payor if the latter takes possession of the instrument and cancels it.

In situations (2) and (3), wherein the owner lacks possession, the risk of paying a non-holder owner cannot be so easily avoided, because of the possibility that the instrument might already be in the hands of a holder in due course. To enable the owner of the instrument who is out of possession to obtain payment without subjecting him to unreasonable inconvenience and, at the same time, to enable the obligor to make the payment without subjecting him to an unreasonable risk that he might have to pay a second time, Section 3–804 provides:

> The owner of an instrument which is lost, whether by destruction, theft or otherwise, may maintain an action in his own name and recover from any party liable thereon upon due proof of his ownership, the facts which prevent his production of the instrument and its terms. The court may require security indemnifying the defendant against loss by reason of further claims on the instrument.

B. WHEN PAYMENT TO HOLDER DOES NOT EFFECT DISCHARGE

It is the general rule that payment to the holder discharges the liability of the payor and of any subsequent parties even though the payor knows that someone other than the holder asserts a superior right to the instrument. There are, however, four exceptions to the general rule. [3–603 (1)] The first exception is recognized when a non-holder, claiming to be owner, furnishes adequate *indemnity* against the risk that a holder will later sue the payor and require him to pay a second time. The second exception occurs when payment or satisfaction to the holder is *enjoined* by a court having jurisdiction over the parties. The third exception occurs when someone other than an intermediary or payor bank pays a holder in a manner inconsistent with the terms of a *restrictive indorsement.* (See pages 114–125) The final exception occurs when a party *in bad faith* pays a holder who acquired the instrument by *theft,* or, unless he has the rights of a holder in due course, holds through someone who acquired the instrument by theft. Usually, the fact that a payor knows of the theft is sufficient to establish bad faith unless he has good reason to believe that the party being paid has the rights of a holder in due course.

Case 1.   P holds M's note. By fraud, D induces P to negotiate the note to him. Before maturity, P notifies M of the fraud and orders him not to pay D. Nonetheless, at maturity M pays D. M is discharged. He paid the holder. It would have been otherwise if, instead of merely ordering M not to pay, P had obtained and served a court order forbidding M to pay D or if P had supplied indemnity deemed adequate by M.

Case 2.   P holds M's note. Planning to negotiate it, P indorses in blank. T steals the note. Unaware of the theft, M pays T. M is discharged because he paid the holder in good faith without knowledge of the theft. It would have been otherwise if, before M paid T, P had advised M of the theft and requested him not to pay.

Case 3.   P holds M's demand note payable to bearer. It is stolen by T who negotiates it to H, a holder in due course. P advises M of the theft and demands payment. Nonetheless M pays H. Although

M knew of the theft, his liability was discharged when he paid H because H was a holder in due course and was entitled to payment regardless of the theft.

Case 4. P holds a draft accepted by A. P indorses "Pay H for collection. P," and delivers the draft to H. When H demands payment, A pays the draft by satisfying an obligation owed to him by H. A remains liable. Although A paid the holder, the value he gave was not consistent with P's restrictive indorsement.

Case 5. H holds M's demand note. M pays H but does not obtain the note. Later H negotiates the note to HDC. M is liable to HDC. M's obligation was discharged when he paid the holder, but it was revived when the note later was acquired by a holder in due course.

§ 6. Tender of Payment

If the obligor on a negotiable instrument makes a proper tender of payment in full to the holder at or after maturity, but the holder improperly refuses to accept the payment, the obligation of the party making the tender is *not* discharged. His obligation continues, but the holder's refusal of a proper tender completely discharges any party who has a right of recourse against the party making the tender. [3–604(2)] Furthermore, the party making the tender is discharged to the extent of all *subsequent* liability for interest, costs, and attorney's fees as long as he keeps his tender open. [3–604(1)]

The underlying reason for discharging a person who has a right of recourse against the person whose tender is refused is that if the tender had been accepted, the party having the right of recourse would have been completely discharged from liability. It would be unjust to weaken his position because the holder chooses to refuse payment.

> P negotiates a note to H. At maturity M tenders payment but H refuses it. M's liability is discharged to the extent of future interest, costs and attorney's fees so long as he keeps his tender open. P is completely discharged. However slight the inconvenience or loss caused by requiring P to pursue M, it would have been avoided if H had taken the payment. It is fair that H rather than P suffer this inconvenience or loss.

An instrument frequently is made or accepted to be payable at a particular place—typically the place of business of the maker or acceptor or a bank. *Unless the instrument is payable on demand,* the fact that the instrument's maker or acceptor is able and ready to pay at the place of payment specified when the instrument falls due is equivalent to tender. [3–604(3)] (See pages 184–186)

§ 7. Reacquisition

When an instrument is returned to or reacquired by one who previously had been a party to the instrument, any *intervening party* is discharged from liability as against the reacquiring party and any subsequent parties who are not holders in due course without notice of the discharge. [3–208]

> By successive unqualified indorsements, P, the payee of a draft negotiates it to A who negotiates it to B who negotiates it back to P. A and B are automatically discharged from liability. The reason is that if P were to sue either A or B on that person's secondary liability, the party sued would in turn have a right to sue P. The result would be two unnecessary lawsuits. If, however, after reacquiring the draft, P negotiates it to H, a holder in due course, and the instrument is dishonored, H normally may recover from P, A or B on their secondary liability. The result would be otherwise if, before negotiating the draft to H, P strikes out the indorsements of A and B. In that case H is charged with notice of the discharge of A and B. [3–208 and Comment] Even though notice of the discharge would not prevent H from being a holder in due course, it does subject him to the defense of discharge.

If the instrument is reacquired by one who has himself no right of action or recourse on the instrument against anyone, the liability of all parties is discharged. [3–601(3)(a)] The instrument is not, however, completely sterile. It may still be reissued or renegotiated so as to create new liability; and if it is acquired by a holder in due course without notice of a prior discharge, he may enforce it without regard to the prior discharge. [3–602]

> M signs a demand note for the accommodation
> of P. The note is promptly negotiated from P
> to A to B to H by successive unqualified indorsements. H promptly obtains payment from P.
> The liability of M, P, A and B is discharged.
> P has no right against A and B later indorsers;
> and he has no right against M who signed for
> his accommodation. But if P, having paid H,
> promptly negotiates the note to HDC who does
> not have notice of the prior discharges, the liability of M, P, A and B on the instrument is revived. No discharge of any party under Article 3
> is effective against a holder in due course unless
> he has notice of it when he acquires the instrument.

§ 8. Discharge of Party with No Right of Action or Recourse

In the preceding paragraph it was stated that
if an instrument is *reacquired* by a party who has
no right of action or recourse on the instrument
against anyone, the liability of all parties is discharged. Reacquisition is, of course, one way in
which such person might obtain a discharge. The
same result normally follows, however, if he is
discharged in any other way provided by Article
3. [3–601(3)(b)]

> P, payee of a note made by M, negotiates it to
> A by unqualified indorsement. A negotiates the
> note to H by unqualified indorsement. H obtains

payment from M whose liability is discharged
pursuant to Section 3–603(1). (See page 304).
The secondary liability of P and A is automatically discharged. The liability of P and A would
not have been discharged if M's liability had
been discharged by bankruptcy pursuant to Federal statute rather then by payment or some
other act or event pursuant to Article 3.

An exception is recognized when a holder releases
a party who has no right of recourse but expressly
reserves his rights against a party who has rights
against the party being released.   [3–606(2)]
(See page 315)

§ 9. Impairment of Right of Recourse or Collateral

If A owes B $1,000 and C binds himself to pay
the $1,000 if A does not, there is a simple surety-
ship relationship in which A is the principal debt-
or, B is the creditor, and C the surety.

A well established principle of suretyship law
is that if the creditor releases the principal debt-
or the creditor is treated as if he intended also to
release the surety. This intention is not attrib-
uted to him if, when he releases the principal debt-
or, he expressly reserves his rights against the
surety; therefore the surety is not discharged.
And, so far as the surety is concerned, neither is
the principal debtor.

The same general principles are applied by the Code to the more involved relationships that exist between and among the holder and the various parties who incur liability on a negotiable instrument. In a simple case involving only a maker, an unqualified indorser and a holder, the maker is viewed as the principal debtor, the holder as the creditor, and the unqualified indorser as the surety. The case becomes more complicated where there are a number of secondary parties because each indorser has a right of recourse with respect to each prior unqualified indorser; and among them a later party is a creditor, any unqualified indorser who precedes him is a surety, and the primary party is deemed to be the principal debtor.

The Code applies a general principle of suretyship law to the holder and to the various parties who are liable on a negotiable instrument by providing that, "the holder discharges any party to the instrument to the extent that without such party's consent the holder * * * releases or agrees not to sue any person against whom the party has to the knowledge of the holder a right of recourse." [3–606(1)(a)]

> H holds a note made by M and indorsed without qualification by A, B and C in that order. If H releases C, the liability of the other parties is unchanged because none of them has a right of recourse against C. If H releases B, however, C is discharged because C has a right of recourse

against B; but A is not discharged because A has no right of recourse against B. If H releases M, then A, B and C are discharged because each of them has a right of recourse against M.

The Code provides also that if a holder wishes to do so, he can release a party against whom, to the knowledge of the holder, another has a right of recourse, and at the same time expressly reserve his rights against the person having the right of recourse. [3–606(2)(a)] If the holder does so, the reservation of rights is effective; but the party against whom the right of recourse is preserved also retains his right against the party being released. [3–606(2)(a)(c)]

P negotiates a note to A by unqualified indorsement. A negotiates the note to H by unqualified indorsement. H releases M, the maker, but expressly reserves his rights against A. A is not released and insofar as A is concerned, neither is P or M. If A pays H, A has a right of recourse against P or M. If A recovers from P, P has a right of recourse against M. The net effect of H's release of M is the same as if he had made an express covenant not to sue M.

The same principles that apply to the complete *release* of a party against whom a person has recourse apply also to a binding agreement by the creditor merely to *extend the time* for the payment of the debt.

Also in accordance with broad principles of suretyship law, the Code provides that any party to an instrument is discharged to the extent that without his consent the holder "unjustifiably impairs any collateral for the instrument given by or on behalf of the party or any person against whom he has a right of recourse." [3–606(1)(b)]

> M borrows $10,000 from P and delivers to P his interest bearing note for that amount and bonds worth $15,000 as security. By an unqualified indorsement, P negotiates the note to H for $10,-000 and also delivers the bonds to H. M asks H to return the bonds. Feeling that he can rely on P's secondary liability, H complies. M meets with market reverses and dishonors the note. H gives P prompt notice of dishonor. P is not liable to H. If H had retained the bonds, he could have foreclosed on them or proceeded against P on his secondary liability. If H had required P to pay, P would have been entitled to foreclose on the bonds. By returning the bonds to M, H impaired the collateral to which P was entitled, and therefore P is discharged.

§ 10. Cancellation

The holder of an instrument may discharge the obligation of any party on it by cancelling it in any manner apparent on the face of the instrument. Cancellation may be effected "by intentionally cancelling the instrument or the party's signature by destruction or mutilation, or by striking out the party's signature." [3–605(1)(a)] Instruments are cancelled most frequently by marking them "Paid." Although striking out the signature of a party to the instrument discharges the person's liability, it does not affect the holder's title to the instrument even though that signature was essential to his chain of title. [3–605 (2)]

To be effective a cancellation must be (1) by the holder and (2) intentional. In Liesemer v. Burg, 106 Mich. 124, 63 N.W. 999 (1895) it was held that there was no effective cancellation when the *maker* of a note, who had requested possession to compute the amount due, marked the note "paid" without making full payment.

§ 11. Renunciation

The holder of a negotiable instrument also may discharge any party by renunciation, which may occur in either of two ways: (1) by a separate writing signed and delivered by the holder or (2) by the surrender of the instrument to the party to be discharged. [3–605(1)(b)] Since a renunciation does not appear on the face of an instrument, it is possible that a holder in due course will not be bound by it because he is unaware of it when he takes the instrument. Neither cancellation nor renunciation requires consideration. [3–605(1)] Consider this case.

> H holds M's note to which M has no defense. Shortly before maturity, H telephones M and

states that he releases him from his liability on the note and that he considers the note to be void. Later that day H has a change of heart and sells the note to A. At maturity, M refuses to pay. A sues. Defense: Renunciation by H. Judgment for A. The defense of renunciation requires that the holder either deliver to the obligor a signed writing containing the renunciation or surrender the instrument. It makes no difference whether or not A was a holder in due course, since M had no defense. In fact, M would have had no defense even if *H* had retained the note and sued. Even if the renunciation had been in writing, it would not have been binding on A if A could have established that he was a holder in due course without notice of it.

Suppose that the holder of a note writes the maker, "I will surrender my notes in the amount of $8500 to (the maker). (signed) Holder." Was this an effective renunciation? In Gorham v. John F. Kennedy College, Inc., 191 Neb. 790, 217 N.W.2d 919 (1974), it was held that it was not. It was merely a promise and not an outright renunciation so it was ineffective even though in writing.

CHAPTER 13

SPECIAL CHARACTERISTICS OF CHECKS AND RELATIONSHIP BETWEEN BANK AND ITS CHECKING ACCOUNT CUSTOMER

Although a check is a special type of draft in the sense that it must be drawn on a bank and payable on demand, with a few minor exceptions it is governed by the same principles governing other drafts. There are, however, a number of important problems which arise primarily because of the unique relationship between the checking account depositor and his bank.

§ 1. Contract between Bank and Checking Account Customer

The relationship between a bank and its checking account customer is the result of a contract voluntarily entered for the mutual benefit of the parties. Such a contract usually is made in an informal manner with a minimum of express terms defining the rights of the parties. Typically, an application to open an account is made by the customer to the appropriate officer at the bank, the customer's needs and the size of the initial deposit are discussed, identification and references are submitted, signature cards are signed, the deposit is made, and a receipt is issued to the customer. Usually, by signing the signature card, the customer agrees to be bound by the rules of the bank. These rules are usually stated on the deposit receipt or on a separate card delivered to the customer. There is no other express contract setting forth the other terms of the relationship. Generally, these terms are supplied by law and custom. In fact, apart from statements relating to bank charges, even the rules which are expressly set forth normally are merely statements of the prevailing law and custom.

Although the parties have much freedom in determining the terms of their agreement, the Code expressly provides that no bank can effectively disclaim responsibility for its lack of good faith or failure to exercise ordinary care, nor can it limit the measure of damages for such lack or failure. But the parties may by agreement determine the standards by which the bank's responsibility is to be measured if such standards are not manifestly unreasonable. [4–103(1)]

§ 2. Checking Account Bank Deposit

The deposit made by the checking account customer sets up a debtor-creditor relationship between the bank and the customer. The identity of each deposit is lost; the funds become part of the general assets of the bank and the bank becomes a debtor of the customer. In case the bank becomes insolvent, the customer is only a general creditor although he normally has the advantage of his account being insured by the Federal Deposit Insurance Corporation. Sometimes special accounts in the nature of trust accounts are deposited in banks creating relationships other than debtor-creditor.

§ 3. Issuance of Check is Not an Assignment

Normally, if a creditor makes an assignment of money owed to him, the debtor becomes legally bound to pay the assignee as soon as the assignee gives him notice of the assignment. If the debtor refuses to pay the assignee, the latter can sue and obtain a judgment against the debtor. As with other drafts, however, merely issuing a check does not operate as an assignment of funds in the drawee's hands. Consequently, even though a bank has adequate funds on deposit to pay checks, it is not liable to the holder of the check unless it accepts the check by certifying it. [3–409(1)] The holder has no recourse against the bank. The bank's only obligation is to its customer if it fails to pay when funds are available. The usual remedy of a holder of a dishonored check is against the drawer and indorsers on their secondary liability. (For some theories on which a drawee might be held liable to a holder in *unusual* circumstances, see pages 148–149)

§ 4. Certification of Check

Certification is the acceptance of a check by the drawee bank. [3–411(1)] By certification, the bank, as an acceptor, becomes primarily liable. Since certification of a check involves the assumption of a new obligation by the bank, it rests in the bank's discretion. Unless otherwise agreed, the bank has no obligation to either the depositor or a third party to certify. [3–411(2)] Nevertheless the practice of certifying checks for *drawers* is rather widespread. Even when they are willing to cash checks, however, many banks are unwilling to certify them for *holders*. Some banks certify checks for holders only with the drawer's approval. Many banks charge when certifying a check for either a drawer or a holder; some charge only a holder; and some charge neither. Many banks charge for certifying only checks drawn on special accounts.

In most cases wherein the certification is obtained by the *drawer*, the reason is that it is required by the payee who is unwilling to rely on the credit of the drawer alone. Contracts commonly provide that payment must be made by certified check, particularly if the amount is large and the payee cannot afford to take the risk that the check will be dishonored.

Normally, when the *drawer* obtains the certification, the payee obtains both the primary obligation of the bank and the secondary obligation of the drawer who stands behind the certification warranting that the certification is good and agreeing to make good if the bank does not. [Comment 1, 3–411(1)] When a holder procures certification, the situation is different; the obligation of the bank remains the same but the drawer is relieved of secondary liability. [3–411 (1)] Also, any indorsers who have indorsed prior to certification are discharged when the holder obtains certification because they are deprived of rights against the drawer who has been discharged. [3–411(1)]

§ 5. Bank's Liability for Wrongful Dishonor

Under the contract between the bank and its customer, the bank has a number of duties, but its primary duty is to honor the depositor's checks when he has sufficient funds on deposit for this purpose.

A bank is liable to its customer for the wrongful dishonor of his check. [4–402] Since liability attaches only if the dishonor is wrongful, it does not attach to a refusal to pay when there are insufficient funds in the drawer's account, when a necessary indorsement is missing, or for any other good reason.

Before the Code the legal theories on which banks were held liable to a drawer whose check was wrongfully dishonored included breach of contract, negligence, wilful wrong, libel, and slander. The damages recoverable have varied depending largely on the theory adopted. The Code does not adopt any single theory, but does distinguish between cases in which dishonor is the result of mistake and other cases. Most wrongful dishonor results from mistake. In such cases prior to the Code, merchants or traders sometimes were allowed to recover substantial damages without proof of actual damages, but others were required to prove actual damages. The Code limits recovery to *actual* damages in all cases involving innocent mistake. It recognizes, however, that actual damages may include damages from injury to credit, damages resulting from arrest or prosecution for uttering bad checks, and other consequential damages.

§ 6. Charging Customer's Account

As a special kind of draft, a check is an order to pay. When a customer issues a check he orders his bank to pay it according to its terms. Therefore, if the check is in proper form and the bank carries out the order in good faith, the bank may properly charge the customer.

A.   OVERDRAFT

When a bank pays a check issued by its customer in proper form, it properly may charge his account even though it is an overdraft. [4–401(1)] Although a customer normally has no right to overdraw his account and the bank is not obliged to pay an overdraft, a check that overdraws an account is nonetheless an order to pay.

The order carries with it an implied authorization to charge the customer's account and an implied promise by the customer to reimburse the bank. [Comment 1, 4–401) Allowing the bank to charge the drawer's account becomes especially important when it pays an overdraft to a holder in due course or to one who later changes his position in good faith in reliance on the payment because in those circumstances there is no breach of any of the presenters' warranties and the payment is final. [3–418 and 3–417(1)] If the bank could not charge the drawer's account, it would have nowhere to go for relief.

B.   DRAWER'S SIGNATURE
UNAUTHORIZED

A bank normally can charge its depositor's account only if his signature was authorized; for otherwise he did not give the order to pay. If the bank pays when the drawer's signature is unauthorized, the bank normally can recover the payment from the forger or anyone else who broke the presenters' warranty that he had no knowledge that the drawer's signature was unauthorized or from anyone else who did not qualify for the benefit of the doctrine of finality provided by Section 3–418, regardless of whether he had knowledge of the unauthorized signature. (See pages 210–212)

C. PAYMENT TO NON–HOLDER

The drawer's order to pay is qualified. To be effective so as to give the bank the right to charge the depositor's account, the bank's payment normally must be made to the *holder* or someone authorized by the holder to receive payment. The bank, therefore, must determine who is the holder. If the instrument has not been indorsed, this usually presents no problem so long as the bank is acting in good faith. If such an instrument was issued as bearer paper (typically "pay to bearer" or "pay to the order of cash"), the holder is anyone in possession of the instrument. If the instrument was issued as order paper, the payee is the holder if he has possession. If the instrument has been indorsed, however, the bank must make certain that all indorsements in the "chain of title" to the presenting party are authorized. If any one of these indorsements is not authorized, the presenter is not the holder and the bank cannot properly charge the drawer's account if it pays the presenter. The bank's remedy is to proceed on the presenters' warranty of title given by the presenter and all transferors back to and including the wrongdoer all of whom lacked title. Whether or not the bank collects on the basis of the presenters' warranty of title, it may be held liable for conversion to the party whose indorsement was forged. [3–419(1)(c)] But in this case the bank normally will be entitled to charge the drawer's account on the theory that the bank is subrogated to the rights of the party whose indorsement was forged. [4–407] (See subrogation, pages 337–340)

D. AMOUNT TO BE CHARGED

If the bank pays a proper party on a check which has *not* been altered, it may, of course, charge the depositor's account the full amount of the check.

Instruments which have been altered, however, present a special problem. If an instrument is materially altered by the holder with a fraudulent intent, each party whose contract is affected is discharged from liability except as against a subsequent holder in due course. (See page 140) Accordingly when a check is so altered, the drawer is discharged.

If the check thereafter is transferred to a holder in due course, however, the latter is entitled to recover according to its original tenor if it was complete when issued, or as completed, if it was incomplete when issued.

If the bank acts in *good faith* when making a payment to a holder, the bank is entitled to charge the drawer's account according to the original tenor of the altered check if it was complete when issued, and according to the tenor of the completed instrument if it was incomplete. [4–401 (2)] The bank is so entitled whether payment was made to a holder in due course who is entitled to the payment or to the defrauder or some other holder who is not.

At first glance, it may seem unfair to the drawer to allow the bank to charge his account when it pays a holder other than a holder in due course after the drawer has been discharged by an alteration. It does not seem unfair, however, when seen through the eyes of the bank which pays in good faith. If the instrument was complete when issued, the drawer really suffers no loss when he is required to pay according to the original tenor of the check; he is merely prevented from getting a windfall at the expense of the bank. If the check is incomplete when issued, requiring the drawer to pay more than he intended seems fairer than thrusting any part of the loss on the bank. The drawer signing an incomplete instrument should realize that he is courting trouble whereas the bank is merely doing what is expected of it—paying a holder, in good faith.

In a case wherein a bank is not entitled to charge a drawer's account for the full amount it has paid on an altered check, it is entitled to recover its loss from the wrongdoer or any other party who broke the presenters' warranty against alteration.   (See pages 220–223)

§ 7.   Drawer's General Duty of Care

The drawer loses the right to bar the drawee from charging his account for a payment made on an altered instrument in excess of the amount originally provided or on an unauthorized signature of his own or of an indorser in the chain of title if the drawer's own negligence substantially contributed to the alteration or unauthorized signature and the drawee bank paid in good faith and in accordance with reasonable commercial standards of the banking business.   [3–406]

§ 8.   Customer's Duty to Discover and Report Unauthorized Signature or Alteration

In addition to the general duty of care described above that is imposed on a drawer who wishes to bar the drawee bank from charging his account on the basis of an alteration or unauthorized signature, the Code imposes a more precise duty in handling his bank statements.

Most banks furnish their checking account customers with periodic statements of account accompanied by cancelled checks and other items in support of debit entries. It is to the interest of the customer to check the cancelled checks against his check stubs and verify the balance. If he does so, he is almost certain to detect any alterations made in the checks he has issued and any checks he did not sign or authorize.

If he finds that the bank has paid and charged a check on which his signature was unauthorized, the customer is entitled to have the bank re-credit his account unless he has ratified or is precluded by his negligence from asserting the unauthorized signature. Similarly, if he finds that an item has been altered by being raised, he may be entitled to require the bank to re-credit him for any excess paid over the original tenor of the check. Also, if the bank has paid someone other than the holder, relying on a forged indorsement in the chain of title, the customer is entitled to have the bank credit his account for the amount of the payment.

A customer should act with reasonable promptness in discovering and reporting any such discrepancies. If he fails to do so, his bank may be injured in two ways. First, it may be deprived of the opportunity to intercept the wrongdoer and obtain restitution. Second, through lack of knowledge of the wrongdoing, it may be unable to prevent future losses at the hands of the same wrongdoer.

To protect the bank from incurring losses which can be expected to flow from a customer's careless handling of his bank statements and to induce the customer to exercise care the Code provides in Section 4–406(1):

> When a bank sends to its customer a statement of account accompanied by items paid in good faith in support of the debit entries or holds the statement and items pursuant to a request or instructions of its customer or otherwise in a reasonable manner makes the statement and items available to the customer, the customer must exercise reasonable care and promptness to examine the statement and items to discover his unauthorized signature or any alteration on an item and must notify the bank promptly after discovery thereof.

If the customer fails to exercise reasonable care and promptness in discovering and reporting these discrepancies, he is precluded from asserting against his bank either *his own* unauthorized signature or any alteration on any item on which the bank can show that it suffered loss because of his failure. [4–406(2)(a)]

In addition, by failure to perform this duty, the bank's customer is precluded from asserting against the bank any alteration or unauthorized signature—*an indorser's as well as his own*—by the same wrongdoer on any item paid by the bank in good faith and without notice *after* the first item and statement are available to the customer for a reasonable period not exceeding fourteen days. [4–406(2)(b)] Losses resulting from alterations and forgeries by the same wrongdoer on these later items usually can be traced directly to the negligent customer. If he had done his duty in the first place, the bank would have been alerted to stop payment on the later items and the wrongdoer would have been taken out of circulation or at least deprived of the opportunity to continue his misdeeds. [Comment 3, 4–406]

Further justification for penalizing a customer who fails to discover and report his unauthorized signature or alteration with reasonable promptness is the fact that the bank's liability for paying forged or altered checks is, with few exceptions, absolute and without regard to fault on the bank's part. As long as the bank is free from fault, it is considered fair to protect it against the customer's carelessness.

However, if the customer can show that the bank, itself, failed to exercise ordinary care in paying an item, the customer is not precluded from asserting against his bank any unauthorized signature or alteration even though he has failed to exercise the required care. [4–406(3)]

Even if the customer was not at fault and the bank was negligent in paying an item, the customer nevertheless is barred from asserting either *his own unauthorized signature* or an alteration unless he does so within one year after the statement charging it is made available to him; and he is barred from asserting that the signature of an *indorser* was unauthorized unless he does so within three years.   [4–406(4)]   The time limits differ because of the assumption that there is far less excuse for a drawer not to detect an alteration or a forgery of his own signature than for failing to detect a forgery of an indorser's signature.

§ 9.   Effect of Death or Incompetence

As a general rule, death or an adjudication of incompetency of his principal has the effect of terminating an agent's authority even before the agent learns of it.

As applied to the agency aspects of the bank-customer relationship, prior to the Code this rule was relaxed both by statute and by the cases. This relaxation of the general rule is reflected in the Code which provides that "neither death nor incompetence of a customer revokes * * * authority to accept, pay, collect or account until the bank *knows* of the fact of death or of an *adjudication* of incompetence *and has reasonable opportunity to act on it.*"   [4–405(1)]   (Emphasis

added.)   The Code further liberalizes the rule by
providing that "even *with knowledge* a bank may
for ten days after the date of death pay or certify
checks drawn on or prior to that date unless ordered to stop payment by a person claiming an
interest in the account."   [4–405(2)]   (Emphasis
added.)

One reason for not binding a bank until it actually knows of the death or adjudication of incompetency is that the tremendous volume of
items handled by modern banks makes any rule
requiring a bank to keep track of the life and
competency of its customers very impractical.
[Comment 2, 4–405]   As applied to paying
checks, there is the further reason that a check
is an order to pay which the bank must obey to
avoid the risk of being held for a wrongful dishonor.   [Comment 2, 4–405]

The Code provision allowing a bank to pay or
certify checks *even with knowledge* unless ordered
not to is an innovation intended to permit holders
of checks drawn shortly before death to cash them
without the need for filing a claim in the estate
proceedings.   There is usually no reason why
these checks should not be paid.   Consequently
requiring a holder to file a claim against the estate is a wasteful formality burdensome not only
to the holder but also to the court, the bank, and
the estate.   [Comment 3, 4–405]   To provide for

the unusual case where there actually is reason to question a holder's right to payment, the Code allows a relative, creditor, or any other person with an interest in the account to order the bank not to pay the check.

§ 10. Right to Stop Payment

It sometimes happens that a person who has issued a check discovers that he has been defrauded by the payee, that the check has been lost, that the check was issued by mistake, or that there is some other reason why he does not wish to have the check paid. He may try to protect himself by ordering his bank to stop payment. [4–403 (1)]

Although the stop payment device is often essential to the protection of the customer, it involves difficulty to the bank and it can easily be abused. Therefore, most banks charge for services connected with stop payment. Some banks charge only on special checking accounts and others charge only after a customer has repeatedly used the service.

To bind the bank, the stop payment order must be received by the bank in time to give it a reasonable opportunity to act before the bank has paid the check or has committed itself to recognize it by certifying or settling for it, or in any of several other ways. [4–403(1)]

Because of the need for haste, most stop payment orders normally are given by telephone and later confirmed in writing. An oral stop payment order is binding upon the bank for only fourteen calendar days unless confirmed in writing within that period. A written order is good for six months unless renewed in writing. [4–403(2)]

Only the bank's customer may stop payment; a payee or indorsee has no right to do so. An exception exists in case of the drawer's death when any person having an interest in the account may stop payment. [Comment 3, 4–403, 4–405(2)]

Since the drawer has no right to require a bank to impair its own credit, he has no right to stop payment of a check which has been certified. Even though his check has been certified, however, the drawer might accomplish the purpose of a stop payment order by promptly enjoining the payee's negotiation of the check and attaching the funds in the hands of the bank.

The effect of stopping payment is to hold the money in the drawer's account. It does not prevent the payee or other holder from suing the drawer on the check or on the obligation for which the check was given. Of course, if the drawer has a defense, he may assert it. Even though he has a defense, however, it will not protect him against a holder in due course who acquires the check unless it is one of the few defenses good against a holder in due course.

A payment in violation of an effective direction to stop payment is an improper payment and renders the bank liable for the loss resulting to the depositor even though it is made by mistake or inadvertence. Any agreement between the bank and customer relieving the bank of its duty to exercise good faith and ordinary care in such matters would be invalid. [4–103(1)]

§ 11. Payment of Stale Checks

In banking and commercial circles, a check outstanding more than six months usually is considered to be stale. Banks are not required to pay such checks, and many banks will not pay them without consulting its depositors. However, the bank is not required to consult the drawer, and if it pays an older check in good faith, it is entitled to charge the drawer's account. [4–404] This rule places the burden on the customer to give instructions to the bank regarding uncashed checks. Sometimes, as in the case of dividend checks, the drawer still wants payment made even after a considerable period of time.

§ 12. Bank's Right to Subrogation for Improper Payment

When a bank pays an item and charges the drawer's account despite a stop payment order or under other circumstances giving the drawer reason to object, justice between the bank and drawer may require: (1) recrediting the drawer's account with the full amount of the payment, (2) leaving the charge against the drawer, or (3) recrediting part of the amount paid. In some cases it also may be necessary to permit the bank to obtain some kind of relief against the party who obtained payment.

All of this is reflected in Section 4–407 of the Code which provides:

> If a payor bank has paid an item over the stop payment order of the drawer or maker or otherwise under circumstances giving a basis for objection by the drawer or maker, to prevent unjust enrichment and only to the extent necessary to prevent loss to the bank by reason of its payment of the item, the payor bank shall be subrogated to the rights
>
> (a) of any holder in due course on the item against the drawer or maker; and
>
> (b) of the payee or any other holder of the item against the drawer or maker either on the item or under the transaction out of which the item arose; and
>
> (c) of the drawer or maker against the payee or any other holder of the item with respect to the transaction out of which the item arose.

In Universal C.I.T. v. Guarantee Bank & Trust Co., 161 F.Supp. 790 (D.C.Mass.1958), plaintiff, depositor, drew checks on defendant bank. The payee deposited these checks in Worcester Bank which allowed the payee to draw against them and so became a holder in due course. Learning that the payee was not entitled to payment, the depositor issued a stop payment order to defendant bank. By mistake, defendant bank paid the checks when they were presented by Worcester Bank and charged the depositor's account. When the depositor sued to recover the charges, the court held for the defendant bank on the theory that it was subrogated to the rights of the Worcester Bank which, as a holder in due course, would have been entitled to recover from the depositor even if the defendant bank had refused payment. This is consistent with Section 4–407(a).

Suppose that in the above case the payee had retained the check instead of negotiating it to a holder in due course and that the drawee bank had paid the payee by mistake despite the stop payment order. In this case, the drawee bank's right to charge the depositor would have depended upon what rights the payee had against the depositor. For example, if the payee already had performed all its obligations to the depositor and was entitled to full payment of the check, the bank, being subrogated to the payee's rights, would have been entitled to charge the drawer's account for the check's full amount. [4–407(b)] If the payee had not carried out any part of the obligation for which the check was issued, the bank, as subrogee of the payee, would not have been entitled to charge the depositor's account at all. It would have been entitled, however, to recover from the payee on the theory that it was subrogated to the depositor's rights. [4–407(c)] If the payee had performed only part of his obligation to the depositor, the bank would have been subrogated to the payee's claim and could have charged the depositor's account to that extent. It would have been entitled to recover the balance of the payment from the payee on the theory that it was subrogated to the depositor's claim against the payee. [4–407(c)]

Of course, many cases are far more complicated. However, in all of these cases the right of subrogation is allowed only to the extent that is necessary to prevent loss to the bank and unjust enrichment to some other party.

CHAPTER 14

BEYOND THE LAW OF COMMER-
CIAL PAPER

The importance of the law of commercial paper in the business world should not blind us to the fact that these distinctive legal and financial devices are not ends in themselves but only means of achieving business objectives. To the businessman, the underlying business transaction is of primary importance; often much creative effort goes into it before any thought is given to its legal aspects. Even when attention is directed to the legal side of a transaction, the legal principles relating to commercial paper usually are no more important than those relating to contracts, agency, security, corporations, or other branches of the law that fix the guidelines within which business must be conducted. As desirable as it might be, however, it is not possible for any book to deal effectively with the law of commercial paper in terms of the multifaceted business transactions to which this law may relate. It follows that anyone aspiring to a sound understanding of the many legal and law-related aspects of business not only must grasp the principles of the law of commercial paper but also must develop his capacity to apply

[*341*]

these principles in a variety of transactions and to integrate them with the many other legal principles that may be applied. This is no easy task, but anyone genuinely interested in law and the business process will find the effort rewarding.

INDEX

References are to Pages

INDEX

CONSIDERATION
Compared with value, 230–233, 239–240
Lack of as defense, 282–284

CONSUMERS
Special treatment,
      Courts, 264–268
      Federal Trade Commission, 270–271
      Legislatures, 16, 18, 268–269
      Need for, 262–263

CONTRACT
Checking account customer and bank, 319–320
Commercial paper as, 2

CONTRIBUTION
Accommodation party, 161

CONVERSION
Drawee's refusal to return draft, 149
Liability for, 157–158

COUNTERCLAIMS
Assignee subject to, 16
Notice of, 252–253

DEATH
Effect on bank as agent, 333–335

DEFENSES
Against holder in due course, 272–282
Alteration, 280–281
Discharge against holder in due course, 279–280
Discharge in insolvency, 279
Jus tertii, 287–288
Lack of consideration, 282–284
Meaning, 250–251
Nondelivery, 284
Outside agreement, 284–286
Person lacking rights of holder in due course, 282–288
Proving, 293
Unauthorized signature, 281–282

INDEX

INDEX

References are to Pages

[*349*]

INDEX

EXECUTORY PROMISE
Notice of defense or claim, 253
Value, 235–236

EXONERATION
Accommodation party, 161

EXTENSION CLAUSE
Effect on negotiability, 60–61

FEDERAL DEPOSIT INSURANCE CORPORATION
Insures checking account, 321

FICTITIOUS PAYEE PROBLEM, 99–104

FIDUCIARY
Notice of, 256
Restrictive indorsement to, 125–128

FINALITY
Doctrine, 210–212

"FIRST IN, FIRST OUT"
When bank gives value, 237–238

FOREIGN BILL
Defined, 192
Protest required, 192

FORGERY
See Unauthorized Signatures

FORGOTTEN NOTICE, 245

FORMS
Certificate of deposit, 30
Check, 28
Draft, 27
Promissory note, 24

FRAUD
Defense against holder in due course, 277–279
In factum or essence, 278–279
In inducement or procurement, 277–278

INDEX

INDEX

INDEX

INDEX

References are to Pages